God Without Being

Religion and Postmodernism
A series edited by Mark C. Taylor

JEAN-LUC MARION

God Without Being

Hors-Texte

Translated by
Thomas A. Carlson

With a Foreword by
David Tracy

The University of Chicago Press
Chicago and London

The University of Chicago Press, Chicago 60637
The University of Chicago Press, Ltd., London
 Published 1991
Paperback edition 1995
Printed in the United States of America
07 06 05 04 03 02 01 00 99 98   3 4 5 6 7 8

ISBN 0-226-50541-3 (paper)

Originally published as *Dieu sans l'être: Hors-texte,*

Library of Congress Cataloging-in-Publication Data

Marion, Jean-Luc, 1946-
[Dieu sans l'être. English]
God without being : hors-texte / Jean-Luc Marion ; translated by Thomas A. Carlson ; with a foreword by David Tracy.
p. cm. —(Religion and postmodernism)
Translation of : Dieu sans l'être.
1. God. 2. Ontology. 3. Philosophical theology. I. Title. II. Series.
BT102.M299 1991
211—dc20   91-19425
CIP

∞ The paper used in this publication meets the minimum requirements of the American National Standard for Information Sciences—Permanence of Paper for Printed Library Materials, ANSI Z39.48-1992.

To Grégoire

From all bodies and minds we could not draw one movement of true charity, that is impossible, and of another, supernatural order.

—Pascal

If I were yet to write a theology—to which I sometimes feel inclined—then the word *Being* would not occur in it. Faith does not need the thought of Being.

—Heidegger

CONTENTS

FOREWORD

It is a pleasure to introduce Jean-Luc Marion's *God Without Being* to an American audience. Much of that audience already knows Marion's deeply influential works on the interpretation of Descartes as well as his work on Husserl and Heidegger, Levinas and Derrida. Moreover, Marion's preface to this English edition nicely focuses on his critical relationship to these complex philosophical influences on his thought. His original preface also clarifies his readings of Nietzsche, Wittgenstein, and Gilson. My responsibility, therefore, is to speak less of the philosophical than of the theological context of Marion's work, for *God Without Being* is clearly both a philosophical and a theological text.

Christian theology today is marked by a great divide. The traditional historical divides within Christianity—Protestant, Catholic, Orthodox—remain intact but have become far less significant than they have been historically. Rather, a peculiarly modern conflict now crosses all the major Christian theological traditions, whether Catholic, Protestant, or Orthodox. Since Schleiermacher and Hegel, Christian theology has been in intense internal conflict over its proper response to modernity (and more recently, as in Marion, to postmodernity). There are many ways to describe this pervasive modern theological conflict. For present purposes, we may name it a conflict between two basic theological strategies on the proper Christian response to modernity.

One classic modern theological strategy wants to correlate the claims of reason and the disclosures of revelation. The other strategy believes that reason functions best in theology by developing rigorous concepts and categories to clarify theology's sole foundation in revelation. On this second view, since revelation alone is theology's foundation, any attempt at correlation is at best a category mistake—at worst, an attempt to domesticate the reality of God by means of reason and being. As the title *God Without Being* suggests, Professor Marion embraces the second, revelation-based strategy for Christian theology. A further discussion of each strategy and the conflict set in motion between them should help orient the reader into the fuller theological context and the controversies of this unsettling and properly provocative book.

First, the strategy of "correlating" reason and revelation. Many theologians, in fidelity to the early modern strategies of classic liberal theologies, believe that the principal task of contemporary Christian theology is to correlate an interpretation of the Christian tradition with an interpretation of the religious questions or "religious dimension" of the contemporary situation. When this typically modern strategy of theological correlation is confident about both Christianity and modernity (as in liberal Protestant theologies and Catholic modernist theologies), the interpretations of the meaning, meaningfulness, and truth of both the tradition and the contemporary situation will often prove a claim to a virtual identity of meaning between Christianity and modernity. In its most famous or infamous form, Christianity can then be viewed as the "absolute religion," now finding its proper conceptual self-understanding in the "absolute knowledge" available to modernity (Hegel).

When this strategy of correlation becomes more troubled (as in such great "correlational" or "mediating" theologians as Paul Tillich in Protestant theology or Karl Rahner in Catholic theology), the "correlation" between "reason" and "revelation" will claim far fewer virtual identities between the essential meanings of modernity and Christianity and something more like a pervasive set of analogies-in-difference between these two distinct phenomena.

When this same kind of correlational strategy becomes less

hopeful about one or another side of the correlation, then the strategy of correlating interpretations of modernity and Christianity will disclose more and more nonidentities, differences, oppositions, interruptions, confrontations. This is clearly the case in many radical critiques of "modernity" and turns away from "theory" to "praxis" in contemporary political, liberation, and feminist theologies.

In these latter theologies, the basically correlational strategy of modern Christian theology continues. However, modernity is now viewed with as much suspicion as hope, and Christianity is viewed as more eschatological (even apocalyptic) in its more self-interruptive essence than reconciling of all reality. In sum, within many correlational theologies, the self-confidence of modernity and the Eurocentrism of Christian liberal theologies have eroded and, at times, exploded into sheer confrontational apocalypse. Hegelian reconciliation is abandoned in favor of liberation from the oppressions and unconscious but systemic distortions (racism, sexism, classism) present in both Christian tradition and secular Enlightenment modernity.

It is clear that Marion's model for theology does not partake of *any* form of this more familiar correlational stance of most modern Christian theologies. Therein lies its great interest and provocation—even for basically correlational theologians like myself. Instead, Marion, in this brilliant book, moves outside all correlational strategies. In Marion's judgment, revelation is the only possible and necessary foundation of any theology worthy of the name. Revelation, centered in forms of visibility, can become an icon for thought. For Marion, reason, although crucial for developing rigorous philosophical-theological concepts for understanding the "gift," even "excess," of God's self-disclosure as "agape," is, on its own, not an icon but an "idol." Reason, for Marion, is capable of thinking Being. But reason is not capable of iconically disclosing God, except within the confinements of Being. For Marion, true theology, focused iconically on God's excessive self-revelation as Love, needs to abandon all the metaphysics of the subject which have defined modernity. Genuine theology needs to abandon as well the onto-theo-logical horizon which may confine even Thomas Aquinas to understanding God in terms of "Being." Contemporary philosophical theology for Marion needs new thought-ful concepts (gift, excess, face, icon) to understand with conceptual rigor the reality of God's self-disclosure as Love.

True theology needs, therefore, "God without Being." Theology needs to cease being modern theo-*logy* in order to become again *theo*-logy (like the theologies of such ancient and medieval Christian Platonists as Pseudo-Dionysius and Bonaventure). Marion has clearly forged a new and brilliant postmodern version of the other great alternative for theology: a revelation-centered, noncorrelational, postmetaphysical theology. Like his great predecessor in Catholic theology, Hans Urs von Balthasar, and like his natural ally in Protestant theology, Karl Barth, Marion has developed a rigorous and coherent theological strategy focused on the reality of God's revelation as pure gift, indeed as excess. This new strategy, in Marion's able philosophical and theological hands, yields a series of profound theological (or, as he would prefer, *theo*-logical) reflections on categories, tendencies, and tensions familiar in much French postmodern thought. The reader will witness Marion's highly original reflections on such categories as the "face," "excess," "gift," "idol," "icon," "agape," "onto-theo-logy," and "goodness" over "Being." Here and elsewhere in his most characteristic moves, Marion yields a rare kind of thoughtfulness on the question of God for all theology and philosophy: a reflection on God without Being.

Readers familiar with contemporary French philosophy (and, therefore, inevitably familiar with Marion's influential readings of Descartes) will also find how accurate Marion is to describe the "horizon" of his own thought as Nietzsche, Heidegger, and Wittgenstein—meaning, of course, contemporary French philosophical appropriations of these thinkers. Readers familiar with the work of Levinas and Derrida will find Marion in an occasionally explicit but pervasively implicit critical conversation with them throughout this book. But throughout this strangely compelling series of highly reflective meditations on seemingly familiar themes and questions of postmodern thought, Marion's voice is distinctive. For Marion is the thinker who raises anew, in this horizon of thought, the question of God.

Theological readers will perhaps be surprised to find French postmodern philosophical reflections bearing such affinities with an apparently premodern theological insistence on "revelation" as the only proper focus for contemporary Christian theology. Theo-logically construed, all other understandings of theology are, for Marion, idols. Levinas and Barth, von Balthasar and Derrida, even Nietzsche and Pseudo-Dionysius: such disparate thinkers all appear in this present text. They clearly do not mean the same, but Marion shows how their differences can co-inhabit a new space of reflection, at once premodern and postmodern: a philosophy and theology of God without Being. Several disparate thinkers unite in this text in their distrust of "modernity," of "metaphysics," and of any "correlation" between "reason" and "revelation." They unite to undo any attempt to totality for reason and Being.

To keep faithful in one's rigorous conceptual thought to that foundation-gift of God's self-revelation as love is, for Marion, to allow God to be God and not some idol created by modern or ancient reflection on "Being." Hence the need to call into question any appeal to the Scholastic tradition of "common being" for understanding God. Hence, far more radically and originally, Marion's insistence that even Thomas Aquinas's understanding of God as *ipsum esse subsistens* with its famous metaphysics of exodus (Gilson) may not be the best route for understanding God revealed as Love. Hence, and more originally still, Marion argues that even Heidegger's anti-onto-theological thought on the "ontological difference" may be a more subtle but finally no less fatal attempt to keep God within the confines of *Sein.*

To approach the question of God, with Heidegger, only through the question of the Holy; to approach the question of the Holy only through the question of Being: surely this post-metaphysical strategy does liberate the question of God from the question of common being and even from any transcendental metaphysics of esse (e.g., K. Rahner, E. Coreth). But—and here Marion is at his most original and daring—may not even Heidegger's strategy confine God within our understanding of *Sein?*

The most original and provocative thoughts of Marion in this rigorous book present the reader, time after time, with a relentlessness that comes from genuine philosophical thoughtfulness. The reader will need to face again, and perhaps as if for the first time, the question of God freed from our usual philosophical reflections on the God of reason (Kant), the God of Being (Aquinas) or the God of morality (Nietzsche). This book forces the reader at one and the same time into two usually conflicting paths away from modernity. One path leads to a premodern space of reflection on God and the Good—to the Christian Platonists starting with the classical theology of divine names in Pseudo-Dionysius. Here, as in Plato, the Good is beyond Being. Marion's other path away from modernity leads into a path of postmodernity, a postmetaphysical and post-Heideggerian attempt to think of God outside the horizon of *Sein* altogether, that is, within the horizon of God's own self-revelation as Agape.

The deeply French Catholic theological sensibility in Marion's philosophy and theology will take even most Catholic theological readers, whether conservative or liberal, on paths they may not usually choose to tread. Conservatives will be led to wonder whether the familiar paths of thought for understanding God in terms of Being from Thomas Aquinas to modern Thomism (Gilson) is a path that genuinely allows the theologian or the philosopher to understand the priority of goodness over being in God's self-revelation as Love. Liberals will be led to question, in more postmodern than antimodern terms, their own commitments to modernity, and thereby to the modern subject, to metaphysics, and to a correlational model for theo-logy. Even those (again like myself) who may not find themselves persuaded to go the full route with Marion will think differently, thanks to Marion, every time they try to think theologically and philosophically of God, Being, Goodness, and Love. For, after Marion, every route to thinking God via Being or Becoming must be thought again—and thought excessively to see if God can be thus understood in terms of Being without being radically misunderstood as somehow constricted by Being, as somehow less than God. Is Platonic "goodness," or Christian "agape," or postmodern "excess" appropriately understood through any notion of Being—whether

Scholastic "common being," Thomist *esse,* or even Heideggerian *Sein?* That disturbing question—disturbing to so many forms of philosophical theology in our period—will come to haunt any serious theological reader of *God Without Being.*

The need for all serious theology to be what Marion nicely names *theo*-logy not theo-*logy* has never been clearer than in a theological landscape littered with idols (whether theist, atheist, or agnostic) of God-talk. The need to recover the unsettling theology of "divine names" from Pseudo-Dionysius forward is clear. The need to question whether any transcendental or metaphysical reflection is the correct route forward for theology finds renewed impetus from this book. Indeed, this book should reopen that question for the contemporary horizon of philosophical theology. Moreover, Heideggerian manifestation (*Offenbarheit*) of *Sein* is not equivalent to Christian revelation (*Offenbarung*), that is, of God's disclosure of God's reality as radically, excessively, Agape beyond Being.

In this book, Marion has moved the discussion of the proper model for contemporary theology and philosophy beyond the usual conservative-liberal impasse (for example, in Catholic terms in France and elsewhere, the *Concilium-Communio* differences). On some ecclesial issues (witness Marion's intriguing reflections here on bishops as theologians), his sympathies are clearly with the Catholic journal *Communio* and not (as are mine) with the Catholic journal *Concilium.* What is stunning and heartening in this text, however, is the absence of any inner-ecclesial polemics and the enlivening, indeed, exhilarating, reality of genuine thoughtfulness for all serious theology. Beyond all ecclesial controversies lies true thoughtfulness and genuine theology: reflection on and with icons of God's self-revelation.

David Tracy

TRANSLATOR'S ACKNOWLEDGMENTS

This translation could not have been completed without the generosity of several friends, teachers, and colleagues. Expressions of gratitude may not suffice to acknowledge all that has been received, but they do constitute a necessary and appropriate beginning. I am indebted in countless ways to Mark C. Taylor, who first encouraged me to undertake the project. The time of that undertaking would not have been what it was without the warm support and unfailing patience of Ashley Tidey. For their willingness to read and discuss various sections of various drafts, I extend my thanks to Jeffrey Kosky, Herman Rapaport, Paul Ricoeur, Clifford Ruprecht, and David Tracy. I owe my deep appreciation to Allan Stoekl, whose close reading of the entire manuscript led to substantial improvements and corrections. Kerry Batchelder and Douglas Johnson were extremely kind to read and correct the final proofs, for which I thank them. Thanks are due also to the staff of the University of Chicago Press, with whom it has been a pleasure to work. As for my parents, Rosanne Lee Carlson and Joseph Carlson II, gratitude simply cannot measure up to all that they have given. Finally, I would like to express my warm thanks to Jean-Luc Marion, both for his assistance and encouragement during work on the translation and for his most generous friendship.

Chicago
April 1991

T.A.C.

PREFACE TO THE ENGLISH EDITION

Since my book has the good fortune of being offered a new life in the New World, I owe it to my English-speaking readers, who, though traditionally indulgent, might find the work rather surprising, to make it as easy as possible to read.

Written at the border between philosophy and theology, this essay remains deeply marked by the spiritual and cultural crisis in which it was thought and written. That crisis, shared by an entire generation (at least), had a time and a stake. A time: the test of nihilism which, in France, marked the years dominated by 1968. A stake: the obscuring of God in the indistinct haze of the "human sciences," which at the time were elevated by "structuralism" to the rank of dominant doctrine. Later I shall have to say what this field of passions, discoveries, strife, and work actually was—this field in which I struggled like many others, having as close teachers Beaufret, Derrida, but also Althusser; as masters, Alquié and Levinas, but also Gilson, Daniélou, and H. U. von Balthasar; and, as horizon, Nietzsche, Wittgenstein, and Heidegger. For the moment, it is sufficient to understand that, in a confused and sometimes unpolished form, the issue was a confrontation between the philosophical prohibitions of nihilism and the demanding openings of Christian revelation in a debate so close that it sometimes brought the antagonists together on a common course.

At the time of its first publication, *God Without Being* provoked some fairly animated debates, in France and elsewhere. Curiously, its theses were better received by the philosophers and academics than by the theologians and believers. The whole book suffered from the inevitable and assumed equivocation of its title: was it insinuating that the God "without being" is not, or does not exist? Let me repeat now the answer I gave then: no, definitely not. God is, exists, and that is the least of things. At issue here is not the possibility of God's attaining

but, quite the opposite, the possibility of Being's attain-
God. With respect to God, is it self-evident that the first
on comes down to asking, before anything else, whether
Does Being define the first and the highest of the divine names? When God offers himself to be contemplated and gives himself to be prayed to, is he concerned primarily with Being? When he appears as and in Jesus Christ, who dies and rises from the dead, is he concerned primarily with Being? No doubt, God can and must in the end also be; but does his relation to Being determine him as radically as the relation to his Being defines all other beings? To be or not to be—that is indeed the first and indispensable question for everything and everyone, and for man in particular. But with respect to Being, does God have to behave like Hamlet? Under the title *God Without Being,* I am attempting to bring out the absolute freedom of God with regard to all determinations, including, first of all, the basic condition that renders all other conditions possible and even necessary—for us, humans—the fact of Being. Because, *for us,* as for all the beings of the world, it is first necessary "to be" in order, indissolubly, "to live and to move" (Acts, 17:28), and thus eventually also to love. But *for God,* if at least we resist the temptation to reduce him immediately to our own measure, does the same still apply? Or, on the contrary, are not all the determinations that are necessary for the finite reversed for Him, and for Him alone? If, to begin with, "God is love," then God loves before being, He only is as He embodies himself—in order to love more closely that which and those who, themselves, have first to be. This radical reversal of the relations between Being and loving, between the name revealed by the Old Testament (Exodus, 3:14) and the name revealed, more profoundly though not inconsistently, by the New (First Letter of John, 4:8), presupposes taking a stand that is at once theological and philosophical.

The philosophical decision takes place within the framework, perhaps, of what is conventionally called "postmodernity." If we understand by modernity the completed and therefore terminal figure of metaphysics, such as it develops from Descartes to Nietzsche, then "postmodernity" begins when, among other things, the metaphysical determination of God is called into question. Following the thematic elaborated by Heidegger, I admit that metaphysics imposes on what it still designates under the disputable title of "God" a function in the onto-theo-logical constitution of metaphysics: as supreme being, "God" assures the ground (itself grounded according to the Being of beings in general) of all other derived beings. In two studies on Descartes,[1] I have examined in more detail the construction of the system of the metaphysical names imposed on "God." Inevitably, though it did not become apparent for three centuries, these names reflect purely metaphysical functions of "God" and hide that much more the mystery of God as such. Nietzsche not only proclaimed the "death of God," he brought the grounds for it to light: under the conceptual names of "God" only metaphysical "idols" emerge, imposed on a God who is still to be encountered. A few years before *God Without Being,*[2] I had noted this paradox in the framework of the short-lived "new philosophers" movement: the "death of God" exclusively concerns the failure of the metaphysical concepts of "God"; in taking its distance from all metaphysics, it therefore allows the emergence of a God who is free from onto-theology; in short, the "death of God" immediately implies the death of the "death of God." But, according to the logic of "postmodernity," the critique thus initiated had to be made deeper: to release God from the constraints of onto-theo-logy can still signify that Being, thought as such, without its metaphysical figure, in the way that Heidegger attempted, is still imposed on him. This second idolatry—"God according to Being"—only appears once one has unmasked the first—"God" according to onto-theo-logy. In *God Without Being,* therefore, I no longer play Heidegger and Nietzsche against metaphysics, but rather, playing against Heidegger and the primacy of the *Seinsfrage,* I shoot for God according to his most theological name—charity. My enterprise remains "postmodern" in this sense, and, in this precise sense, I remain close to Derrida.[3]

My enterprise does not remain "postmodern" all the way through, however, since it claims in the end to be able to refer to charity, the *agape* properly revealed in and as the Christ, according to an essential anachronism: charity belongs neither to pre-, nor to post-, nor to modernity, but rather, at once abandoned to and removed from historical destiny, it dominates any situation of thought. The thematic of destitution, which strikes all beings and all Being with vanity (chap. 4), develops an a-historical "deconstruction" of the history of metaphysics. At least it claims to outline this "deconstruction" within the framework of a phenomenology that is pushed to its utmost possibilities.[4]

A theological decision supports the philosophical decision. In rejecting the denomination of God by Being, am I not colliding with one of Thomas Aquinas's major theses? Am I not distancing myself from one of the most explicit benchmarks of properly Catholic theology (since *Aeterni Patris* in 1879, but even at Vatican II in 1965)? This of course is exactly what I was reproached for by a number of theologians, "Thomist" or not.[5] There is certainly a serious question here that no quick answer can satisfy. Without prejudicing other research, I will limit myself to sketching a few arguments.

First argument: the Being from which God is liberated in *God Without Being* is defined in terms of two different domains. On the one hand, we have the metaphysical tradition of the *ens commune*, then of the objective concept of being, of its abstract univocity, such as it collapses under the critiques of Hegel and Nietzsche; but then, according to so incontestable a Thomist as E. Gilson, this "Being" no longer has anything to do with the *esse* that Saint Thomas assigns to the Christian God. So my thesis does not oppose but, rather, confirms the antagonism between the Thomistic *esse* and the "Being" of nihilism by disqualifying the claim of the latter to think God.[6] On the other hand, we have Being such as Heidegger understands it, as a phenomenological horizon, and then as *Ereignis;* in both cases, the enthusiastic naïveté of the beginnings has largely given way, among the theologians, to great caution: Heidegger could indeed run the risk of a gnostic drift, even of an "ontologist" idolatry, whose famous "God alone who can save us" bears all the ambiguities. Within this perspective, *God Without Being* would offer a warning against a danger that is still to come, but already threatening for Christian faith.

Hence the second argument. In supposing (as certain passages in this book indisputably suggest) that it is necessary to liberate God from *esse* in the very sense that Saint Thomas understood it, this conflict would still have to be resituated within the wider theological debate of the divine names. Historically, in the tradition of Denys's treatise *On Divine Names* and its commentaries, Saint Thomas certainly marks a rupture: contrary to most of his predecessors (including Saint Bonaventure), as well as to several of his successors (including Duns Scotus), he substitues *esse* for the good (*bonum, summum bonum*) as the first divine name. This intitiative is not self-evident. In order to confirm it, we must first locate and meditate on it, which is what I attempted by sketching the path that Saint Thomas did *not* take and by stressing that that path also offers a solution. One last argument follows from this: even when he thinks God as *esse,* Saint Thomas nevertheless does not chain God either to Being or to metaphysics.

He does not chain God to Being because the divine *esse* immeasurably surpasses (and hardly maintains an *analogia* with) the *ens commune* of creatures, which are characterized by the real distinction between *esse* and their essence, whereas God, and He alone, absolutely merges essence with *esse:* God is expressed as *esse,* but this *esse* is expressed only of God, not of the beings of metaphysics. In *this* sense, Being does not erect an idol before God, but saves his distance.

Saint Thomas doesn't chain God to metaphysics either, since he explicitly stresses that "res divinae non tractantur a philosophis, nisi prout sunt rerum omnium principia": divine things do not belong to metaphysics as one of its objects; rather, they only intervene in metaphysics indirectly in the capacity of principles for its objects, "non tanquam subjectum scientiae, sed tanquam principia subjecti."[7] Between metaphysics (with its domain, common Being) and God, the relation, even and especially for Saint Thomas, has to do not with inclusion but with subordination: God, as principle, subjugates the subjects of philosophy to himself. Consequently, since the subjects of philosophy belong to Being, we must go so far as to conclude that their cause, God, also causes Being itself: "Deus est causa universalis totius esse."[8] But if God causes Being, wouldn't we have to admit that, for Saint Thomas himself, God can be expressed without Being? At the very least, we should have to grant that Thomism does not amount to the identification of the *esse commune* with God, and that, if *esse* characterizes God in Thomism, *esse* itself must be understood divinely, thus having no common measure with what Being can signify in metaphysics—and especially in the onto-theo-logy of modern metaphysics.

These debates, animated as they may have been, nevertheless do not get at the heart of the question, where something entirely different is at stake: can the conceptual thought of God (conceptual, or rational, and not intuitive or "mystical" in the vulgar sense) be developed outside of the doctrine of Being (in the metaphysical sense, or even in the nonmetaphysical sense)? Does God give himself to be known according to the horizon of Being or according to a more radical horizon? *God Without Being* barely sketches an answer, but does sketch it: God gives Himself to be known insofar as He gives Himself—according to the horizon of the gift itself. The gift constitutes at once the mode and the body of his revelation. In the end the gift gives only itself, but in this way it gives absolutely everything. The approach and reception of the gift are only described here with difficulty. First in a negative way: the experience of vanity indicates that even that which is finds itself disqualified as if it were not, so long as it does not have added to its status as a being the dignity of that which finds itself loved. Next in a dogmatic way: I attempt a pure and simple description of two emblematic figures of the gift, which Christian theology offers without being able or having to justify them—the Eucharist and the confession of faith. We describe these as two facts that are absolutely irreducible to Being and to its logic, facts that are only intelligible in terms of the gift. In conclusion, *agape* appears only as a pure given, with neither deduction nor legitimation. But in this way the given appears all the more as a given.

To give pure giving to be thought—that, in retrospect it seems to me, is what is at stake in *God Without Being*. It is also the task of my future work and, I expect, of the work of many others.

Paris
January 1991

J. L. M.

ENVOI

One must admit that theology, of all writing, certainly causes the greatest pleasure. Precisely not the pleasure of the text, but the pleasure—unless it have to do with a joy—of transgressing it: from words to the Word, from the Word to words, incessantly and in theology alone, since there alone the Word finds in the words nothing less than a body. The body of the text does not belong to the text, but to the One who is embodied in it. Thus, theological writing always transgresses itself, just as theological speech feeds on the silence in which, at last, it speaks correctly. In other words, to try one's hand at theology requires no other justification than the extreme pleasure of writing. The only limit to this pleasure, in fact, is in the condition of its exercise; for the play from words to the Word implies that theological writing is played in distance, which unites as well as separates the man writing and the Word at hand—the Christ. Theology always writes starting from an other than itself. It diverts the author from himself (thus one can indeed speak of a diversion from philosophy with all good theology); it causes him to write outside of himself, even against himself, since he must write not of what he is, on what he knows, in view of what he wants, but in, for, and by that which he receives and in no case masters. Theology renders its author hypocritical in at least two ways. Hypocritical, in the common sense: in pretending to speak of holy things—"holy things to the holy"—he cannot but find himself, to the point of vertigo, unworthy, impure—in a word, vile. This experience, however, is so necessary that its beneficiary knows better than anyone both his own unworthiness and the meaning of that weakness (the light that unveils it); he deceives himself less than anyone; in fact, here there is no hypocrisy at all: the author knows more than any accuser. He remains hypocritical in another, more paradoxical sense: if authenticity (remembered with horror) consists in speaking of oneself, and in saying only that for which one can answer, no one, in a theological discourse, can, *or should,* pretend to it. For theology consists precisely in saying that for which only another can answer—the Other above all, the Christ who himself does not speak in his own name, but in the name of his Father. Indeed, theological discourse offers its strange jubilation only to the strict extent that it permits and, dangerously, demands of its workman that he speak beyond his means, precisely because he does not speak of himself. Hence the danger of a speech that, in a sense, speaks against the one who lends himself to it. One must obtain forgiveness for every essay in theology. In all senses.

It will be necessary, however, to justify a few points in what follows. Under the title *God Without Being* we do not mean to insinuate that God is not, or that God is not truly God. We attempt to meditate on what F. W. Schelling called "the freedom of God with regard to his own existence."[1] Put a different way, we attempt to render problematic that which seems obvious, about which the philosophers descending from metaphysics agree with the theologians descending from Neo-Thomism: God, before all else, has to be. Which means at one and the same time that before other beings, he would have to be, and that before every other initiative, he would have also to take that of being. But does Being relate, more than anything, to God? Does God have anything to gain by being? Can Being—which whatever is, provided that it is, manifests—even accommodate any(thing of) God? Just to approach this question, to render it conceivable and audible, one must treat Being starting from that instance which provokes all bedazzlements and

makes them appear insurmountable, the idol. Thus we attem
first to contrast the idol and the icon, one reinforcing the oth
in a common antagonism, in order to advance to Being—the
name of God that in theology is assumed to be the first, just as
in philosophy God, as first being, supposedly invests Being.[2]
For as soon as Being itself acts as an idol, it becomes thinkable
to release oneself from it—to suspend it. Hence, without
Being, the two new instances where an opening to God is destined: vanity and, conversely, charity. And what if God did not
have first to be, since he loved us first, when we were not? And
what if, to envisage him, we did not have to wait for him within
the horizon of Being, but rather trangress ourselves in risking
to love love—bare, raw. As love, however, remains essentially
inaccessible to us, the suspension that delivers God from Being
becomes feasible for us only in its negative aspect—the vanity
that melancholy pours over the world of beings. Hence Dürer.
Hence the experimental rigor to which we aspire here for charity—for love: even he who does not love experiences more
than nothing in this disaster; he experiences vanity through
melancholy. He experiences the irreducibility of love, by default. In short, melancholy opens (to) distance.

Because God does not fall within the domain of Being, he
comes to us in and as a gift. "God who is not, but who saves the
gift";[3] the poet speaks correctly, with one slight reservation:
God saves the gift precisely inasmuch as he is not, and does not
have to be. For the gift does not have first to be, but to pour out
in an abandon that, alone, causes it to be; God saves the gift in
giving it before being. The horizon that Being clears by its retreat opens on the gift, or, negatively, on vanity. The highest
question becomes love or, what amounts to the same thing,
charity. It long remains before us, unquestioned and redoubtable.

Where, however, does this lead? Obviously, love is made
more than it is analyzed. One way of proceeding, as far as God
is concerned, stems from the Eucharist: in it the Word leaves
the text to be made flesh. *Outside the text*[4] indicates less an
addition than a deliverance, or rather a final *corps-à-corps,*
where love makes the body (rather than the reverse). The Eu-

charastic gift consists in the fact that in it love forms one body with our body. And if the Word is also made body, surely we, in our body, can speak the Word. The extreme rigor of charity restores us to speech that is finally not silent.

The book that follows I wrote in solitude, but not alone. All these texts result from questions, debates, and lectures, all for particular circumstances (literally—surrounded by others); they owe to those who occasioned them their unity, their objectivity, and, I hope, their rigor. I am therefore perfectly aware of returning here—with slight editing—what was given to me—in the mode of inquiry. There again, the gift preceded the fact of being. I want to acknowledge my debt to the insistence of Maurice Clavel in making me attack head-on the great struggle of Being with the cross. What follows constitutes a way of keeping my promise without truly fulfilling its vows. I would like also to recognize, among many others, two friends without whom this book—and many other things as well—would not have seen the light of the day, Jean Duchesne and Robert Toussaint. As for Rémi Brague, who, with his philological probity, preferred to correct our proofs rather than suffer by finding too many errors, I offer him all my gratitude. The insufficiencies are my own, and I, more than others, am aware of them.

Paris, March 25, 1982

God Without Being

1

THE IDOL AND THE ICON

That the idol can be approached only in the antagonism that infallibly unites it with the icon is certainly unnecessary to argue. The two concepts most certainly belong to two distinct, and in many ways competing, historical moments: *eidōlon* presupposes the Greek splendor of the visible, whose polychromy gives rise to the polysemy of the divine, whereas *eikōn,* renewed from the Hebrew by the New Testament and theorized by patristic and Byzantine thought, concentrates—and with it the brilliance of the visible—on the sole figure of the one whom Hölderlin named *Der Einzige,* The Only One, only by comparing and finally integrating him with Dionysus and Heracles. But such a conflict unfolds in a dimension far more essential than any possible polemic between "pagan art" and "Christian art"; rather, this very formulation covers (and dissimulates in rendering banal) a much more essential issue. For the historical succession of two models of "art" permits one to disclose a phenomenological conflict—a conflict between two phenomenologies. The idol does not indicate, any more than the icon, a particular being or even class of beings. Icon and idol indicate a manner of being for beings, or at least for some of them. Indeed, a determination that would limit itself to opposing the "true God" (icon) to the "false gods," in extending the polemic of the vetero-testamentary prophets, would not be suitable here. For the Christian iconoclasts of the eighth century gave the name "idol" to that which had been conceived and venerated as icon of the true God, and the Jews of the Old Covenant rejected all representation as idolatrous, even representation of the God of the Covenant (the "Golden Calf," it has been argued, perhaps only personalized the God of the Covenant, and the very Temple of Jerusalem could have been deserted by the divine *Shekinah* only insofar as it foundered in idolatry). Fortunately, every effort to take seriously the destinal momentum (*Geschick*) and initial support of Greece implies that a more receptive interpretation dismisses the accusation of pure and simple idolatry, and tries—in vain or successfully, it hardly matters here—to acknowledge the authentically divine dignity of that which, in the monuments of that age, offers itself for veneration (Hegel, Schelling, Hölderlin). In short, the icon and the idol are not at all determined as beings against other beings, since the same beings (statues, names, etc.) can pass from one rank to the other. The icon and the idol determine two manners of being for beings, not two classes of beings.

Their interference thus becomes all the more problematic and seems to demand attention all the more urgently. But, one can rightly object, even if certain beings can pass from the idol to the icon, or from the icon to the idol, only changing thus in status when venerated, not every being is able to do so: indeed, not just any being can give rise to, still less demand, veneration. Even if the number of those that demand veneration and the mode of that veneration vary, all admit nevertheless to certain common, minimal characteristics: it is a question of *signa* concerning the divine.

Signa: the Latin term means much here. The only works that can pretend to the contradictory status of idol and/or icon are those that art has so worked that they no longer restrict their visibility to themselves (as in what are so rightly called the "pleasurable arts" [*arts d'agrément*]), but, as such and by thus remaining absolutely immanent in themselves, that they signal indissolubly toward another, still undetermined term. More specifically, this referral does not signal toward another instance than that which the work of art itself constitutes, coming to overdetermine the work from the outside by some "symbolic value"; on the contrary, this referral constitutes the most essential dignity of the work. The work appears as such only in signaling, because it is only in signaling that the work has the value of a *signum.* One thus would have to interrogate the *signa* concerning their mode of signaling, suspecting that the idol and the icon are distinguishable only inasmuch as they signal in different ways, that is, inasmuch as each makes use of its visibility in its own way. The diversity of these ways for signaling and becoming *signa* no doubt, however, decides everything between the idol and the icon.

Signa, but also concerning the divine: without even pretending to approach the most extreme difficulty (would the being that accedes to visibility only as *signum* be able to signal a referent other than the divine itself and itself alone?), one must at least note that the divine comes into play here only with the support of visibility. But in having to do with the divine, visibility is expressed in several manners. Or rather, variations in the mode of visibility indicate variations in the mode of apprehension of the divine itself. The same mode of visibility would not suit just any figure of the divine, but maintains with the divine a rigorous and undoubtedly constitutive relation: the manner of seeing decides what can be seen, or, at least negatively, decides what in any case could not be perceived of the divine.

In outlining the comparative phenomenology of the idol and the icon, it is therefore a question of specifying not any particular matter of aesthetics or art history, but two modes of apprehension of the divine in visibility. Of apprehension, or also, no doubt, of reception.

1—First Visible

The idol never deserves to be denounced as illusory since, by definition, it is seen—*eidōlon,* that which is seen (**eidō, video*). It even consists only in the fact that it can be seen, that one cannot but see it. And see it so visibly that the very fact of seeing it suffices to know it—*eidōlon,* that which is known by the fact that one has seen it (*oïda*). The idol presents itself to man's gaze in order that representation, and hence knowledge, can seize hold of it. The idol is erected there only so that one see it: the monumental statue of Athena shone from the Acropolis to the gaze of the sailors of the Piraeus, and if the darkness of a *naos* shaded the chryselephantine statue, it followed that in order to divine it, the worshiper experienced that much more of its fascination when, approaching, he could finally lift his eyes to it. The idol fascinates and captivates the gaze precisely because everything in it must expose itself to the gaze, attract, fill, and hold it. The domain where it reigns undividedly—the domain of the gaze, hence of the gazeable [*regardable*]—suffices as well for reception: it captivates the gaze only inasmuch as the gazeable comprises it. The idol depends on the gaze that it satisfies, since if the gaze did not desire to satisfy itself in the idol, the idol would have no dignity for it. The most common criticism of the idol asks with amazement how one can adore as a divinity that which the hands that pray have just forged, sculpted, decorated—in a word, fabricated. "Delivered from idols," Claudel acknowledges in the idol no more than the aberration of "the savage who builds himself a canoe and who with the one superfluous board fabricates Apollo."[1] This criticism, however, misses the essential: for the fabricated thing becomes an idol, that of a god, only from the moment when the gaze has decided to fall on it, has made of it the privileged fixed point of its own consideration; and that the fabricated thing exhausts the gaze presupposes that this thing is itself exhausted in the gazeable. The decisive moment in the erection of an idol stems not from its fabrication, but from its investment as gazeable, as that which will fill a gaze. That which characterizes the idol stems from the gaze. It dazzles with visibility only inasmuch as the gaze looks on it with consideration. It draws the gaze only inasmuch as the gaze has drawn it whole into the gazeable and there exposes and exhausts it. The gaze alone makes the idol, as the ultimate function of the gazeable.

Since the gaze alone characterizes the idol, how are we to understand the multiplicity of idols, their variable validities, their contingent figures, their disparate dignities? The gaze makes the idol, not the idol the gaze—which means that the idol with its visibility fills the intention of the gaze, which wants nothing other than to see. The gaze precedes the idol because an aim precedes and gives rise to that at which it aims. The first intention aims at the divine and the gaze strains itself to see the divine, to see it by taking it up into the field of the gazeable. The more powerfully the aim is deployed, the longer it sustains itself, the richer, more extensive, and more sumptuous will appear the idol on which it will stop its gaze. To stop the gaze: we could not do better than to say, to stop a gaze, allow it to rest (itself) in/on an idol, when it can no longer pass beyond.[2] In this stop, the gaze ceases to overshoot and transpierce itself, hence it ceases to transpierce visible things, in order to pause in the splendor of one of them. No longer transpiercing itself, the gaze no longer pierces things, no longer sees them in transparency; at a certain point, it no longer experiences things as transparent—insufficiently weighted down by light and glory—and a last one finally presents itself as visible, splendid, and luminous enough to be the first to attract, capture, and fill it. This first visible will offer, for each gaze and in the measure of its scope, its idol. Idol—or the gaze's landing place.[3] What, then, does the idol indicate?

2—Invisible Mirror

Before presenting the idol's characteristic visibility and its intrinsic meaning, one must interpret its very appearance. When the idol appears, the gaze has just stopped: the idol concretizes that stop. Before the idol, the gaze transparently transpierced the visible. To be exact, the gaze did not see the visible, since it did not cease to transpierce it—to transpierce it piercingly. In each visible spectacle, the gaze found nothing that might stop it; the gaze's fiery eyes consumed the visible so that each time the gaze saw nothing.[4]

But here the idol intervenes. What shows up? For the first (and last) time, the gaze no longer rushes through the spectacle stage without stopping, but forms a stage in the spectacle; it is fixed in it and, far from passing beyond, remains facing what becomes for it a spectacle to *re*-spect. The gaze lets itself be filled: instead of outflanking the visible, of not seeing it and rendering it invisible, the gaze discovers itself as outflanked, contained, held back by the visible. The visible finally becomes visible to the gaze because, again literally, the visible dazzles the gaze. The idol, the first visible, from the beginning, dazzles a gaze until then insatiable. The idol offers to, or rather imposes on, the gaze, its first visible—whatever it may be, thing, man, woman, idea, or god. But consequently, if in the idol the gaze sees its first visible, it discovers in it, more than just any spectacle, its own limit and proper place. As an obstacle to a transmitter sends back waves and indicates the transmitter's location in relation to that obstacle, the idol returns the gaze to itself, indicating to it how many beings, before the idol, it has transpierced, thus also at what level is situated that which for its aim stands as first visible above all. The idol thus acts as a mirror, not as a portrait: a mirror that reflects the gaze's image, or more exactly, the image of its aim and of the scope of that aim. The idol, as a function of the gaze, reflects the gaze's scope. But the idol does not at once manifest its role and status as mirror. For the idol, precisely because it fixes upon itself the light and the scope of the gaze, shines immediately with a brilliance by definition equal (at least) to what this gaze can see; since the idol fills the gaze, it saturates it with visibility, hence dazzles it; the mirror function obscures itself precisely by virtue of the spectacle function. The idol masks the mirror because it fills the gaze. The mirror lets its function be obfuscated by the glare of the gazeable, which is finally visible. Because it offers to the gaze its first visible, the idol itself remains an invisible mirror. That the mirror remains invisible, since the visible dazzles the gaze, makes it so that the idolater never dupes, nor finds himself duped: he only remains—ravished.

The idol, as invisible mirror, gives the gaze its stopping point and measures out its scope. But the idol would not fix any gazeable object if the gaze by itself did not first freeze. The divine, like the sun that Valéry evokes (in an involuntary echo of Aristotle), can be fixed in a thousand and one idols, where its splendor is visibly reflected:

> Yes, gigantic sea delirium-dowered,
> Panther-hide, and chlamys filled with holes
> By thousands of the sun's dazzling idols . . . [5]

But, in order for an idol to appear and, fixedly, draw the attention of a gaze, the reflection of a stable mirror must accommodate it. Instead of the gaze floating along unstable waves of "the sea, the sea perpetually renewed,"[6] it must present itself in a mirror, a gaze as mortally immobile as coagulated blood: "The sun drowned in its blood which coagulates" (Baudelaire).[7] In order that the idol may fix it, the gaze must first freeze. Thus the invisible mirror that the first visible offers it does not only indicate to the gaze how far its most distant aim extends, but even what its aim could not have in view. When the gaze freezes, its aim settles (in the sense that when a wine settles it attains maturity), and hence the not-aimed-at disappears. If the idolatrous gaze exercises no criticism of its idol, this is because it no longer has the means to do so: its aim culminates in a position that the idol immediately occupies, and where every aim is exhausted. But that which renders a gaze idolatrous could not, at least at first, arise from an ethical choice: it reveals a sort of essential fatigue. The gaze settles only inasmuch as it rests—from the weight of upholding the sight of an aim without term, rest, or end: "to sleep with the sleep of the earth." With the first visible and the invisible mirror, the idol offers the gaze its earth—the first earth upon which to rest. In the idol, the gaze is buried. The idol would be disqualified thus, vis-à-vis a revelation, not at all because it would offer the gaze an illegitimate spectacle, but first because it suggests to the gaze where to rest (itself). With the idol, the invisible mirror admits no beyond, because the gaze cannot raise the sight of its aim. The invisible mirror thus marks, negatively, the shortcoming of the aim—literally, the *invisable*.[8] The visible begins where the aim stops. The invisible mirror is concealed in the first visible, which thus marks the *invisable*. The idol allows no invisible, first because it conceals its function as invisible mirror, in the brilliance of its light, and then because, beyond it, even more than the invisible, the *invisable* opens, or rather closes up. For an invisible would imply first that a yet obscure aim stretches toward it in order to open it.

Consequently, the genuineness and the limits of the idol can be defined: in the idol, the divine actually comes into the visi-

ity for which human gazes watch; but this advent is mea-
ed by what the scope of particular human eyes can support, by what each aim can require of visibility in order to admit itself fulfilled. In short, the advent of the divine is fixed in an idol only if the human gaze is frozen and, thus, opens the site of a temple. The idol is measurable by the *templum,* which, in the heavens, the gaze of man each time delimits to its own measure—"deus is, cujus templum est omne id quod conspicis"—"that God, whose temple is everything that you see."[9] That god whose space of manifestation is measured by what portion of it a gaze can bear—precisely, an idol.

3—Dazzling Return

Thus the idol consigns the divine to the measure of a human gaze. Invisible mirror, mark of the *invisable,* it must be apprehended following its function and evaluated according to the scope of that function. Only then does it become legitimate to ask what the material figure given to the idol by human art represents, what it resembles. The answer is that it represents nothing, but presents a certain low-water mark of the divine; it resembles what the human gaze has experienced of the divine. The idol, such as any archaic *kouros,* obviously does not claim to reproduce any particular god, since the idol offers the only materially visible original of it. But consigned to the stone material is what a gaze—that of the artist as religious man, penetrated by god—has seen of the god; the first visible was able to dazzle his gaze, and this is what the artist tries to bring out in his material: he wants to fix in stone, strictly to solidify, an ultimate visible, worthy of the point where his gaze froze. Rock, wood, gold, or whatever, tries to occupy with a fixed figure the place marked by the frozen gaze. Terrorizing as much as ravishing, the emotion that froze the gaze would have to invest the stone as it invested the gaze of the religious artist. Thus the spectator, provided that his attitude become religious, will find in the materially fixed idol the brilliance of the first visible whose splendor freezes the gaze. That his attitude should become religious means that, to the brilliance fixed by the material idol, the scope of his gaze exactly corresponds, and hence his gaze, with that brilliance, will receive the first splendor that might stop, fill, and freeze it. The idol consigns and conserves in its material the brilliance where a gaze froze, in the expectation that other eyes will acknowledge the brilliance of a first visible that freezes them in their ultimate scope. The idol serves as a materially fixed relay between different brilliancies produced by the same first visible; it becomes the concrete history of the god and the memory of it that men do or do not keep. For this very reason, no one, not even a modern of the age of distress, remains sheltered from an idol, be he idolatrous or not: in order for the idol to reach him it is sufficient that he recognize, fixed upon the face of a statute, the splendid brilliance of the first visible where, one day, his gaze was frozen in its scope. Robert Walser recorded this threat and described this invasion of the divine with quasi-clinical precision in an unforgettable prose poem.[10] Because the idol allows the divine to occur only in man's measure, man can consign the idolatrous experience to art and thus keep it accessible, if not to all and at all times, at least to the worshipers of the god, and as long as the gods have not fled. Art no more produces the idol than the idol produces the gaze. The gaze, by freezing, marks the place where the first visible bursts in its splendor; art attempts, then, to consign materially, on a second level, and by what one habitually calls an idol, the brilliance of the god. That only this brilliance should merit the name of idol is proved by the necessity, in order to recognize this brilliance on the material face, of a corresponding gaze, hence also of a gaze whose aim settles and freezes with such a first visible. In short, the fact that idols do not coincide with their pure and simple statues is proved by the ease with which we desert idolatry, when our gaze takes off from work, visiting a particular temple or museum—to the extent that these visits lack the aim whose expectation could let itself be fulfilled and hence frozen, the signs of stone and color must wait, as mute gazes, for some animated eyes to reach them and be dazzled once again by the still-confined brilliance. Often we do not have, or no longer have, the means for such a splendid idolatry.

4—Conceptual Idol

If we occidentals, dated (and endowed) by the completion of metaphysics, lack the aesthetic means to grasp the idol, others remain or even open up for us. Thus the concept. The concept consigns to a sign what at first the mind grasps with it (*concipere, capere*); but such a grasp is measured not so much by the amplitude of the divine as by the scope of a *capacitas,* which can fix the divine in a specific concept only at the moment when a conception of the divine fills it, hence appeases, stops, and freezes it. When a philosophical thought expresses a concept of what it then names "God," this concept functions exactly as an idol. It gives itself to be seen, but thus all the better conceals itself as the mirror where thought, invisibly, has its forward point fixed, so that the *invisable* finds itself, with an aim suspended by the fixed concept, disqualified and abandoned; thought freezes, and the idolatrous concept of "God" appears, where, more than God, thought judges itself. The conceptual idols of metaphysics culminate in the *causa sui* (as Heidegger indicates)[11] only insofar as the figures of onto-theo-logy have all undertaken to consign to a concept the ultimate low-water mark of their advance toward the divine (Plato, Aristotle), and after that toward the Christian God: thus the conceptual idol of the "*moralischer Gott,* the God of 'morality'" (Heidegger)[12] limits the horizon of the grasp of God by Kant—"the presupposition of a moral author of the world"[13]—just as it does that of the "death of God," since, by the very admission of Nietzsche himself, "Im Grunde ist ja nur der moralische Gott überwunden, At bottom it is only the moral God that has been overcome."[14] In both cases, in that of theism as in that of so-called "atheism," the measure of the concept comes not from God but from the aim of the gaze. So here also Feuerbach's judgement stands: "it is *man* who is the *original model* of his idol."[15] Perhaps we could then glimpse why it belongs constitutively to the idol to prepare its twilight. We could have experienced this twilight twice: first aesthetically, once the oracles were silenced, in the period when the brilliance of the Enlightenment obfuscated that of the *signa* forged by hand; and today, when in the black sun of nihilism we seem delivered, or simply deprived and disinherited, "of books and of Ideas, of Idols and of their priests."[16]

5—Icon of the Invisible

The icon does not result from a vision but provokes one. The icon is not seen, but appears, or more originally seems, looks like, in the sense that, in Homer, Priam is stupefied by Achilles, *hossos eēn hoios te; theoisi gar anta eōkei (Iliad* 24:630): Achilles is not counted among the gods, but he seems like a god, like the semblance of a god. In him, so to speak, something characteristic of the gods rises to visibility, though precisely no god is thus fixed in the visible. Whereas the idol results from the gaze that aims at it, the icon summons sight in letting the visible (here, Achilles) be saturated little by little with the invisible. The invisible seems, it appears in a semblance (**eikō/*eoika*)[17] which, however, never reduces the invisible to the slackened wave of the visible. Far from the visible advancing in search of the invisible, like quarry not—yet—seen, which the gaze would flush out, one would say rather that the invisible proceeds up into the visible, precisely because the visible would proceed from the invisible. Or even, not the visible discerning [*discernant*] between itself and the invisible, hemming in [*cerner*] and reducing it, but the invisible bestowing [*décernant*] the visible, in order thus to deduce the visible from itself and to allow itself to appear there. In this sense, the formula that Saint Paul applies to Christ, *eikōn tou theou tou aoratou,* icon of the invisible God (Col. 1:15), must serve as our norm; it even must be generalized to every icon, as, indeed, John of Damascus explicitly ventures: *pasa eikōn ekphantorikē tou kruphiou kai deiktikē.*[18] For what is said here of Christ and of God must be understood for every icon (unless this should be the inverse, as we will see)—icon not of the visible, but indeed of the invisible. Hence this implies that, even presented by the icon, the invisible always remains invisible; it is not invisible because it is omitted by the aim (*invisable*), but because it is a matter of rendering visible this invisible as such—the unenvisageable. That the invisible should remain invisible or that it should become visible amounts to the same thing, namely, to the idol, whose precise function consists in dividing the invisible into one part that is reduced to the visible and one part that is obfuscated as *invisable*. The icon, on the contrary, attempts to render visible the invisible as such, hence to allow that the visible not cease to refer to an other than itself, without, however, that other ever being reproduced in the visible. Thus the icon shows, strictly speaking, nothing, not even in the mode of the productive *Einbildung*. It teaches the gaze, thus does not cease to correct it in order that it go back from visible to visible as far as the end of infinity, to find in infinity something new. The icon summons the gaze to surpass itself by never freezing on a visible, since the visible only presents itself here in view of the invisible. The gaze can never rest or settle if it looks at an icon; it always must rebound upon the visible, in order to go back in it up the infinite stream of the invisible. In this sense, the icon makes visible only by giving rise to an infinite gaze.

6—The Face Envisages

But what does it mean to render visible the invisible as such? Unless the concept of the icon simply fails, is this not just a great deal of verbal clatter taking the place of a concept? The invisible as such could not render itself visible; no doubt if the invisible and, above all, the divinity of the gods or of God are understood in (metaphysical) terms of *ousia:* either *ousia* becomes visible (sensible, intelligible—which for our purposes are one) or it does not, and the idol, which itself produces the dichotomy, can decide. It remains that *ousia,* at least for theology, does not exhaust what can occur. Indeed, the conciliar definition, definitively confirming the theological status of the icon, bases the icon on *hupostasis:* "He who venerates the icon venerates in it the hypostasis of the one who is inscribed in it."[19] Reverence conveyed to the icon concerns in it the hypostasis of the one from whom the traced face arises. *Hupostasis,* which the Latin Fathers translate by *persona,* does not imply any substantial presence, circumscribed in the icon as in its *hupokeimenon* (and this as opposed to the substantial presence of Christ in the Eucharist); the *persona* attested its presence only by that which itself most properly characterizes it, the aim of an intention (*stokhasma*) that a gaze sets in operation. The icon lays out the material of wood and paint in such a way that there appears in them the intention of a transpiercing gaze emanating from them. But, a superficial listener may object, in defining the icon by the aim of an intention, hence by a gaze, do we not rediscover exactly the terms of the definition of the idol? Absolutely, but in a nearly perfect inversion: the gaze no longer belongs here to the man who aims as far as the first visible, less yet to an artist; such a gaze here belongs to the icon itself, where the invisible only becomes visible intentionally, hence by its aim. If man, by his gaze, renders the idol possible, in reverent contemplation of the icon, on the contrary, the gaze of the invisible, in person, aims at man. The icon regards us—it *concerns* us, in that it allows the intention of the invisible to occur visibly. Moreover, if man's gaze envisages the blind side of the first visible, or of its material consignment in the icon, he who sees it sees in it a face whose invisible intention envisages him. The icon opens in a face, where man's sight envisages nothing, but goes back infinitely from the visible to the invisible by the grace of the visible itself: instead of the invisible mirror, which sent the human gaze back to itself alone and censured the *invisable,* the icon opens in a face that gazes at our gazes in order to summon them to its depth. One even must venture to state that only the icon shows us a face (in other words, that every face is given as an icon). For a face appears only inasmuch as the perfect and polished opacity of a mirror does not close it; that a face closes up implies nothing but its enclosure in a radiant mirror: precisely, nothing closes a face by a mask more than a radiant smile. The icon alone offers an open face, because it opens in itself the visible onto the invisible, by offering its spectacle to be transgressed—not to be seen, but to be venerated. The reference from the perceived visible to the invisible person summons one to travel through the (invisible) mirror, and to enter, so to speak, into the eyes of the icon—if the eyes have that strange property of transforming the visible and the invisible into each other. To the invisible mirror where the gaze freezes succeeds the opening of a face where the human gaze is engulfed, invited to see the invisible.

The human gaze, far from fixing the divine in a *figmentum* as frozen as itself, does not cease, envisaged by the icon, there to watch the tide of the invisible come in, slack on immense visible shores. In the idol, the gaze of man is frozen in its mirror; in the icon, the gaze of man is lost in the invisible gaze that visibly envisages him.

7—Visible Mirror of the Invisible

The possibility of rendering visible the invisible as such now becomes conceivable: in the idol, the reflex of the mirror distinguishes the visible from that which exceeds the aim, the invisible because *invisable;* in the icon, the visible is deepened infinitely in order to accompany, as one may say, each point of the invisible by a point of light. But visible and invisible thus coexist to infinity only insofar as the invisible is not opposed to the visible, since it consists only of an intention. The invisible of the icon consists of the intention of the face. The more the face becomes visible, the more the invisible intention whose gaze envisages us becomes visible. Better: the visibility of the face allows the invisibility that envisages to grow. Only its depth, that of a face that opens to envisage, permits the icon to join the visible with the invisible, and this depth is joined itself with the intention. But the intention here issues from infinity; hence it implies that the icon allows itself to be traversed by an infinite depth. However, whereas the idol is always determined as a reflex, which allows it to come from a fixed point, an original from which, fundamentally, it returns (the idol as specter, *un revenant—Gespenst* indeed covers certain uses of *eidōlon*)—the icon is defined by an origin without original: an origin itself infinite, which pours itself out or gives itself throughout the infinite depth of the icon. This is why its depth withdraws the icon from all aesthetics: only the idol can and must be apprehended, since it alone results from the human gaze and hence supposes an *aisthesis* that precisely imposes its measure on the idol. The icon can be measured only on the basis of the infinite depth of the face; the intention that envisages in this manner depends only on itself—for *aisthesis* is substituted an apocalypse: the invisible disengages itself in the visible, along an intention, only by the pure grace of an ad the heavens can be rent only of themselves, for the face t[illegible] scend from them (Isa. 63:19). The icon recognizes no other measure than its own and infinite excessiveness [*démesure*]; whereas the idol measures the divine to the scope of the gaze of he who then sculpts it, the icon accords in the visible only a face whose invisibility is given all the more to be envisaged that its revelation offers an abyss that the eyes of men never finish probing. It is, moreover, in this sense that the icon comes to us from elsewhere: certainly not that it should be a question of recognizing the empirical validity of an icon "not made by the hands of men" but indeed of seeing that *ackeiropoiēsis* in some way results necessarily from the infinite depth that refers the icon back to its origin, or that characterizes the icon as this infinite reference to the origin. What characterizes the material idol is precisely that the artist can consign to it the subjugating brilliance of a first visible; on the contrary, what characterizes the icon painted on wood does not come from the hand of a man but from the infinite depth that crosses it—or better, orients it following the intention of a gaze. The essential in the icon—the intention that envisages—comes to it from elsewhere, or comes to it as that elsewhere whose invisible strangeness saturates the visibility of the face with meaning. In return, to see, or to contemplate, the icon merely consists in traversing the depth that surfaces in the visibility of the face, in order to respond to the apocalypse where the invisible is made visible through a hermeneutic that can read in the visible the intention of the invisible. Contemplating the icon amounts to seeing the visible in the very manner by which the invisible that imparts itself therein envisages the visible—strictly, to exchanging our gaze for the gaze that iconistically envisages us. Thus, the accomplishment of the icon inverts, with a counfounding phenomenological precision, the essential moments of the idol. As an astonishing sequence from Saint Paul shows: "We all, with face unveiled and revealed [*anakekalummenō prosōpō*], serving as optical mirror to reflect [*katoptrizomenoi*] the glory of the Lord, we are transformed in and according to his icon [*eikona*], passing from glory to glory, according to the spirit of the Lord" (2 Cor. 3:18). It seems practically useless (and impossible as well) even to outline a commentary. Let us briefly point out the reversal: here our gaze does not designate by its aim the spectacle of a first visible, since, inversely, in the vision, no visible is discovered, if not our face itself, which, renouncing all grasping (*aisthesis*) submits to an apocalyptic exposure; it becomes itself visibly laid out in the open. Why? Because, as opposed to the idol that is offered in an invisible mirror—invisible because dazzled as much as dazzling for and by our aim—here our gaze becomes the optical mirror of that at which it looks only by finding itself more radically looked at: we become a visible mirror of an invisible gaze that subverts us in the measure of its glory. The invisible summons us, "face to face, person to person" (1 Cor. 13:12), through the painted visibility of its incarnation and the factual visibility of our flesh: no longer the visible idol as the invisible mirror of our gaze, but our face as the visible mirror of the invisible. Thus, as opposed to the idol which delimited the low-water mark of our aim, the icon displaces the limits of our visibility to the measure of its own—its glory. It transforms us in its glory by allowing this glory to shine on our face as its mirror—but a mirror consumed by that very glory, transfigured with invisibility, and, by dint of being saturated beyond itself from that glory, becoming, strictly though imperfectly, the icon of it: visibility of the invisible as such.[20]

8—The Icon in the Concept

Holding its qualification only from the distance of infinite depth, the icon is not the concern, any more than is the idol that here at least it confirms, of the artistic domain. The painter presents one of the possible media—the perceptible—to the opening of a face, just as the sculptor, who consigns to stone the brilliance of the god—the first visible—mobilizes the memory by a perceptible medium. But, as the idol can exercise its measure of the divine by concept, since the gaze as well can invisibly reflect its own aim and in it dismiss the *invisable,* the icon also can proceed conceptually, provided at least that the concept renounce comprehending the incomprehensible, to ...mpt to conceive it, hence also to receive it, in its own excessiveness. But precisely, *can* such concepts be conceived? The only concept that can serve as an intelligible medium for the icon is one that lets itself be measured by the excessiveness of the invisible that enters into visibility through infinite depth, hence that itself speaks or promises to speak this infinite depth, where the visible and the invisible become acquainted. When Descartes establishes that the *idea Dei* would be given as *idea infiniti,* and that this "ut sit vera nullo modo debet comprehendi, quoniam ipsa incomprehensibilitas in ratione formali infiniti continetur,"[21] he indicates a path that is at least similar: the icon obliges the concept to welcome the distance of infinite depth; obviously this distance is valid only as infinite, hence indeterminable by concept; however, it is not a question of using a concept to determine an essence but of using it to determine an intention—that of the invisible advancing into the visible and inscribing itself therein by the very reference it imposes from this visible to the invisible. The hermeneutic of the icon meant: the visible becomes the visibility of the invisible only if it receives its intention, in short, if it refers, as to intention, to the invisible; that is, the invisible envisages (as invisible) only in passing to the visible (as face), whereas the visible only presents to sight (as visible) in passing to the invisible (as intention). Visible and invisible grow together and as such: their absolute distinction implies the radical commerce of their transferences. We find again, at work in the icon, the concept of distance: that union increases in the measure of distinction, and reciprocally. Without here taking up again the intrinsic relation of the icon to distance, let us simply indicate some of the perspectives that one opens on the other. (*a*) Valid as icon is the concept or group of concepts that reinforces the distinction of the visible and the invisible as well as their union, hence that increases the one all the more that it highlights the other. Every pretension to absolute knowledge therefore belongs to the domain of the idol. (*b*) The icon has a theological status, the reference of the visible face to the intention that envisages, culminating in the reference of the Christ to the Father: for the formula *eikōn tou theou tou aoratou* concerns first the Christ. It would remain to specify in what measure this attribution has a normative value, far from simply constituting just one application of the icon among others. (*c*) As much as idolatry, because it measures the divine according to the scope of a gaze that freezes, can nevertheless attain to an actual experience of the divine only at the cost of being reduced to one of the "so-called gods" (René Char),[22] so the icon, as it summons to infinity—strictly—contemplation in distance, could not but overabundantly subvert every idol of the frozen gaze—in short, open the eyes of the frozen gaze (as one opens a body with a knife), open its eyes upon a face. The idol places its center of gravity in a human gaze; thus, dazzled as it may be by the brilliance of the divine, the gaze still remains in possession of the idol, its solitary master.

The idol always moves, at least potentially, toward its twilight, since already in its dawn the idol gathers only a foreign brilliance. The icon, which unbalances human sight in order to engulf it in infinite depth, marks such an advance of God that even in times of the worst distress indifference cannot ruin it. For, to give itself to be seen, the icon needs only itself.

This is why it indeed can demand, patiently, that one receive its abandon.

2

DOUBLE IDOLATRY

In homage to Maurice Clavel

1—The Function of the Idol

One would have to begin, of course, with a dialogue with Nietzsche, and with the madman of *Fröhliche Wissenschaft,* hence first by a more essential concept of the idol. This more essential concept of the idol, in fact, must be developed in such a way that it may rightly accommodate the intellectual representation of the divine and offer the framework of an interpretation, or better, of a reinterpretation, of the "death of God." One therefore must trace, at least in outline, the contours of a figure of the idol—figure the figure, schematize the schema. This redoubling, which comes quite naturally and as if inevitably to the pen, betrays in advance the fact that the idol summons the ambivalence of its domains of application, perceptible and intelligible, or rather "aesthetic" and conceptual.

Does figuring the idolatrous figure imply returning to it the caricature with which one so often reproached it for imposing on the divine? But the idol has nothing caricatural, deceitful, or illusory about it. It shows only what it sees; that *eidōlon* remains directly invested by, and tied to **eidō,* does not simply indicate to us a neutral or insignificant etymological fact, but exactly reflects a founding paradox. The idol shows what it sees. It shows that which, indeed, occupies the field of the visible, with neither deceit nor illusion, but which indissolubly invests it only on the basis of vision itself. The idol supplies vision with the image of what it sees. The idol produces (itself) in actuality (as) that at which vision intentionally aims. It freezes in a figure that which vision aims at in a glance. Thus does the mirror close the horizon, in order to offer sight the only object at which sight aims, namely, the face of its very aim: the gaze gazing at itself gazing, at the risk of seeing no more than its own face, without perceiving in it the gaze that gazes. Except, for the idol, no mirror precedes the gaze, nor, as if accidentally, encloses its space of vision; to be reflected, and upon itself alone, idolatrous vision mobilizes no other instance than itself. In the future of its aim, at a certain point that nothing could foresee, the aim no longer aims beyond, but rebounds upon a mirror—which otherwise never would have appeared—toward itself; this invisible mirror is called the idol. It is not invisible in that one cannot see it, since to the contrary one sees nothing but it; it is invisible because it masks the end of the aim; starting with the idol, the aim no longer progresses, but, no longer aiming, returns upon itself, reflects itself, and by this reflex, abandons as unbearable to live—not visible because neither aimed at nor *visable*—the invisible.

The invisible mirror therefore does not produce the reflexive return of the aim upon itself, it results from it: it only offers, so to speak, the trace of the bounce, the imprint of the absorption of the aim, then of its takeoff, in return, upon itself. This wooden board, the idol, has the quasi value of a springboard for vision that, having advanced so far, returns from it toward itself. As the sediment in a wine indicates maturation and the fact that no further change is possible, so the idol constitutes only a sedimentation of the aim of the invisible and of the divine, hence what remains once the aim is stopped by its reflection. In the idol, as a statue or painting, the aim settles. The inversion of the aim determines the point of invisibility, and the reflection gives rise to the mirror. The invisible mirror is not so much the unseen cause of the reversal of vision as it is this reversal of vision that fixes, on a limit, the invisible. Thus, the idol only freezes itself in the firmness of a figure startin from the instance of a reversal. The figure results from the re versal upon/before the invisible, and not the inverse. The idol therefore appears as a reflection on the individual: an aim toward the *visable* that, at a certain point of the aim, is inflected upon itself, is reflected upon itself in order to characterize as invisible that at which it no longer can aim. The invisible is defined by the reflection whose defection abandons the visible as not *visable,* hence not visible—in short, invisible.

So the idol all the more masks the invisible when it is marked with visibility. The more it misses, by default, the invisible, the more it can be remarked as visible. The statue of one of these *kouroï* that, even in a room of the National Museum of Athens, still overcome us with their powerful and well-balanced splendor, indeed bears the sign of the divine. No one has the authority to deny that the divine marked the sacred sites, temples, and statues. Above all, no one has the power to do so. The fact is that the idol registers, as a low-water mark signals a rise in the water level, a certain advance of the aim at the divine, to the point of a certain reflection and defection. The testimony of the idols indeed may have lost its pertinence for us: but it is not thereby disqualified as such, namely, as divine, but simply struck with insignificance. For if the idols forged by the Greeks no longer show us the divine, the fault (if fault need be indicated) comes back neither to the divine nor to the Greeks. Simply, among us there are no longer any Greeks for whom alone these stone figures could indicate by their invisible mirror a reflection upon the invisible, whose visible low-water mark well corresponds to that particular experience of the divine attained only by the Greeks. The idols of the Greeks betray, silently and incomprehensibly, an absolutely actual experience of the divine, but an experience that was realized only for them. What renders the Delphic Oracle mute stems, not from any fraud finally exposed (Fontenelle), but from the disappearance of the Greeks. The idol always marks a true and genuine experience of the divine, but for this very reason announces its limit: as an experience of the divine, starting in this way with the one who aims at it, in view of the reflex in which, through the idolatrous figure, this aim masks and marks its defection with regard to the invisible, the idol always must be read on the basis of the one whose experience of the divine takes shape there. In the idol, the divine indeed has a presence, and it indeed offers itself to an experience, but only starting from an aim and its limits. In a word, the divine is figured in the idol only indirectly, reflected according to the experience of it that is fixed by the human authority—the divine, actually experienced, is figured, however, only in the measure of the human authority that puts itself, as much as it can, to the test. In the idol, the divine function of *Dasein* is thus betrayed and calibrated. Which means that the idol never reaches the divine as such, and that, for this very reason, it never deceives, deludes, or misses the divine. As a divine function of *Dasein,* it offers the index of an always-real experience of *Dasein.* Only foolishness could doubt that the idol reflects the divine, and that in a way it may yet incite us to evoke for ourselves the experience of which it remains the sediment. But for this validity and this innocence, the idol pays the price of its limitation: it is an experience of the divine in the measure of a state of *Dasein.* What renders the idol problematic does not stem from a failure (e.g., that it offers only an "illusion") but, on the contrary, from the conditions of its validity—its radical immanence to the one who experiences it, and experiences it, rightly so, as impassable. To each epoch corresponds a figure of the divine that is fixed, each time, in an idol. In fact, it is not by chance that Bossuet risks the term *epoch* in a universal history that, from one end to the other, meditates on the succession of idols.[1] Only the genuineness of the idol, as a limited and hence real (real because limited) way of taking the divine into view, allows one to conceive the fraternity that Hölderlin recognizes between Heracles, Dionysus, and Christ.[2] The idol indeed testifies to the divine, from the point of view of the aim that produces it as its reflection. Each time, therefore, the idol testifies to the divine, but each time the divine thought starting from its aim, limited to a variable scope by *Dasein.* Therefore, the idol always culminates in a "self-idolatry," to speak like Baudelaire.[3] The idol: less a false or untrue image of the divine than a real, limited, and indefinitely variable function of *Dasein* considered in its aiming at the divine. The idol: the image of the divine that *Dasein* forms, hence that much less God than, in a more real way, a figure of the divine. Form an image of the divine? Usage instead says: "form an idea of . . ."; could this be because, preeminently, the idea would constitute the culmination of the idol?

2—The Ambivalence of the Conceptual Idol

The concept, when it knows the divine in its hold, and hence names "God," defines it. It defines it, and therefore also measures it to the dimension of its hold. Thus the concept on its part can take up again the essential characteristics of the "aesthetic" idol:[4] because it apprehends the divine on the basis of *Dasein,* it measures the divine as a function of it; the limits of the divine experience of *Dasein* provoke a reflection that turns it away from aiming at, and beyond, the invisible, and allows it to freeze the divine in a concept, an invisible mirror. Notably, the "death of God" presupposes a determination of God that formulates him in a precise concept; it implies then, at first, a grasp of the divine that is limited and for that reason intelligible. One therefore must add quotation marks to what is thus named God—"God"—that indicate less a suspicion than a delimitation: the "death of God" presupposes a concept equivalent to that which it apprehends under the name of "God." It is on the basis of this concept that the critique exerts its polemic: if "God" includes alienation in its concept (Feuerbach, Stirner, Marx), or a nimble figure of the will to power (Nietzsche), then it will—to the point of absolute disappearance—undergo the consequences of this concept. Which implies, obviously, the equivalence of God to a concept in general. For only this equivalence renders "God" operative as a concept. Which means that an atheism (conceptual, naturally, and not every atheism—even though the tie between conceptual atheism and sociological atheism may be of consequence) is worth only as much as the concept that contains it. And, as this concept of "God" accedes to the precision that will render it operative only by remaining limited, one must say that a conceptual atheism can assure its rigor, demonstrativeness, and pertinence only because of its regionalism; not *in spite of* it, *but indeed because of*

lism indicates that for the term, by definition unde-
od, the concept substitutes some precise definition,
:r which, through the determining definition, under-
vill exercise its logic. Thus the conceptual atheisms imply the substitution for *God* of a given regional concept—called "God"; therefore they bear only on concepts each time fostering this "God" that they announce. The "so-called gods" (René Char) substitute for *God* the "gods" that, conceptually, we are limited to expressing. This "God," that a concept suffices to express, nevertheless has nothing illusory about it. It clearly exposes what *Dasein,* at the moment of a particular epoch, experiences of the divine and approves as the definition of its "God." Only such an experience of the divine is not founded so much in God as in man: and, as L. Feuerbach says exactly, "man is the original of his idol"[5]—man remains the original locus of his idolatrous concept of the divine, because the concept marks the extreme advance, then the reflected return, of a thought that renounces venturing beyond itself, into the aim of the invisible.

It now becomes possible to ask what concept—rigorous because regional—offers the "death of God" its idolatrous support. To this question, Nietzsche himself, explicitly and in advance, responds: "Does morality make impossible this pantheistic affirmation of all things too? At bottom [*im Grunde*], it is only the moral god that has been overcome. Does it make sense to conceive a 'god beyond good and evil'?"[6] Only the "moral God" can die or even be discovered as already dead; for he alone, as "*moral* God," is amenable to the logic of value: he himself operates and is comprehensible only in the system of values of morality as counternature; thus does he find himself directly hit the moment that, with nihilism, "the highest values are devalued." Nihilism would have no hold over "God" if, as "moral God," he were not exhausted in the moral domain, itself taken as the ultimate figure of "Platonism." Recognizing, according to the very letter of the Nietzschean text, that only the "moral God" dies, does not amount to dulling the radicality of his argument, but, on the contrary, to disengaging its condition of possibility. This condition of possibility presupposes, obviously, the equivalence between God and an idol (the regional concept), here the "moral God." Hence a double question. (*a*) What scope are we to acknowledge in this idol? (*b*) What origin are we to attribute to it?

We can fix its scope, provisionally, by reference to what it does not exclude: the "death of God" as "moral God" leaves intact, even more opens and provokes, the coming of the "new gods," whose affirmative function upholds this world, which becomes the only world. Thus even within the Nietzschean argument, the death of God is valid only as far as the idol that renders it thinkable aims, since, beyond this *Götzendämmerung,* there is another dawn of the divine. As for the status of this new rising of the divine, only later can we conduct an examination of it. As to the origin of this idol, it is easily located. Feuerbach, in construing the whole of philosophy of religion as an idolatry—not in order to denounce its bankruptcy, but indeed to consecrate in it a finally legitimate appropriation—remarks that in it idolatry deploys all of its rigor in thinking "God" as moral: "Of all the attributes which the understanding assigns to God, that which in religion, and especially the Christian religion, has the pre-eminence, is moral perfection. But God as a morally perfect being is nothing else than the realised idea, the fulfilled law of morality. . . . The moral God requires man to be as he himself is."[7] But, here as often, Feuerbach is hardly valid except as a relay in the direction of Kant, who explicitly thinks of God as "a moral author of the world."[8] To show that this equivalence acts as an idol, in the strict sense that we defined it, does not present, at least in one sense, any difficulty. The apprehension of "God" as moral author of the world implies an actual experience of God (who would risk doubting the religious authenticity of Kant's practical philosophy?) but founded on a finite determination of "God" (from the sole practical point of view), starting not from the nature—if there is one—of God, but indeed from human *Dasein*'s experience of it. This last characteristic Kant explicitly introduces: "This idea of a moral Governor of the world is a task presented to our practical reason. It concerns us not so much to know what God is in Himself (in His nature) as what He is for us as moral beings";[9] thus indeed it is uniquely for us, without regard for his own nature, that "God" can be expressed "as moral essence," "moral being." Even more than Kant, Fichte brutally formulates the idolatrous reduction of the "moral God": "This living and effective moral order is identical with God. We do not and cannot grasp any other God."[10] Thus, either Nietzsche has nothing precise in view, and his argument regresses from conceptual rigor to foundering in a pathos one might call "poetic," to spare it any more ambiguous qualifiers, or else he denounces as a crepuscular idol the Kantian (and thereby "Platonic") identification of God with the "moral God." Such an identification calls for two criticisms.

One is developed by Nietzsche's whole argument—namely, that this idea is equivalent to an idol: *Götzendämmerung,* so that, if, as according to Schelling's statement, "God is something much more real than a simple moral order of the world,"[11] then the crepuscular idol releases, by its disappearance, the space of an advent of the divine other than the moral figure. Because by its idolatrous disposition it holds a strictly regional validity, conceptual atheism is even more valid here as a liberation of the divine. The true question, concerning Nietzsche, does not concern his so-called (and vulgar) atheism; it asks if the liberation of the divine, which it attempts, accedes to a true liberation or fails along the way.

However, another infinitely more radical critique arises here—it no longer asks simply whether conceptual atheism, since it has rigor only in remaining regional, must necessarily be recognized as idolatrous, hence to be rejected; it wonders whether idolatry does not affect as much, or more, the conceptual discourse that pretends to accede positively to God. In the end Kant and Nietzsche equally admit the equivalence of God with the "moral God," so that the same idolatry affects the thinker of the categorical imperative as much as the thinker of the "death of God." Hence the suspicion that idolatry, before characterizing conceptual atheism, affects the apologetic attempts that claim to prove, as one used to say, the existence of God. Every proof, in fact, demonstrative as it may appear, can lead only to the concept; it remains for it then to go beyond itself, so to speak, and to identify this concept with God himself. Saint Thomas implements such an identification by an "id quod omnes nominunt," repeated at the end of each of his *viae*

(*Summa theologica* Ia,q.2,a.3), as Aristotle concluded the c onstration of *Metaphysics* (A:7) by *touto gar ho theos* "for t the god" (1:072b29–30), and as, above all, Leibniz ended at the principle of reason asking, "See at present if that which we have just discovered must not be called God."[12] Proof uses positively what conceptual atheism uses negatively: in both cases, equivalence to a concept transforms God into "God," into one of the infinitely repeatable "so-called gods." In both cases, human discourse determines God. The opposition of the determinations, the one demonstrating, the other denying, does not distinguish them as much as their common presupposition identifies them: that the human *Dasein* might, conceptually, reach God, hence might construct conceptually something that it would take upon itself to name "God," either to admit or dismiss. The idol works universally, as much for denegation as for proof.

3—Metaphysics and the Idol

The first idolatry can be established rigorously starting from metaphysics to the extent that its essence depends on ontological difference, though "unthought as such" (Heidegger). The result that we have just obtained raises, by its very radicality, a question that is delicate because universal. We went from idolatry to conceptual atheism in order to bring to light the idolatrous presupposition of every conceptual discourse on God, even the positive. But in showing too much we no longer show anything: in extending the suspicion of idolatry to every conceptual enterprise concerning the divine, do we not run the risk of disqualifying this very suspicion? The localization of idolatry can assure its claims only by limiting itself, that is, by marking off precisely the field of its application. To suppose that such a field could be defined without contradiction implies a universal characteristic of metaphysical thought as such, or even a characteristic of thought that makes it appear as universally metaphysical. Heidegger was able to bring this characteristic to light as ontological difference. We admit therefore, without arguing or even explaining it here, the radical anteriority of ontological difference as that through and as which the *Geschick* of Being deploys beings, in a retreat that nevertheless saves a withdrawn proximity. We also admit that ontological difference is operative in metaphysical thought only in the forgetful figure of a thought of Being (thought summoned to and by Being) that, each time, keeps ontological difference unthought as such: "The thinking of metaphysics remains involved in the difference which as such is unthought . . ."[13] Thus Being never finds itself thought as such, but always and only as the unthought of being [*das Seiendes*] and its condition of possibility. Such that the thought of Being is obscured even in the question *"ti to on?"* where the *on hē on* indicates more the beingness of beings (*Seiendheit, ousia, essentia*) than Being as such. Beingness thus transforms the question of Being as well into a question of the *ens supremum,* itself understood and posited starting from the requirement, decisive for being, of the foundation. In this way, the two questions lead the interrogation concerning Being back to the assurance of the foundation: "The onto-theological constitution of metaphysics stems from the prevalence of that difference which keeps Being as the ground, and beings as what is grounded and what gives account, apart from and related to each other."[14] The divine appears thus only in ontological difference unthought as such, hence also in the figure of the founding funds required for the securing of beings, funds having to be placed in security, hence to found. Onto-theo-logy disengages, of itself, a function and hence a site for every intervention of the divine that would be constituted as metaphysical: the theo-logical pole of metaphysics determines, as early as the setting into operation of the Greek beginning, a site for what one later will name "God." Such that "God can come into philosophy only insofar as philosophy, of its own accord and by its own nature, requires and determines that and how God enters into it."[15]

The advent of something like "God" in philosophy therefore arises less from God himself than from metaphysics, as destinal figure of the thought of Being. "God" is determined starting from and to the profit of that of which metaphysics is capable, that which it can admit and support. This anterior instance, which determines the experience of the divine starting from a supposedly unavoidable condition, marks a primary characteristic of idolatry. Nevertheless, it does not yet suffice to interpret the theological discourse of onto-theo-logy as an idolatry. For it is suitable also to determine the scope, limited but positive, of the concept that idolatry sets in equivalence with "God." In order to do so, we will admit with Heidegger, but also as a historian of philosophy, that this concept finds a complete formulation, in modernity (Descartes, Spinoza, Leibniz, but also Hegel), with the *causa sui:* "The Being of beings is represented fundamentally, in the sense of the ground, only as *causa sui.* This is the metaphysical concept of God. . . . The cause [*Ur-Sache*] as *causa sui.* This is the right name for the god of philosophy."[16] In thinking "God" as *causa sui,* metaphysics gives itself a concept of "God" that at once marks the indisputable experience of him and his equally incontestable limitation; by thinking "God" as an efficiency so absolutely and universally foundational that it can be conceived only starting from the foundation, and hence finally as the withdrawal of the foundation into itself, metaphysics indeed constructs for itself an apprehension of the transcendence of God, but under the figure simply of efficiency, of the cause, and of the foundation. Such an apprehension can claim legitimacy only on condition of also recognizing its limit. Heidegger draws out this limit very exactly: "Man can neither pray nor sacrifice to this God. Before the *causa sui,* man can neither fall to his knees in awe nor can he play music and dance before this god.

"The god-less thinking which must abandon the God of philosophy, God as *causa sui,* is thus perhaps closer to the divine God. Here this means only: god-less thinking is more open to Him than ontotheologic would like to admit."[17] The *causa sui* offers only an idol of "God" so limited that it can neither aspire to worship and adoration nor even tolerate them without immediately betraying its insufficiency. The *causa sui* says so little about the "divine God" that to assimilate it with the latter, even with the apologetic intention of furnishing a supposed proof, amounts to speaking crudely, even in blasphemy: "a God who must permit his existence to be proved in the first place is ultimately a very ungodly God. The best such proofs of existence can yield is blasphemy."[18] Blasphemy, here, barely constitutes the obverse of an idolatry of which conceptual atheism would present the reverse. In both cases, God is second to "God," that

ıcept that is limited—to the cause as foundation—
.ıs cost only, operative at the heart of metaphysics. Idol-
:mpts to speak the good side of that of which *blas*phemy
.s the *bad;* of that which blasphemy speaks *bad*ly idolatry
.gines itself to speak well. Each fails to see that they speak
.e same name; well or badly hardly matters, since the whole question consists in deciding whether a proper name can appropriate God in a "God"; the unconscious blasphemy of idolatry thus can be denounced authentically only by also unveiling the thoughtless idolatry of blasphemy. Only on the basis of a concept will "God" be, equally, refuted or proved, hence also considered as a conceptual idol, homogeneous with the conceptual terrain in general.

What have we gained so far? Have we not simply come back to our point of departure, the suspicion of idolatry applied to the concept? We have come back to it, but with a determination that characterizes it in a decisive manner: the conceptual idol has a site, metaphysics; a function, the theo-logy in onto-theology; and a definition, *causa sui.* Conceptual idolatry does not remain a universally vague suspicion but inscribes itself in the global strategy of thought taken in its metaphysical figure. Nothing less than the destiny of Being—or, better, Being as destiny—mobilizes conceptual idolatry and assures it a precise function. We therefore end up, in a reading of Heidegger, inverting word for word the imprudent and hasty formula of Sartre, speaking of "the *Ens causa sui* which the religions name God."[19] Now, only metaphysics is willing and able to name the *Ens causa sui* by the name of God, because to begin with only metaphysics thinks and names the *casua sui.* On the contrary, "the religions," or, to remain precise, the Christian religion, does not think God starting from the *causa sui,* because it does not think God starting from the cause, or within the theoretical space defined by metaphysics, or even starting from the concept, but indeed starting from God alone, grasped to the extent that he inaugurates by himself the knowledge in which he yields himself—reveals himself. Bossuet says some very wise things; under the deliberately nonelaborated triviality of his remarks he states that "our God . . . is infinitely above that first Cause and prime mover known by philosophers, though they did not worship it."[20] To reach a nonidolatrous thought of God, which alone releases "God" from his quotation marks by disengaging his apprehension from the conditions posed by onto-theo-logy, one would have to manage to think God outside of metaphysics insofar as metaphysics infallibly leads, by way of blasphemy (proof), to the twilight of the idols (conceptual atheism). Here again, but in the name of something like God and no longer of something like Being, the step back out of metaphysics seems an urgent task, although not a noisy one. But in view of what, this step back? Does the overcoming of idolatry summon us to retrocede out of metaphysics, in the sense that *Sein und Zeit* attempts a step back toward Being as such by the meditation of its essential temporality? Does retroceding from metaphysics, supposing already that in doing so there arrives the thought devoted to Being as Being, suffice to free God from idolatry—for does idolatry come to completion with the *causa sui*, or, on the contrary, does the idolatry of the *causa sui* not refer, as an indication only, to another idolatry, more discrete, more pressing, and therefore all the more threatening?

4—The Screen of Being

Thus far, in what way have we advanced? Have we not simply taken up the Heideggerian meditation on the figure that the divine assumes in the onto-theo-logy of metaphysics, to identify it, with some violence, with our own problematic of the idol? Does not this perhaps forced identification simply offer a new case of a deplorable but persistent mania—that of taking up within a theological discourse, in spite of them, the moments of the Heideggerian discourse, in a game where one and the other party lose infinitely more than they gain? Precisely, we must now indicate how the problematic of idolatry, far from falling here into disuse, finds the true terrain of a radical discussion when it encounters the attempt of a thought of Being as Being.

However, before outlining this paradox, and in order better to take it into view, let us look back to Nietzsche. The "death of God," as death of the "moral god," confirms the twilight of an idol; but, just because it has to do with an idol, the collapse entails, even more essentially than a ruin, the clearing of a new space, free for an eventual apprehension, other than idolatrous, of God. This is why Nietzsche announces "new gods" as an authentic possibility that their ardent expectation renders foreseeable. But these new gods can never be rendered visible unless their apprehension is submitted to the will to power, which controls the horizon of all beings, as the beingness of beings—"höchste Macht—das genügt!" Freed from moral idolatry, the gods nevertheless remain subject to other instances, to another unique instance of which they are the function, the will to power; for they constitute, purely and simply, states and figures of it. The new gods depend on "the religious, that is to say god-forming [*gottbildende*] instinct."[21] Thus, one idolatrous apprehension succeeds another: the manifestation of the divine only passes from one (moral) condition to another (*Wille zur Macht*), without the divine's ever being freed as such. Just as we were able to venture that Nietzsche, because he carries metaphysics to completion, constitutes its last moment, so must we suggest that Nietzsche renders the twilight of the idols crucial only by himself consummating a new (final?) development of the idolatrous process. The will to power forges "gods" at every instant: there is nothing, in the modern sense, more *banal* than a "god"; we never stop seeing ourselves, to the point of obsessional disgust, surrounded by them: each instant not only furnishes them but even demands and produces them. For, to a universal domination of the will to power that gives the seal of the eternal to becoming, there must correspond, according to the rigor of onto-theo-logy, the triumphant brilliance of a unified figure of the divine, hence of the maximum become actual of a state and of a figure of the will to power. The barbarous surging forward of terrible and trivial "idols" (for we very rightly name them "idols"), of which our nihilistic age ceaselessly increases the consumption, marks the exasperation of idolatry and not, to be sure, the survival of some natural—then delinquent—desire to see God.

It does not suffice to go beyond an idol in order to withdraw oneself from idolatry. Such a reduplication of idolatry, which even Nietzsche cannot avoid, we can suspect in Heidegger in a way even more vast and hence more dangerous than in Nietzschean expectation. For Nietzsche the "death of God" opens in nihilism, and it is through endured nihilism that the will to power accedes to a figurative production of new gods. The essence of technology, culminating in Enframing (*Gestell*), completes nihilism, but in such a way that nihilism opens to the possibility of a salvation. In fact, by carrying the interpretation of the Being of beings as present and presence (*Anwesenheit*) to its insurmountable end, hence by declaring the privilege of beings over their beingness and also by forgetting that, in ontological difference, what does not cease to be forgotten is precisely Being, Enframing carries ontological difference to its height, manifesting it all the more clearly that it does not think it as such. Where danger increases, salvation increases also. Enframing poses ontological difference as a problem by the fact that, with a massive and equal force, it both produces and fails to recognize it. Thus, as and because nihilism does not cease to aim at the advent of "new gods," and in a sense provokes that advent, so "with the end of philosophy, thinking is not also at its end, but in transition to another beginning."[22] The other beginning attempts to think ontological difference as such, hence to think being as Being. To this "other beginning" Heidegger designates a precise function and stake, in opposition to ontological difference, and does not burden it with any problematic character, future or fantastic. The "new beginning," which is compelled to think Being as such and hence accomplishes a step back from philosophy, is realized in *Sein und Zeit* or at least in its *aim*. The "new beginning," just like the "new gods," belongs to no future, since it can only open a future without prospect that the repeated pretension of the present does not immediately govern. In short, it is carried out before us and, one must hope, with us. And thus, the "new beginning" that breaks with unthought ontological difference, hence with the *causa sui* of onto-theo-logy, undertakes to conceive the "divine god," or at least does not close itself to this possibility or, better, opens it. We therefore conclude that the "new beginning," in charge of Being as Being, attempts to approach the god qua god. Hence the decisive declaration, which with its harmonics we must now hear: "Only from the truth of Being can the essence of the holy be thought. Only from the essence of the holy is the essence of divinity to be thought. Only in the light of the essence of divinity can it be thought or said what the word 'God' is to signify. . . . Being.

"In such nearness, if at all, a decision may be made as to whether and how God and the gods withhold their presence and the night remains, whether and how the day of the holy dawns, whether and how in the upsurgence of the holy an epiphany of God and the gods can begin anew [*neu beginnen*]. But the holy, which alone is the essential sphere of divinity, which in turn alone affords a dimension for the gods and God, comes to radiate only when Being itself beforehand and after extensive preparation has been illuminated and is experienced in its truth."[23] Each of these texts obeys a strictly regulated superposition of conditions that imply each other and interweave with one another. Thus does Being determine beings by the clearing of its retreat; the advance of beings, which Being (*das Heile*) maintains intact, crowns in its turn the most protected among them by the glory of the holy (*das Heilige*); yet only the brilliance of the holy can assure the opening of something like a divine being (*das Gottliche*); and only the virtue of the divine can charter and support the weight of beings, at this point notable because one must recognize on their countenances the face of the gods (*die Götter*). Finally, only the tribe of the gods can yield and guarantee a sufficiently divine abode so that someone like the God of Christianity or another (only the claim to unicity being in question here) can have the leisure to render itself manifest. These interwoven conditions all gather together in the play of that which elsewhere (in his strange lecture, *The Thing*) Heidegger names the Fourfold or the Square (*Geviert*), of which the four instances, Earth and Sky, mortals and the divinities, buttress one another, hence confirm and repel one another, in an immobile and trembling tension where each owes its advent only to the combat with the others, and where their mutual struggles owe the harmonious equilibrium of their (dis)entanglement(s) only to Being, which convokes, mobilizes and maintains them. The gods need only play their part here, in a Fourfold; as one barely can say that God suffices to maintain the role of the gods, even less could one envisage him withdrawn from the Fourfold; neither withdrawn nor, of course, initiator or master.[24]

To the thought that is attached to thinking Being as Being, outside of metaphysics, in the definite confrontation with ontological difference meditated as such, the question of "the existence of God" inevitably will appear misplaced, hasty and imprecise. Imprecise, for what does it mean *to exist,* and is this term suitable to something like "God"? Hasty, since before coming to "God," even as a hypothesis, one must pass through the dazzling but trying multiplicity of the gods, then through the miraculous simplicity of the divine and of the holy, in order finally to end at the very question of Being. The "marvel of all marvels" consists no more in the existence of "God" than in the existence of any other being, or even in what "existence" (metaphysically) means, but in the fact, more simple and therefore more difficult to think, *that* what-is *is.*[25] What is essential in the question of "the existence of God" stems less from "God" than from existence itself, therefore from Being. Thus, in the end, this question appears misplaced—at once unsuitable and dislodged from its proper site: the truth on "God" could never come but from where truth itself issues, namely from Being as such, from its constellation and from its opening. The question of God must admit a preliminary, if only in the form of a preliminary question. In the beginning and in principle, there advenes neither God, nor a god, nor the *logos,* but the advent itself—Being, with an anteriority all the less shared in that it decides all the rest, since according to and starting from it there literally remain only beings, and nothing other than beings and the nothing. The very question of the ontic priority of "God" can be posed only at the heart of this advent. But what is more decisive, in the order of thought, than, precisely, the order of questions that provoke it?

We therefore posit that here again, a second time, and beyond the idolatry proper to metaphysics, there functions *another* idolatry, proper to the thought of Being as such. This affirmation, as blunt as it may seem, derives nevertheless directly from the indisputable and essential anteriority of the ontological question over the so-called ontic question of "God." This anteriority suffices to establish idolatry. We furnish nevertheless two confirmations, which permit us to connect two of the moments of the idol to two of Heidegger's decisions. (*a*) The idol determines the "god" on the basis of the aim, hence of an anterior gaze. But in the texts examined above, the dependence of "God" on the gods, then on divinity, on the holy, and finally on Being, does not seem to have its origin in an ontically identifiable gaze; thus Heidegger would not satisfy one of the conditions of the idol. In fact, one should not forget, in reading the texts subsequent to the "turn," the (in fact *definitive*) accomplishment of earlier texts having to do with the analytic of *Dasein* and the fundamental essence of phenomenology. To say Being/*Sein* quite simply would not be possible if man were not able to attain his dignity of *Dasein; Dasein* here indicates what is peculiar to the human being, which consists in the fact that, in this being, not only *its* Being is an issue (as *Sein und Zeit* repeats in 1927), but more essentially, as Heidegger says in 1928, Being itself and its comprehension: "Human *Dasein* is a being with the kind of being [*Seinsart*] to which it belongs essentially to understand something like Being [*dergleichen wie Sein zu verstehen*]."[26]

The later isolated anteriority of *Sein* is secured concretely by *Dasein* over itself; phenomenologically, the anteriority of Being can be developed and justified only by the anteriority of the analytic of *Dasein*. Therefore, one must admit the absolute phenomenological anteriority of *Dasein*, as comprehension of Being, over all beings and over every regional ontic investigation. Heidegger characterized this privileged situation of *Dasein* when he spoke of its "peculiar neutrality."[27]

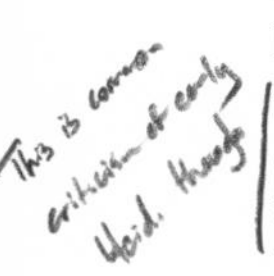

Related to a religious law, or to the ontic existence of "God," the phenomenological privilege of *Dasein* lays itself open to "the semblance of an extremely individualistic, radical atheism, *Schein eines extrem individualistischen, radikalen Atheismus*." Doubtless it is a question only of appearance, if one bears in mind an existential option: certainly Heidegger himself does not belong among those whom he later will name the "public scoundrels." Still, taken in its phenomenological definition, hence as *Kategorienforschung*, "philosophical research is and remains an atheism";[28] atheism here indicates less a negation than a suspension. But such a suspension—phenomenologically inevitable—implies theologically an instance anterior to "God," hence that point from which idolatry could dawn. No doubt "the ontological interpretation of *Dasein* as Being-in-the-world tells neither for nor against the possible existence of God [*ein mögliches Sein zu Gott entschieden*],[29] but the very possibility of this indecision implies a suspension. This suspension in turn implies, from an anterior because exterior point of view, an aim that suspends every ontic position; *Dasein* exerts this aim, and no term could appear unless aimed at and seen by it. *Dasein* precedes the question of "God" in the very way that Being determines in advance, according to the gods, the divine, the holy, "God," his life and his death. "God," aimed at like every other being by *Dasein* in the mode of a placement in parentheses, submits to the first condition of possibility of an idolatry.

The idol is constituted by the thrust of an aim anterior to any possible spectacle, but also by a first visible, where, settling, it attains, without seeing, its invisible mirror, low-water mark of its rise. Does one find in the Heideggerian text a thesis that confuses the first visible with the invisible mirror? The thought that thinks Being as such cannot and must not apprehend anything but beings, which offer the path, or rather the field of a meditation, of Being. Any access to something like "God," precisely because of the aim of Being as such, will have to determine him in advance as a being. The precomprehension of "God" as being is self-evident to the point of exhausting in advance "God" as a question. Heidegger often repeats that the believer, because of his certainty of faith, can well conceive the philosophical question of Being but can never commit himself to it, held back as he remains by his certainty. The remark can at the least be reversed: assured of the precomprehension of every possible "God" as being and of his determination by the anterior instance of Being, Heidegger can well conceive and formulate the question of God (without quotation marks) but can never seriously commit himself to it. Precisely because in advance and definitively, "God," whatever his future figure may be, strictly *will be:* "The Gods only signal simply because they *are*"; "God is a being who, by his essence, cannot not be"; "that being which can never not be. Thought 'theologically,' this being is called 'God' "; "And the gods likewise: to the degree that they *are,* and however they are, they too all stand *under 'Being.'*"[30] In short, "God" first becomes visible as being only because he thus fills—at least in one sense—and reflexively refers (invisible mirror) to itself an aim that bears first and decidedly on Being. In other words, the proposition "God is a being" itself appears as an idol, because it only returns the aim that, in advance, decides that every possible "God," present or absent, in one way or another, has to be. Which is formulated strictly by the sequence: "For the god also is—if he is—a being and stands as a being within Being and its coming to presence, which brings itself disclosingly to pass out of the worlding of the world [*auch der Gott ist, wenn er ist, ein Seiender*]."[31]

But is it self-evident that God should have to be, hence to be as a being (supreme, plural—however one wants) in order to give himself as God? How is it that Being finds itself admitted without question as the temple already opened (or closed) to every theophany, past or to come? And could one not even suspect, on the other hand, that, by the definition and axiom of the thought of Being as such, the temple of Being could in no way assist, call for, admit, or promise whatever may *be* concerning what one must not even *name*—God? And if this suspicion need not be confirmed, at least one can raise it legitimately, and one has to be amazed that it does not amaze more both the believers and the readers of Heidegger. Undoubtedly, if "God" is, he is a being; but does God have to be?

In order not to have to avoid this question, and because it appears to us incontestable that the texts of Heidegger do avoid it, we would say that in this precise sense, one must speak of a second idolatry. That it bears on the "more divine god"[32] does not invalidate but confirms this idolatry: for what "God" thus allows that an aim should decide his greater or lesser divinity, if not that "God" which results from a gaze that is both pious and blasphemous? What assurance would permit the introduction of a more legitimate equivalence between God and Being (where he still would play the role of a being) than the one obtaining between God and the *causa sui* "God" of metaphysics? Or again, does not the search for the "more divine god" oblige one, more than to go beyond onto-theo-logy, to go beyond ontological difference as well, in short no longer to attempt to think God in view of a being, because one will have renounced, to begin with, thinking him on the basis of Being? To think God without any conditions, not even that of Being, hence to think God without pretending to inscribe him or to describe him as a being.

But what indeed can permit and promise the attempt at a thinking of God without and outside of ontological difference?—The danger that this critical demand may in fact render thought on the whole immediately impossible cannot be minimized. Indeed, to think outside of ontological difference eventually condemns one to be no longer able to think at all. But precisely, to be no longer able to think, when it is a question of God, indicates neither absurdity nor impropriety, as soon as God himself, in order to be thought, must be thought as "id quo majus cogitari nequit," in other words, as that which surpasses, detours, and distracts all thought, even nonrepresentational. By definition and decision, God, if he must be thought, can meet no theoretical space to his measure [*mesure*], because his measure exerts itself in our eyes as an excessiveness [*démesure*]. Ontological difference itself, and hence also Being, become too limited (even if they are universal, or better: because they make us a universe, because in them the world "worlds") to pretend to offer the dimension, still less the "divine abode" where God would become thinkable. Biblical revelation seems, in its own way, to give a confirmation of this, or at least an indication, when it mentions, in the same name, what one *can* (but not must) comprehend as *Sum qui sum,* hence God as Being, and what one *must,* at the same time, understand as a denegation of all identity—"I am the one that I want to be." Being says nothing about God that God cannot immediately reject. Being, even and especially in Exod. 3:14, says nothing about God, or says nothing determining about him. One therefore must recognize that the impossibility, or at least the extreme difficulty, of thinking outside of ontological difference could, in some way, directly suit the impossibility—indisputable and definitive—of thinking God as such. Ontological difference, *almost* indispensable to all thought, presents itself thus as a *negative* propaedeutic of the unthinkable thought it is the ultimate idol, the most dangerous but also the ducational and, in its way, profitable, since it offers itself obstacle that, beaten down and trampled, becomes an imate scaffolding—*scabellum pedibus tuis*—without entering into the unthinkable, the indispensable unthinkable. For the unthinkable here has no provisional or negative acceptation: indispensable, indeed, the unthinkable offers the only appraised face of the one of whom it is question of thinking. Concerning God, let us admit clearly that we can think him only under the figure of the unthinkable, but of an unthinkable that exceeds as much what we cannot think as what we can; for that which I may not think is still the concern of *my* thought, and hence to *me* remains thinkable. On the contrary, the unthinkable taken as such is the concern of God himself, and characterizes him as the *aura* of his advent, the glory of his insistence, the brilliance of his retreat. The unthinkable determines God by the seal of his definitive indeterminateness for a created and finite thought. The unthinkable masks the gap, a fault ever open, between God and the idol or, better, between God and the pretension of all possible idolatry. The unthinkable forces us to substitute the idolatrous quotation marks around "God" with the very God that no mark of knowledge can demarcate; and, in order to say it, let us cross out G~~o~~d, with a cross, provisionally of St. Andrew, which demonstrates the limit of the temptation, conscious or naive, to blaspheme the unthinkable in an idol. The cross does not indicate that G~~o~~d would have to disappear as a concept, or intervene only in the capacity of a hypothesis in the process of validation, but that the unthinkable enters into the field of our thought only by rendering itself unthinkable there by excess, that is, by criticizing our thought. To cross out G~~o~~d, in fact, indicates and recalls that G~~o~~d crosses out our thought because he saturates it; better, he enters into our thought only in obliging it to criticize itself. The crossing out of G~~o~~d we trace on his written name only because, first, He brings it to bear on our thought, as his unthinkableness. We cross out the name of G~~o~~d only in order to show ourselves that his unthinkableness saturates our thought—right from the beginning, and forever.

To think G~~o~~d, therefore, outside of ontological difference, outside the question of Being, as well, risks the unthinkable, indispensable, but impassable. What name, what concept, and what sign nevertheless yet remain feasible? A single one, no doubt, love, or as we would like to say, as Saint John proposes—"God [is] *agape*" (1 John 4:8). Why love? Because this term, which Heidegger (like, moreover, all of metaphysics, although in a different way) maintains in a derived and secondary state, still remains, paradoxically, unthought enough to free, some day at least, the thought of God from the second idolatry. This task, immense and, in a sense, still untouched, requires working love conceptually (and hence, in return, working the concept through love), to the point that its full speculative power can be deployed. We could not undertake here, even in outline, to indicate its features. May it suffice to indicate two decisive traits of love, and their speculative promise.

a) Love does not suffer from the unthinkable or from the absence of conditions, but is reinforced by them. For what is peculiar to love consists in the fact that it gives itself. Now, to give itself, the gift does not require that an interlocutor receive it, or that an abode accommodate it, or that a condition assure it or confirm it. This means, first, that as love, God can at once transgress idolatrous constraints; for idolatry—especially the second—is exercised by the conditions of possibility (Being, if "God" is a being, the "divine abode," if "God" depends on the divine, etc.) which alone arrange for God a place worthy of him, and thus, if the conditions of that worthiness cannot be brought together, close his domain to his heirs, and hence assign him to marginality. If, on the contrary, God is not because he does not have to be, but loves, then, by definition, no condition can continue to restrict his initiative, amplitude, and ecstasy. Love loves without condition, simply because it loves; he thus loves without limit or restriction. No refusal rebuffs or limits that which, in order to give itself, does not await the least welcome or require the least consideration. Which means, moreover, that as interlocutor of love, man does not first have to pretend to arrange a "divine abode" for it—supposing that this very pretension may be sustained—but purely and simply to accept it; to accept it or, more modestly, not to steal away from it. Thus, even the inevitable impotence of man to correspond to the destiny that love gratuitously imposes upon him is not enough to disqualify its initiative or its accomplishment. For, in order to accomplish the response to love, it is necessary and sufficient to will it, since will alone can refuse or receive so that man cannot impose any condition, *even negative,* on the initiative of God. Thus no aim can any longer decide idolatrously on the possibility or impossibility of access to and from "God."

b) There is more: to think God as agape equally prohibits ever fixing the aim in a first visible and freezing it on an invisible mirror. Why? Because, as opposed to the concept that, by the very definition of apprehension, gathers what it comprehends, and, because of this, almost inevitably comes to completion in an idol, love (even and especially if it ends up causing thought, giving rise—by its excess—to thought) does not pretend to comprehend, since it does not mean at all to take; it postulates its own giving, giving where the giver strictly coincides with the gift, without any restriction, reservation, or mastery. Thus love gives itself only in abandoning itself, ceaselessly transgressing the limits of its own gift, so as to be transplanted outside of itself. The consequence is that this transference of love outside of itself, without end or limit, at once prohibits fixation on a response, a representation, an idol. It belongs to the essence of love—*diffusivum sui*—to submerge, like a ground swell the wall of a jetty, every demarcation, representational or existential, of its flux: love excludes the idol or, better, includes it by subverting it. It can even be defined as the movement of a giving that, to advance without condition, imposes on itself a self-critique without end or reserve. For love holds nothing back, neither itself nor its representation. The transcendence of love signifies first that it transcends itself in a critical movement where nothing—not even Nothingness/Nothing—can contain the excess of an absolute giving—absolute, that is, the defeat of all that is not exercised in that very abandon.

The second idolatry therefore can be surpassed only in letting God be thought starting from his sole and pure demand. Such a demand goes beyond the limit of a concept—even that of metaphysics in its onto-theo-logy—but also the limit of every condition whatsoever—even that of Being conceived in ontological difference. God can give himself to be thought without idolatry only starting from himself alone: to give himself to be thought as love, hence as gift; to give himself to be thought as a thought of the gift. Or better, as a gift for thought, as a gift that gives itself to be thought. But a gift, which gives itself forever, can be thought only by a thought that gives itself to the gift to be thought. Only a thought that gives itself can devote itself to a gift for thought. But, for thought, what is it to give itself, if not to love?

5—Note on the Divine and Related Subjects

The first version of the present text appeared in 1980 in a collection dedicated entirely to Heidegger and the question of God, *Heidegger et la question de Dieu* (Paris: Grasset, 1980). That collection took up the proceedings of a private colloquium, organized a few months before by the Irish College in Paris, where my text had been discussed. J. Beaufret and F. Fédier were kind enough to react to my theses and to offer those valuable remarks in the printing of the same volume. I would like to offer here a few points in response to their respective statements.

"All the same one would have to learn to read otherwise than in the bind of 'someone who is at a complete loss'[33] this passage from the *Letter on Humanism*" ("Heidegger et la théologie," p. 30) which I analyzed above (pp. 39 ff.) and which poses as preliminary to any manifestation of "God" that of the "gods," of the divine, of the holy, of the safe, and finally of Being. Playing, on that occasion, the role of the "someone," I would like to speak about the "loss." To begin, let us clear up a misunderstanding: if "monotheism is the point of view of those who declare false what would inspire in others the highest veneration" (J. Beaufret, p. 34), then I am not "monotheistic"; or rather, my personal attempt to *accede* to monotheism does not imply any declaration of falsification with regard to other venerations, since the theory of the idol that I outline has precisely no other consequence than to give legitimacy to other venerations and for that very reason to explain their multiplicity, hence to limit their dignity. For one can ground the legitimacy of multiple "venerations" only by a doctrine that limits them; one will have the generosity to grant me that, as to grant me that the reading of Hölderlin does not remain totally foreign to me. I wonder moreover how one can defend the reduction of the divine without presenting a doctrine of the idol—my own or, if it may be found, a better one. After this pointless reproach, let us get to the essential. Beaufret underlines that Heidegger simply wants to allow this to be thought: "Even more sacred than every God is consequently the world" (p. 33); consequent to what? "Quite simply," consequent to this: "The Deity, without belonging to the holy, is no longer even the Deity, but a vain pretension of a being, reputed to be All-Powerful, to usurp the center of that of which he represents only one region" (p. 31). In this authoritative exegesis of the contested passage of the *Letter,* I would like to raise two points. (*a*) "a being, reputed to be All-Powerful": the commentator takes up again, without questioning it, Heidegger's assumption: every "God," by precomprehension, is defined as a being, and, if one holds to the discourse of metaphysics, a being characterized by omnipotence. These two assumptions I indeed had mentioned in the initial text. I simply ask: just as the metaphysical determination of "God" as all-powerful is not self-evident (Heidegger himself having allowed us to glimpse this), must one admit that the determination of "God" as "a being" is itself self-evident? How is it that this question arouses no other response than the implicit accusation of misinterpretation or the assurance of its banality?

In fact, there is nothing banal about it, in view of its immediate result, to which the authoritative commentary holds, moreover correctly, above all. This result posits (*b*) that once "God" is defined as a "being," his pretension to fix himself as an absolute center becomes a usurpation. "God," playing the character of a "being," usurps the center of the "world," a center that returns to the *Geviert,* which alone makes a world. I had not brought up anything else, in order to found the diagnostic of idolatry; and hence Beaufret concedes my point of departure. I ask for nothing more. Or rather I do, on this basis: is it self-evident that "God," or rather G~~o~~d, should *be,* should have to be, should have to be like one of the "regions" of that of which the *Geviert* alone assures the conjunctions? Do these questions have any foundation with relation to the text of the *Letter?* The exegete at least confirms that they indeed have a basis in it. But then why take them to be inaudible, and degrade them to the realm of gain and loss?[34]

Coming back, in a brief and beautiful text entitled "Heidegger et Dieu," on the same passage from the *Letter,* Fédier remarks inversely that "Heidegger does not at all pretend to submit God to Being. He contents himself with soberly signaling that each time it is a question of thinking God, one will have first to think Being" (p. 44). In fact the distinction is right in a way, since Heidegger invokes only a precedence (*erst, zuvor,* etc.) of Being over "God." We concede this voluntarily, although subject to examination of still unpublished texts. Once this is admitted, is the diagnostic of idolatry put into question? The simple fact that, according to Fédier himself, "God," in order to reveal himself, hence in order to *give himself,* must satisfy preliminary conditions, and even preliminaries of thought, far from invalidating, rather confirms this diagnostic. The declaration of reassuring intentions that follows—"In *this* limited sense, the god depends on Being. The Greeks said: 'even the gods obey Necessity.' In *this* limited sense, the thought of Being is higher than the thought of God" (p. 45)—reconciles nothing. For, beside the fact that Greek thought concerning the gods does not constitute an absolute reference by itself, and especially beside the fact that it is not a question of thought as preliminary (an anterior aim), but rather of envisaging the hypothesis of an unthinkableness that goes beyond all thought, "*this* limited sense" was defined a few lines above: "All that is in the world, and even that which *comes* into it, like the god, is lit up by the light of Being." This sequence would merit word-for-word examination. I ask, among other things: (1) On what rests the definition and legitimacy of "All"? (2) In what sense can one think "to come" into the world, and do all the "gods" come into it in the same sense as the Johannine *erkhomenos?* (3) Does that which Being projects in matters of light illuminate with glory the "gods" as such, or, on the contrary, does it not sometimes obfuscate precisely that by which it/they reveal(s) itself/themselves as "God," or G~~o~~d? In short, does the light of Being glorify the G~~o~~d who, according to the Apostle Paul, only reveals himself as a folly? In illuminating this being, a Jew on the cross, does the light of Being permit one to recognize more than an ignominious death? And if not, can one still affirm that Being accommodates all the gods as such by the simple fact that it allows them to be seen as beings? We simply ask, is the "light of Being" qualified to accommodate every revelation?

If we renounce the untenable positions of Beaufret and Fédier—which consist in minimizing the idolatrous violence of the text of the *Letter,* at the risk of rendering their respective commentaries even *more* indisputably idolatrous—are we condemned to a "condemnation" of Heidegger, with the odiousness and ridiculousness of such a pretension? Not at all. We rediscover the pure and simple way in which Heidegger understood his own text. In fact, we have the good fortune that our question concerning *this* text of the *Letter* was posed to Heidegger, during a session of the Evangelical Academy of Hofgeismar, in December 1953. And Heidegger responded: "With respect to the text referred to from the 'Letter on Humanism,' what is being discussed there is the God of the poet, not the revealed God. There is mentioned merely what philosophical thinking is capable of on its own. Whether this may also be of significance for theology cannot be said because there is for us no third case by which it could be decided."[35] I cannot but fully subscribe to this position, which admits—against the zeal of the exegetes—the irreducible heteronomy, with regard to "God," of that which thought (philosophical or poetic?) can do on the one hand, and that which revelation gives. Revelation (I say, icon) can neither be confused with nor subjected to the philosophical thought of "God" as being (I say, idol). Heidegger says it, and confirms me in a word, there where I wandered about with neither grace nor progress. The G~~o~~d who reveals himself has nothing in common (at least in principle, and provided that he not condescend to it) with the "God" of the philosophers, of the learned, and, eventually, of the poet.

May the exegetes allow me to rely, against or without them, on Heidegger's statement. For, if it surprises one to be at a total loss,[36] some can find themselves "ashamed like a fox taken by a hen," to leave the last word, all the same, to the poet.[37]

3

THE CROSSING OF BEING

Thus, "what we cannot speak about we must pass over in silence—*darüber muss man schweigen.*" In other words, in passing from Wittgenstein to Heidegger, in speaking from the starting point of philosophy (or almost) and not from that of logic (or almost): "Someone who has experienced theology in his own roots, both the theology of the Christian faith and that of philosophy, would today rather remain silent about God [*von Gott zu schweigen*] when he is speaking in the realm of thinking."[1] Within such an improvised consensus, in spite or because of a judicious approximation, the two thinkers who dominate our epoch cross and meet. In it they radically determine, on the one hand, calculative thought and, on the other hand, meditating thought, and each their relations; such a consensus, however, does not restate, despite the evident similarity of terms, the caution that Ignatius of Antioch addressed to the overly prolix Christians: "It is better to keep silence and to be, than to speak without being."[2] If we are summoned to silence—if, as Aristotle says, we are "forced by the truth itself"[3] to keep silent with regard to something like God—this state of affairs nevertheless does not settle the fundamental question. For silence itself is expressed in several ways. We know silences of contempt and of joy, of pain and of pleasure, of consent and of solitude. Afforded by the concrete daily attitude and what it most rightly imposes is what one might call the theological attitude, which only bears on what Origen names the "dogmas to be kept in silence, *ta siōpōmena dogmata*."[4] But what does this silence mean? To what silence are we summoned today? Death, preeminently, imposes silence; the emptiness of infinite spaces opposes its suffocating vacuity like an eternal silence; aphasia, desertlike, grows with its silence. Does this silence, which threatens modernity more than any other, have the least relation, as to something like God, with what Pseudo-Dionysius has in mind when he incites us to "honor the ineffable [things] with a wise silence"?[5]

In other words, the highest difficulty does not consist in managing to reach, with Wittgenstein or Heidegger, a guarded silence with regard to God. The greatest difficulty doubtless consists more essentially in deciding what silence *says:* contempt, renunciation, the avowal of impotence, or else the highest honor rendered, the only one neither unworthy nor "dangerous."[6] But already we pay so much attention to securing the place where only silence is suitable that we do not yet try to determine the stakes and the nature of this silence. The silence concerning silence thus conceals from us that, finally, nothing demands more of interpretation than the nothingness of speech—or even that, to have done with silence, keeping silence does not suffice. Silence, precisely because it does not explain itself, exposes itself to an infinite equivocation of meaning. In order to keep silent with regard to God, one must, if not hold a discourse on God, at least hold a discourse worthy of God on our silence itself.

1—The Silence of the Idol

Let us take a moment to ascertain the seriousness of this new question, for a response is never worth more (and is often worth less) than the question that fostered it with a genuine questioning. A first indication clearly attests that, far from closing off a difficulty, silence opens one—the extreme difficulty that we experience in keeping silent before that about which, nevertheless, we simply cannot speak. There is nothing surprising in the fact that we may not be able to speak of God; for, if speaking is equivalent to stating a well-constructed proposition, then by definition that which is defined as ineffable, inconceivable, and unnameable escapes all speech. The surprising thing, therefore, is not our difficulty in speaking of God but indeed our difficulty in keeping silent. For in fact, with regard to God, overwhelmingly, we speak. In a sense we speak only about that, and much too much, with neither modesty nor precaution. Moreover, not keeping silent concerning God can be taken in several ways. (*a*) First, obviously, it can be taken in the sense of pious chattering, or supposedly such, since it often joins rampant heresy with invalidity; we simply mention this for the record. (*b*) Next, just as obviously, it can be taken in the sense of the discourse, rather enfeebled today, that disqualifies or deconstructs the very notion of God; this discourse consists in speaking of God in order to silence him, in not keeping silent in order to silence him. This discourse manifests two weaknesses: it does not see the difference between silencing and keeping silent, because it does not see that a refutation remains within the field of predication, whereas the very adage of Wittgenstein requires that one bypass predication to reach silence. It does not suffice to refute—even as far as "to reduce" a possible interlocutor "to silence"—in order to arrive at keeping silent. The discourse of refutation especially presupposes a conceptual definition of the very thing that it refutes and must, to display even the appearance of rigor, lend two contradictory characteristics to that thing: on the one hand, the definition must exhaust the individual, for want of which its destruction would not eliminate God, by which it is given as a real definition of an individual which is itself at least possible. On the other hand, the definition must in some way undo itself entirely before its refutation; the possible definition (*exigentia existentiae*) must also deconstruct itself as impossible. This double and contradictory demand is comprehensible only if one distinguishes, within the definition of God thus employed, an idol: namely a representation of God at once inadequate (objectively) and impassable (subjectively).[7] We can conclude that the conceptual idol leads the discourse of refutation to keep silent about God even less in that it seeks more to silence him. (*c*) There remains one final way of not keeping silent about God—the noisiest but, we must admit, the most seductive. It is used on occasions of what it is sometimes possible to call "returns to God." One might consider a recent example, the acknowledged role of God in the historico-theoretical deconstruction of certain figures of Leninism. Let us take an example from the French situation, which can be distinguished quite clearly from the testimony of certain Soviets, whose authentic spiritual experience cannot be disputed. All that matters here is the conceptual treatment to which these testimonies are subject in France. In the face of the annihilation of the individual and his share of liberty, what is very approximately named "transcendence" or Spirit appears as the unique means of returning humanity to man or, more prosaically, of portraying as "beautiful souls"—angels—the militants taken in by revolutions. In these cases the name of God hardly intervenes any longer except to back up another concept with infinity, which alone functions in the real operation of the discourse: whether it be a question of freedom, of the spirit, of the soul, of desire, or even of the Other, God always figures as a figurehead, without one's ever thinking him as such. This is all the more true in that returns to God unravel into extremely interested recourses to God, which unbelief, fundamental or superficial, accomplishes as well as—even better than—sincere and confessed faith. Moreover, only the pompous literary Christians are deceived.[8] In these two last cases (the best illustrated in France recently, by the way) the same nonsense occurs, which alone allows one to keep silent so little and so poorly with regard to God: the idolatry of substitution. On the one hand, one presupposes a concept as exhausting the name of God, in order to reject the one by the other; on the other hand, one presupposes that a God guarantees that which another concept signifies more directly, in order to characterize the one through the other. There is here a double impotence to keep silent about God, which silences him all the more. But whence comes the impotence to silence, or rather, our impotence to guard our silence instead of silencing that which our chattering assails?

Keeping our silence, in order precisely by this reserve to

honor that which we would designate by silence—in other words, in this case, God—this would become thinkable only if God exposed himself to thought. The retreat of our eventual silence implies an absolute pole of reference around which a respectful desert might grow. The common idolatrous treatment of God prohibits straightaway the solitude of such an absolute pole of reference, since between our gaze or our speech and him, the idol interposes the invisible mirror where the first visible sends the thrust of this gaze back to itself. For what is characteristic of modernity, understood as the perfect completion of metaphysics, does not at all consist in a negation of God.

Such theoretical negation can be located easily in preceding centuries. Modernity is characterized first by the nullification of God as a question. Why does God no longer inhabit any process of questioning? Because the response to the question of his essence or existence (according to the strict metaphysical acceptation of these terms) becomes irrelevant. Not, undoubtedly, for ideological debate and according to the yardstick of the movement of ideas, but surely given a phenomenological reduction. What, then, is put at stake in a negation or an affirmation of God? Not God as such, but the compatibility or incompatibility of an idol called "God" with the whole of the conceptual system where beings in their Being make epoch. The gap between compatibility and incompatibility no doubt matters, but it matters infinitely less than the constant substitution, in one case and the other, of an absolute pole by an idol. Theism and atheism bear equally upon an idol. They remain enemies, but fraternal enemies, in a common and impassable idolatry. Of such idolatry Nietzsche gives the best and final illustration, by demonstrating in exemplary fashion the two functions held by the idol.—To begin with, negation. In what way must one refute something that is named "God"? Not vaguely, but very exactly, for as much as " 'The father' in God is thoroughly refuted; likewise 'the judge,' 'the rewarder' "; this is to say that refutation implies an identification between the so-called "God" and the moral uses/names that, de facto, constitute his operative definition: "Question: does morality make impossible this pantheistic affirmation of all things too? At bottom it is only the moral god that has been overcome. Does it make sense to conceive a god 'beyond good and evil'? Would a pantheism in this sense be possible?"[9] Refutation acts in the gap between an overly precise but operative concept of "God" (the "moral God" in the sense of Kant or Fichte) and the undetermined instance of a "God beyond good and evil." This very gap renders problematic the identification of the absolutely autonomous pole with a name/concept, whatever it may be. In fact, the "moral God" functions as an idol, indisputably reflecting the gaze that the man of *ressentiment* directs toward the divine, precisely because he in no way reaches the absolute pole. Where then is the idol that supports atheism fixed? The response to this question fully manifests the modern lack of difference between theism and atheism. In fact, atheism works on an idol of the will to power, as also does the affirmation of "new gods." Atheism denies the "moral God" in having understood the "birth of Christianity out of the spirit of *ressentiment,*" hence for having reconstituted its genealogy on the basis of a reactive state of the will to power; for *"ressentiment* itself becomes creative and gives birth to values."[10] What is peculiar to Nietzsche consists not so much in proclaiming the "death of God" as in thinking it on the basis of the will to power. One certainly must continue to admit what is taken for "God," but as an effect of a (reactive) state of the will to power.

Hence, in perfect continuity with (idolatrous) negation, (idolatrous) affirmation: when, according to another inclination in his thought concerning the divine, Nietzsche opens the horizon of manifestation of the "new gods," he deduces them just as much from the will to power: "And how many new gods are still possible! As for myself, in whom the religious, that is to say god-forming [*gottbildende*] instinct occasionally becomes active at impossible times—how differently, how variously the divine has revealed itself to me each time!" Under what forms? Response: "The sole way of maintaining a meaning for the concept 'God' would be: God *not* as a driving force, but God as a maximal state, as epoch [making]—a point in the evolution of the will to power"; or again: "'God' as the moment of culmination: [*Dasein*] as an eternal deifying and un-deifying. But in that not a high point of value, but a high point of power."[11] The "new gods" receive their justification, their existence, and their meaning from the sole will to power, of which they offer a thousand indefinitely rejected and renascent faces, a thousand idols without twilight because without eternity, if not with repeated births. Henceforth one must ask what still separates them from the "moral God," since, like him, they ensue from the will to power. Or even, why are certain idols extinguished crepuscularly, whereas others open at dawn? Because, simply, some originate in a more active and affirmative figure of the will to power, and others in a less affirmative, more reactive figure. Between the dead and future "gods" the distinction remains one of degree. From the point of view of the multiform will to power, the "gods," whatever they may be, remain idols whose validity faithfully reflects the state of the gaze that aims at them and sees in them its own affirmation or infirmity. Both on the face of the "moral God" and on that of the "new gods," only the will to power shows itself. It alone speaks, in the dithyramb of the "gods" that live as in the silence of the "gods" that are dead.

And so we understand why we manage so poorly to keep silent before that which we cannot express in a statement. What Wittgenstein indicates by the term of *das Mystische*[12] we never have in view for itself, precisely because we always aim at it within our own aim. Nobody demonstrates this better than Nietzsche, who, as by a phenomenological reduction *avant la lettre,* genealogically leads the "gods"—all, without exception—back to the will to power. Now this will to power speaks and produces, even if *das Mystische* appears "dead" since the will to power indeed suffices as well to speak and to produce it. That is, the "gods" can always be expressed, as genealogically recognized idols of the will to power. We never will have to keep silent before that which we cannot say—because we never will have anything to express other than idols of the will to power. Nothing is to be said but the will to power, outside of which nothing *is*, not even the nothing, since becoming itself passes, like being, to the will to power: "Recapitulation: to impose upon becoming the character of Being—that is the supreme will to power."[13] Hence we never will keep silent, occupied with producing and expressing the thousand and one idols at which the will to power, within and outside of us, will aim as so many goals. Hence, not keeping silent, we will not point out, even by a respectful silence, an absolute pole—absolved from the will to power. Hence, by not keeping silent, by covering it with our busy chattering, we silence that which silence alone, possibly, could have honored—by attempting precisely not to say it, or even to aim at it. Either to silence silence, by dint of words busied in declaring all the idols and the thousand and one goals, or else to silence *oneself* in order to let that very thing which silence honors be told.

But if our very silence does not succeed at keeping silent, the fault does not return to some empirical behavior of "a public scoundrel" that the simple measures of an intellectual police would be able to straighten out. Our silence either gives way to an indefinite chattering or no longer manages to honor, but simply passes under silence, because, fundamentally, it belongs, as do all of us, to the domain of nihilism, hence, of the play, finally laid bare, of the will to power. Metaphysics comes to completion in the will to power that does not cease to will itself, as well when it wills "gods" as when it does not will them, and hence which wills only idols of itself, and cannot but will such idols. And in this metaphysical completion, the western destiny of the Being of beings is consummated in its ultimate perfection, since "the innermost essence of Being is the will to power."[14]

We therefore must risk a question, already often approached, that has continued to appeal to us: in order to withdraw "God" from the idol, must we not undertake to think him—should we still say think?—starting from another instance than the one that reduces him to silence, or covers him over with idolatrous chattering? We identify this instance as the will to power, hence metaphysics in its completion, hence finally as Being itself envisaged as the Being of beings. To free "God" from his quotation marks would require nothing less than to free him from metaphysics, hence from the Being of beings. To free silence from its idolatrous dishonor would require nothing less than to free the word "God" from the Being of beings. But can one think outside of Being? And, in order to escape idolatry and to take away its quotation marks, does it suffice precisely no longer to mark them?

2—The Ontological Impediment[15]

In a sense, no one more than Heidegger has aroused the suspicion that it may be necessary to liberate "God" from the question on/of Being, but that this liberation is also contrary to the conditions of thought. The enormity of our proposition—to liberate "God" from Being—can become tolerable, hence simply envisageable, only if it is first formulated rigorously enough to admit precise reservations and to offer a measurable paradox. Thus must one follow the Heideggerian establishment of the chiasmus between "God" and Being, if only to learn to displace it. For if "God" crosses Being, this crossing itself can be understood in several ways.

The first decision made by Heidegger, and maintained down to the last texts, cuts absolutely between theology and the question of—and even more—the word *Being;* the first is constituted as such, hence in conformity with its essence, only by excluding the second. Thus, in 1951 in Zurich, where someone asked him, once again, "Is it proper to posit Being and God as identical?" Heidegger responded,

> Being and God are not identical and I would never attempt to think the essence of God by means of Being. Some among you perhaps know that I come from theology, that I still guard an old love for it and that I am not without a certain understanding of it. If I were yet to write a theology—to which I sometimes feel inclined—then the word *Being* would not occur in it. Faith does not need the thought of Being. When faith has recourse to this thought, it is no longer faith. This is what Luther understood. Even within his own church this seems to be forgotten. One could not be more reserved than I before every attempt to employ Being to think theologically in what way God is God. Of Being, there is nothing here to expect. I believe that Being can never be thought as the ground and essence of God, but that nevertheless the experience of God and of his manifestedness, to the extent that the latter can indeed meet man, flashes in the dimension of Being, which in no way signifies that Being might be

> regarded as a possible predicate for God. On this point one would have to establish completely new distinctions and delimitations.[16]

This complex text joins several theses which it is important not to confuse: (*a*) the nonidentity of God with Being; (*b*) the nonpertinence of the word *Being* in theology; (*c*) the pertinence of the dimension of Being for experiencing "God." At this point on our path, we will engage only the second of these theses, which conveys the incompatability of *Being* with the theological lexicon. In 1953, at Hofgeismar, Heidegger very clearly confirmed it: "The thinker speaks of the 'manifestness [*Offenbarkeit*] of Being'; but 'Being' is an untheological word. Because revelation itself determines the manner of manifestness and because theology does not have to prove or interpret 'Being,' theology does not have to defend itself before philosophy. . . . The Christian experience is so completely different that it has no need to enter into competition with philosophy. When theology holds fast to the view that philosophy is foolishness, the mystery character of revelation will be much better preserved. Therefore, in the face of a final decision, the ways part."[17] The caesura clearly appears: thought, here philosophy, concentrates on the open manifestation (*Offenbarkeit*) of Being, theology is attached to the revelation (*Offenbarung*) of "God"; the piety of the one is due to the rigor of its questioning, the piety of the other, to the vigor of faith. Not only do they remain "separated by an abyss,"[18] but faith, which alone qualifies theology, confronts philosophy as a "mortal enemy, a *Todfeind*."[19] For theology is not limited to distinguishing itself from philosophy; in conformity with the word of Saint Paul, "Has not God distracted [*emōranen*] the wisdom of the world?" and, with Luther's authority, Heidegger gives full weight to faith's apprehension of philosophy as foolishness: "For the original Christian faith, philosophy is foolishness," and asks modern believers, "Will Christian theology make up its mind to take seriously the word of the apostle and thus also the conception of philosophy as foolishness?"[20] As long as faith is not conscious of its own nature, it misses its own basis, namely, faith alone, and in its turn is distracted; distracted, it attempts to fix itself a new ground in calling for Being—despite the abyss that separates the two—going so far as to claim to elaborate a "Christian philosophy" where, in the best of cases, thought can recognize only a "square circle" or some "wooden iron."[21] This caesura admits no reconciliation: if theology refuses to look on philosophy as foolishness, then theology, in return, becomes foolishness in the eyes, this time, of philosophy. "Foolishness" here indicates much more than an error, a divergence, a conflict; foolishness indicates the irreducibility of two logics that neither can nor must, in any case, comprehend one another: faith cannot comprehend thought, or thought faith; no third position will ever present itself to reconcile them, to the extent that "in the face of a final decision, the ways part."[22] Foolishness indicates that the two logics act irreducibly, in solitudes that no mediation can open; or rather, since it depends notably on Being, logic does not cover the field of revelation that the Johannine *Logos* opens to faith. Nothing less than foolishness separates theology from Being.

This disposition of the disciplines is not sufficient, however, for our initial plan—to liberate "God" from the question of Being. It is not sufficient, first, because Heidegger, in full accord with his intention, does not elaborate the modalities of an authentically theological discourse, since it remains to him, by hypothesis, foreign. A single indication comes to us: the word *Being* must not intervene in a theological discourse. This indicates a rule that theologians should, if not respect literally, at least consider with care. Next, this disposition does not suffice because the distinction between the disciplines immediately frees up the possibility of a nontheological discourse on "God." For, if theology does not speak according to Being, and if "God" has been thought nonetheless according to Being, one must immediately deduce that some thoughts of "God" are not the concern of theology. Hence the field of theology does not coincide with that of "God": "God" can also be the concern of theiology, of knowledge concerning the being par excellence: "First philosophy, qua ontology, is also the theology of what truly is. It should more accurately be called theiology. The science of beings as such is in itself onto-theological."[23] The addition of an *i,* which transforms theology into theiology, is not insignificant: the *logos* henceforth bears, more essentially than on "God"/ *ho theos,* on the instance that alone characterizes it as exemplary, the divine itself/*to theion*. Beings are now expressed in their Being according to the double dimension of beings in general and of the being par excellence; the latter defines the possibility of a strictly philosophical science of the divine, theiology. It is only a question here of beings in their Being, and not of that which faith offers to authentically Christian theology; an indisputable proof comes to us in that (the) theiology (of onto-theo-logy), in stating "the existence of God" *positively,* can nevertheless perfectly well blaspheme: "For example, a proof for the existence of God can be constructed by means of the most rigorous formal logic and yet prove nothing, since a god who must permit his existence to be proved in the first place [*erst*] is ultimately a very ungodly god. The best such proofs of existence can yield is blasphemy."[24]

To "degrade" the notion of "God," for example, to that of "highest value" constitutes a "blow" against "God," inasmuch as it is first "the greatest blasphemy imaginable against Being."[25] The theiological discourse on "God," or on any other being par excellence, is the concern of philosophy and more precisely of onto-theo-logy, which characterizes philosophy's metaphysical turn. Metaphysics, in fact, has no need for the theology of faith in order to state divine names: "God" as ultimate foundation, with Leibniz;[26] "God" as "God of morality" with Kant, Fichte, and Nietzsche;[27] "God" finally and above all as *causa sui* with Descartes, Spinoza, and in the end all of metaphysics.[28] These concepts of "God" arise strictly from metaphysics, according to the sole demand of onto-theo-logy. And in addition, if the thought that wants to "destruct" the ontology of metaphysics attempts to reach "a more divine god,"[29] this quest belongs still and always to the meditation of Being, whose theiology touches beings—without relation to the theology touched by faith. In other words, "God" does not enter into philosophy because, from Christian revelation, he would pass into Greek thought; for this passage itself became possible only inasmuch as, first and foremost, the (Greek) thought of Being is constituted as the thought of the Being of beings according to onto-theo-logy.[30]

Thus, the "abyssal" distinction between philosophy and theology appears otherwise more complex than a simple contraposition: theology does not have at its disposal an exclusive domain to which the undivided domain of philosophy would correspond: in fact philosophy, like theology, also reaches something like "God." Over the domain of "God," theiology has as much right, or at least other but indisputable rights, as theology. More than of contraposition, we would have to speak of subordination—unless, with "God," it should be a question, in both cases, of the same stakes.

Such a question can be taken up in another way. We will ask then, if theology does not have "God" for its exclusive formal object, how, vis-à-vis theiology, can theology be defined? Heidegger gives theology as such a precise and—to our knowledge—never retracted definition: "Theology as the interpretation of the divine word of revelation," or, which here amounts to the same thing, "interpretation of man's Being toward God."[31] Theology therefore does not have to do with "God," in whatever sense one understands him. It has to do with the fact (*Faktum/Positivität*) of faith in the Crucified, a fact that only faith receives and conceives: it secures its scientificity only by fixing itself on the positive fact of faith, namely, the relation of the believer to the Crucified. Theology does not elaborate the science of "God," but "the science of faith," and only then the science of the object of faith (*das Geglaubte*), in the strict sense that this object is only elaborated in faith as "believing comportment."[32] If from the very first, as early as section three, *Sein und Zeit* privileges the authority of Luther, this nonetheless is not a question of a choice between several possible theologies (against Catholicism, e.g.); it is a question of a philosophical decision. Luther intervenes to demonstrate the gap between theiological knowledge (according to the later nomenclature) of "God" and theological science, which concerns only the relation of faith to the event of faith. Nevertheless, this distinction between sciences would remain strictly epistemological (taking the expression with all its requisite insignificance), if Christian theology had not in fact historically misunderstood its own definition; for it did not cease, in Heidegger's eyes, to pretend to be a science not of faith and thus only of the *believing* man and then of the "God" *of faith,* but indeed a science, by faith, of man and even of "God." Indeed, one must remark that, more than ten years before Heidegger denounces the confusion between theology and theiology, *Sein und Zeit* denounces before and above all else the confusion between the (phenomenological) analytic of *Dasein* and "the anthropology of Christianity and the ancient world," which, substituting itself for the former, masks its urgency and closes off access to it. "The anthropology of Christian theology, taking with it the ancient definition [namely, of man as *animal rationale*], arrives at an interpretation of beings, which we call *Dasein.*"[33] Instead of understanding itself as a "conceptual self-interpretation of *believing* existence," as an "interpretation of man's Being *toward God,*"[34] theology claims to be an interpretation of *being* itself, whose ontological dignity prescribes that one name it *Dasein.* Theology misses its own authentically theological status by usurping, under the apparently inoffensive title of anthropology, the strictly phenomenological (hence philosophical) task of an analytic of *Dasein.* Theology first loses its way by claiming to treat *Dasein* as such (*schlechthin/überhaupt*), and not, as a science of faith, *Dasein* as believing. In short, one must relativize theology, hence put it back in its place, precisely because it does not keep its place and does not recognize the gap between *Dasein* as such and *Dasein* as believing. Theology, through one and the same wrong move, does not recognize the scientific character that faith assures it and prevents, by its displaced anthropology, the analytic of *Dasein.* Heidegger relativizes the dignity of theology only in the name of the exigencies of what is involved in *Dasein,* the Being of beings, hence in the name of what he even names, at that time, ontology.[35]

On the basis of *Sein und Zeit,* and only thus, the lecture *Phänomenologie und Theologie,* given first in the same year, 1927, at Tübingen, becomes intelligible. In it, a very clearly defined topic opposes philosophy and theology. Philosophy is distinguished from every other science in that, concentrated on the analytic of *Dasein,* of the being with whose being Being itself is an issue,[36] it constitutes "*the* science of Being, the ontological science." On the contrary, theology remains an "ontic science" with the same standing as chemistry or mathematics.[37]

There is no paradox in that: theology is elaborated as a p
science precisely because a *positum* is reserved for it;
itum, this being that becomes a formal object for it, must n
lead to confusion: it is not a question of "God" (who is first the concern of theiology) or of man (who as *Dasein* is the concern of philosophy), but purely and simply of the *Christlichkeit,* namely, of the faith of man in the event of Christ's being put to death. But such a "Christianity," if it affects man, does not allow any anthropology and does not interfere with the analytic of *Dasein,* and for a fundamental reason: as opposed to other existentials and other *Grundbestimmungen,* Christianity, if it indeed marks *Dasein* in a situation of believing existence, nevertheless does not belong to it. Christianity affects *Dasein* but neither issues from it nor characterizes it: "The essence of faith can formally be sketched as a mode of human existence which, according to its own testimony—itself belonging to this mode of existence—*does not* arise from Dasein and *is not* freely temporalized by it, but rather from that which is revealed in and with this mode of existence, from what is believed." To believe, most certainly, concerns *Dasein* as a possibility of existence, but, in the capacity of faith, this possibility can come to it only from an instance other than itself as *Dasein:* "the *Dasein* which is touched by it does not itself have mastery of it (*von sich aus nicht mächtig*)."[38] Theology studies that which only occurs to *Dasein* in a manner not fitted to *Dasein,* since by definition the fact of faith is measured by what the believer believes. In other words, nothing *daseinsmässig* intervenes in the field of theology. Hence it follows that each concept, in order to appear authentically theological, must measure its essential disparity with the "pre-Christian *Dasein,*"[39] which assures the strictly ontological "correction" of the ontic addition that faith carries out in it.[40] Faith introduces a "way"[41] of *Dasein* that can appear only with the measure of the disparity that its believing variant imposes on *Dasein;* hence by reference to the ontological analytic of *Dasein.* Theology, thus justified as the ontic science of "Christianity" and of believing existence, falls outside of the analytic of *Dasein.* The phenomenological reduction of man to *Dasein* undertaken by *Sein und Zeit* excludes theology as much as all the other ontic sciences—it excludes theology even

more, for none has attempted as powerfully as theology to dispense with such an analytic through the efforts of anthropology. Theology must renounce determining *Dasein* and, on the contrary, let itself be "corrected" by its neutrality. Neutrality means the analytic of *Dasein* has nothing to do with something like faith or, especially, "God." In a word, *Dasein* exists—precisely because it ex-sists—without "God": "Philosophical research is and remains an atheism," "The existentiell involvement of fundamental ontology brings with it the semblance of an extremely individualistic, radical atheism."[42] The invariant of *Dasein* appears more essential to man than the ontic variant introduced by faith. Man can eventually become a believer only inasmuch as he exists first as *Dasein*.

To liberate theology from the word *Being* now assumes a precise meaning: it is not in any way a question of unbinding theology from *Dasein* but, on the contrary, of according theology a proper domain—faith—only on condition of submitting it to an ontological "correction." Theology distances itself from *Being* neither more nor less than it distinguishes itself, like the other ontic sciences, from *Dasein*. To be sure, it must not employ the word *Being* but by default, not by excess: theology refers to something greater than itself, to the existential analytic of *Dasein*, and later, to the thought of *Seyn*. The theology of faith must avoid saying the word *Being* because Being expresses itself more essentially than theology can ever glimpse; and for this very reason every theology remains subject to the question of Being, as every ontic variant of *Dasein* refers back to bare *Dasein* itself.[43]

In assigning ourselves the task of liberating "God" from the question of/on Being, we at first believed that we found, following the tracks left by Heidegger, our journey's path. We now glimpse that this is not the case; the situation is defined on the contrary by two relativizations: (*a*) In metaphysics, "God," in the capacity of being par excellence, is the concern of a theiology inscribed in the onto-theo-logy of metaphysics; to the extent that metaphysics in a certain way puts the Being of beings into operation, "God" in metaphysics is the concern of Being; and this without exception. The intervention of the Christian "God" in the concepts of metaphysics constitutes but one par-

ticular case, on the whole not very determining, of ontc
logy. Before such an inclusion of "God" in Being, can on
by a reflex characterized, to simplify, as Lutheran (but als
trated by Pascal or Barth), toward a "God of faith," exempt from
metaphysical determination? (*b*) In this second hypothesis, theology appears as an ontic science of faith, whose perfect independence remains exactly ontic, and which, in that very measure, must be subject to the ontological "correction" of *Dasein,* of which it offers, in its own way, only a variant. We see here the independence most certainly of faith and of its theology, but ontic independence, which implies an irreducible ontological dependence. Hence the theology of faith falls within the domain of *Dasein* and, directly through it, of Being, as the "God" of metaphysics falls within the domain of onto-theo-logy and hence indirectly through it of Being. It seems that the question of "God" never suffered as radical a reduction to the first question of Being as in the phenomenological enterprise of Heidegger.

Does it remain possible to envisage a third route, where the question concerning "God" would be freed from the question of Being? One could indeed argue in this way: the faith of believing man certainly refers, phenomenologically, back to *Dasein,* but its intention aims at a term foreign to *Dasein;* even more, the undetermined term of that aim cannot be reduced to what metaphysics apprehends of it, a *causa sui;* hence, in the capacity of a pure possibility for the believing aim, it is necessary to envisage another name of "God." Heidegger actually does not dismiss this third route—or, at least, he does not dismiss it totally. But he envisages it according to an appreciably different apparatus: a "God" other than the *causa sui* can and even must be envisaged; but to envisage, if the term must have a phenomenological meaning, implies an aim, and hence an aim of *Dasein.* This aim cannot be defined by faith, which remains a factical and ontic determination of *Dasein;* it therefore must be understood on the basis of *Dasein* as such, as the being in which its being, or rather Being itself, is an issue. Consequently, the "more divine god" can be envisaged only within the limit of an aim that determines it in advance as a being, elaborated according to the "Being of the gods, *Seyn der Göt-*

ter."[44] That which, whatever it may *be,* will (would) respond to the aim of "God" will (would) *be* "God" only on the condition of being: "for the god/'God' himself also is—if he is—a being and stands as a being in Being, in the latter's essence, which brings itself disclosingly to pass out of the worlding of the world, *auch der Gott ist, wenn er ist, ein Seiender.*"[45] Every non-metaphysical possibility of "God" finds itself governed from the start by the thesis (hypothesis, impediment [*hypothèque*]?) of Being that will accommodate it only as a being. If there must be a "God" outside of metaphysics, this could *be* only if he *is*—in the capacity of a being elaborated in its being, hence according to Being. Being offers in advance the screen on which any "God" that would be constituted would be projected and would appear—since, by definition, to be constituted signifies to be constituted as a being. To be constituted as being of/in Being, as one surrenders to—literally becomes "the divine prisoner" of—Being? Of course, it seems possible to attenuate this overly violent conclusion by all the concessions and kindness of the world; but this is only the kindness precisely *of the world,* of the Fourfold where the world worlds, between Earth and Sky, the mortals and the divinities. One must still decide whether the worldliness of the world has the right and dignity to take in from among the divinities, gods, or however one would like to name them, something like "God," or more exactly that which must lose the quotation marks of "God" in order to reveal itself, without condition, antecedent, or genealogy, as that which iconistically crosses the rights of the absolute, G~~o~~d? *Whence comes the decision that G~~o~~d should have to be,* like a being that Being manifests, that is manifested according to Being? How is it that the gap between manifestation (*Offenbarkeit*) and revelation (*Offenbarung*), explicitly repeated and traversed, is found to be forgotten and erased, so as to conclude that what determines the one—manifestedness of beings according to the Openness of Being—must necessarily determine revelation as well? In the end, is it self-evident that biblical revelation transgresses neither beings in what they reveal nor Being in the manner [*guise*] of its revelation? Who then decides that the mode of revelation, about which the Bible emphasizes that it speaks *polumerōs kai polutropōs,* "in many refrains, in many different ways" (Heb. 1:1), should have to sacrifice, as a retainer fee, to Being? According to Heidegger's very discourse, the Fourfold defines the world and its worlding. What then of the event that is called G~~o~~d, since it claims not to belong to this world (John 18:36), and asks those who believe to "deal with this world as though they had no dealings with it [*khrōmenoi ton kosmon hōs mē katakhrōmenoi*]. For the figure of this world is passing away" (1 Cor. 7:31)? In other words, if, by an anhypothetical hypothesis that we admit absolutely, the question of Being is determined only in relation to itself, namely, according to the claim that Being exerts over *Dasein* and that defines at the start every world that would be constituted as such, must one not infer *also, according to the same rigor,* that that which, by hypothesis, does not belong to the world and gives itself as such, is not the concern of Being? Can one not uphold the radical irreducibility to the *Anspruch des Seins* of what Heidegger himself does not hesitate—strangely—to name, in parallel, the *Anspruch des Vaters in Christus,*[46] the claim that the Father, in Christ, exerts on man, whose designation as *Dasein* henceforth becomes worthy of question? Or again, can one have done with the specificity of faith, acknowledged, moreover, by imposing on it a purely ontic status, as if it were self-evident that the phenomenological enterprise of an analytic of *Dasein* did not admit, by its very reduction, any exterior and definitively other instance? These questions here remain, for us, questions, and do not mask disguised affirmations. However, a question remains a question, even if it does not come to us from Being. For faith, far from annihilating questions through the idiotic prolepsis of a blunt certitude (as many people, and not the least among them, imagine), can open certain abysses that all the meditation *of the world* would not be able even to glimpse. These interrogations could be gathered into a topical question, modest in appearance: does the name of the G~~o~~d, who is crossed because he is crucified, belong to the domain of Being? We are not at all speaking of "God" in general, or thought on the basis of the divine, hence also of the Fourfold. We are speaking of the G~~o~~d who is crossed by a cross because he reveals himself by his placement on a cross, the G~~o~~d revealed by, in, and as the Christ;

in other words, the G~~o~~d of a rigorously *Christian* theology. But—and we must allow ourselves to be amazed by this—for Heidegger, even *this* G~~o~~d remains enough a "God" to take his name from Being: "in Christian theology, we define God, the *summum ens qua summum bonum,* as the highest value."[47] This statement is at the very least doubly amazing. First, it is amazing in that the nomination of "God" as *ens supremum* is attributed expressly to *Christian* theology and not to the theiology of onto-theo-logy, as would have seemed more suitable; to invoke a *lapsus* here would amount to underestimating in an unworthy manner the steadiness of Heidegger's writing. And if by chance it were necessary nevertheless to concede a *lapsus,* the secret slipping of thought thus betrayed would merit as much attention as the explicitness of a written letter; in fact, *Christian theo*logy passes under the yoke of the question of Being. But this statement is also amazing in a second way. The two terms here evoked, *summum ens* and *summum bonum,* refer, no doubt intentionally, to the problem of divine names, and even more precisely, to the debate over the primacy, among them, of the *ens* or of the *bonum.* In other words, Heidegger takes a position, in a debate that can be historically situated, in favor of the *ens* as the first divine name: the good intervenes now only as a manner of beingness, which alone sets forth the first name of "God." In a sense, everything happens as if the primacy of the question of Being (Heidegger) met, without confusion and with the full disparity that separates a thought that recedes from metaphysics from a thought that remains in it, the primacy of the *ens* over every other divine name (Saint Thomas). Once again, it is not a question of establishing a spurious agreement—a game, we know, too often attempted, and always in vain—but of noting the analogy between two relations of anteriority: to subject the question of "God" first to the question of Being, to subject the naming of "God" to the primacy of the *ens.* In summarily retracing the Thomistic decision, we would have not only to determine how the *ens* acts among the divine names, or how its primacy sets aside other means of access to "God," but perhaps also to anticipate how, by analogy, the Heideggerian decision may not be self-evident and, even, how to open up another side, if not a beyond: that G~~o~~d does not express himself first according to and starting from Being.

3—Being or Else (The Good)

The principal denomination of G~~o~~d as and by Being cannot—let us point out the evidence straightaway—be justified by pure and simple recourse to the verse from Exodus 3:14. Indeed, only one's conceptual weakness permits the attribution to the "metaphysic of Exodus" of the dignity and the merit of a radical innovation. Otherwise, Saint Thomas would have stated only the common, directly biblical thesis—which, as much from the point of view of Gilson as from any other, could not be defended. May a few remarks therefore suffice here to mark the disparity between the biblical text and the "metaphysic of Exodus." (*a*) The formula from the Hebrew, *ehyeh asher ehyeh,* can be understood as a positive statement, of the type, "I am the one who is," but doubtless first as a refusal to specify further of what "Being" it is a question, in the way of a statement of the type, "I am who I am";[48] thus did Gilson himself recognize that, understood literally, Exodus 3:14 offers "the only formula that says absolutely nothing and that says absolutely everything."[49] (*b*) Supposing that this formula offers a positive statement and does not deny the possibility and legitimacy of any statement concerning G~~o~~d, one would still have to determine under what formulation one can understand it. It can be admitted that, as such, the Hebrew verb *hayah* does not suffice to introduce a concept of "Being"; historically, the transition from the biblical register to conceptual debate between philosophers and theologians depends on the translation of the Septuagint: *egō eimi ho ōn.* This translation substitutes a participle, *ho ōn,* for a conjugated form, a present persistence for something unaccomplished; in short, an action can become an attribute, even a name. This modification remains in the background of the Latin formula *Sum qui sum,* as soon as it is interpreted in view of the *ipsum esse* or of the *idipsum esse* (from Saint Augustine on).[50] (*c*) Even when the Greek Fathers rely on Exodus 3:14 to determine categorically the divinity of the Word, for example, and even though they invoke it to define a name for G~~o~~d, they never infer thereby that this name, *ho ōn,* might define the very essence of God as such. Precisely because *ho ōn* returns to the Son, it could not in any way determine the triune divinity, which therefore exceeds Being.[51] (*d*) Finally, supposing that the preliminary difficulties have found a group of satisfying and coherent solutions, one would still have to define whether the name indirectly implied by Exodus 3:14 inevitably precedes other names, like the one that 1 John 4:8 insinuates, *ho theos agapē estin,* "God is love," or we would have to gloss: what allows that "God" should be G~~o~~d consists, more radically than in being, in loving. In short, in supposing that Exodus 3:14 delivers one of the divine names, we still would have to determine whether it is a question of the first. No exegesis, no philological fact, no objective inquiry could accomplish or justify this step; only a theological decision could do so and retrospectively rely on literary arguments. It was Saint Thomas who made this decision in full knowledge of the facts, since he did it in a debate with the *Treatise on Divine Names* by Denys. Undoubtedly, in face of the claim of the *ens/esse* to the title of first divine name, agape as such is not encountered, but only the good, *bonum/agathon;* but precisely, specifies Denys, G~~o~~d himself "charms" all beings at once by "goodness, charity and desire, *agathotēti kai agapēsei kai erōti,*" since he loves "with a beautiful and good *eros* of all things, by the hyperbole of desiring goodness, *erōtikē*"[52]: the good inspires and fosters agape (as also *erōs*). We therefore are justified in reading, in the debate between the *ens* and the good, in a sense, the debate between the *ens* and agape, which crops up therein.

When Saint Thomas postulates that "the good does not add anything to being [the *ens*] either really or conceptually, *nec re nec ratione,*" he does not limit himself to underscoring the largely admitted reversibility of transcendentals, which he later will state by emphasizing that "the goodness of God is not something added to his substance, but his very substance is his goodness."[53] He states a thesis that is directly opposed to the anteriority, more traditionally accepted in Christian theology, of the good over the *ens.* For Saint Bonaventure still, the last instance that permits a contemplation of G~~o~~d is contained in goodness, whereas the *ens/esse* offers only the next-to-last step of speakable elevation. "After considering the essential attributes of God, the eye of our intelligence should be raised to look upon the most blessed Trinity, so that the second Cherub may be placed alongside the first [namely, in order to frame the Ark of the Covenant]. Just as being itself [*ipsum esse*] is the root principle of viewing the essential attributes, and the name through which all the others become known, so the good itself [*ipsum bonum*] is the principal foundation for contemplating the emanations." The first of these two names relies on the word of Moses and was privileged by John of Damascus, whereas the second relies on the Trinitarian word (Matt. 28:19) of Christ; and "Dionysius, following Christ, says that the Good is God's primary name."[54] In going back from *id quo nihil majus cogitari potest* to *id quo nihil melius cogitari potest,* Saint Bonaventure indeed inevitably came upon Denys and the thesis that Saint Thomas confronts. Denys posits that G~~o~~d, namely, that which can be aimed at only by the function (and not the category) of the "Requisite (*aitia*) of all things," is deployed as the "principle of beings whence issues, as well as all beings whatsoever, Being itself, *arkhē aph'ēs kai auto to einai.*" G~~o~~d gives Being to beings only because he precedes not only these beings, but also the gift that he delivers to them—to be. In this way the precedence of Being over beings itself refers to the precedence of the gift over Being, hence finally of the one who delivers the gift over Being. That one, the Requisite, "Being returns to him, but he does not return to Being; Being is found in him, but he is not found in Being; he maintains Being, but Being does not maintain him."[55] Being, *auto to einai,* is only uncovered in being dispensed by a gift; the gift, which Being itself thus requires, is accomplished only in allowing the disclosure in it of the gesture of a giving as much imprescriptible as indescribable, which receives the name, in praise, of goodness. More than for the good, Denys praises G~~o~~d for the (de-) nomination of goodness: the good that gives and gives itself in fact. The ultimate nomination recedes from Being to goodness, whose denomination opens a properly unconditioned field to the Requisite, over all and even over nothing: "for the divine denomination of the good manifests all the processions of the Requisite of all things, and extends as much to beings as to nonbeings, *eis ta onta kai eis ta ouk onta.*"[56] It is this text that Saint Thomas had to confront and bypass when he attempted to establish that the name taken from Exodus 3:14, "who is, the one who is," stands as "the most proper name of God"; his reasoning is stated thus: this name "does not signify form, but simply being itself [*ipsum esse*]. Hence since the being of God is His essence itself [*esse Dei sit ipsa ejus essentia*], which can be said of no other . . ., it is clear that among other names this one specially nominates God [*hoc maxime proprie nominat Deum*]."[57] The whole question consists precisely in determining whether a name can be suitable "maxime proprie" to G~~o~~d, if G~~o~~d can have an essence, and (only) finally if this "essence" can be fixed in the *ipsum esse/actus essendi.* For Denys deploys the primacy of goodness over *auto to einai,* over the *ipsum esse* with particular rigor. To begin with, he does not pretend that goodness constitutes the proper name of the Requisite, but that in the apprehension of goodness the dimension is cleared where the very possibility of a categorical statement concerning G~~o~~d ceases to be valid, and where the reversal of denomination into praise becomes inevitable. *To praise* the Requisite *as* such, hence *as* goodness, amounts to opening distance. Distance neither asks nor tolerates that one fill it but that one traverse it, in an infinite praise that feeds on the impossibility or, better, the impropriety of the category. The first praise, the name of goodness, therefore does *not* offer any "most proper name" and decidedly abolishes every conceptual idol of "God" in favor of the luminous darkness where G~~o~~d manifests (and not masks) himself, in short, where he gives himself to be envisaged by us.

Next, since the Requisite recedes from Being to goodness, it also must advance beyond beings to nonbeings. Goodness advances to meet nonbeings. Denys insists without reservation on this decisive point, in clearly judging the audacity of his thesis: "And if the good surpasses all beings . . . one must say also, if one might dare, that non-being itself also, *kai auto to mē on,* tends towards the good beyond all beings"; and further on: "The discourse must dare even to say that non-being also, *kai to mē on,* participates in the beautiful and the good [namely, *kalon kai agathon*]," "or, to be brief, all beings come from the beautiful and the good, and all non-beings reside beyond every essence in the beautiful and the good."[58] In order to praise G⊗d as being Being itself, it is necessary that whoever thus refers to the Requisite should petition [*requière*] him starting from Being, hence that he be; only beings can aim at G⊗d according to and as *auto to einai.* That which is not cannot, by definition, enter into *this* form of praise. But in order to praise G⊗d as beautiful and good, as goodness, the petitioner [*le requérant*] has no need, if only to be, since the absence of all perfection, even ontic, already designates the place and the instance of a radical desire. The less the nothing has of perfection, the more it will desire perfection. At the extreme, in order to desire, literally less than nothing is required: the less than nothing itself[59] can already petition the Requisite under the denomination of goodness, can praise him as goodness. Ontology concerns being, and if it touches upon nonbeing, this is in view of comprehending it in and as possible being. The discourse of praise is rightfully implemented with nonbeing as such, since its radical imperfection itself offers the motivating forces of desire with a view toward goodness. The less than nothing aims at the Requisite through its absolute desire itself; the specificity of that aim is attested by the specificity of the denomination by which the less than nothing praises the Requisite: as the beautiful and good, and not as Being itself—denomination characterized by another praise and another situation, that of beings (and, for ontology, possible and assimilated ones). Nonbeings as such praise the Requisite by an absolutely singular praise, irreducible to that employed, to give one example among others, by beings.

The modern commentaries (and Saint Thomas) here advance the same reductionist interpretation: by *mē on,* nonbeing, and *ouk onta,* nonbeings, Denys would mean only matter without form, the privation of form, and in no way absolute non-Being.[60] Supposing that such should be the implicit doctrine of the Dionysian *corpus,* one still would have to wonder why Denys chose the "Platonic" terminology, and not another that would have permitted him to avoid having to envisage the hypothesis—delicate, to say the least—of *mē on/ouk onta,* instead of limiting himself to the marked off-field of *onta.* And conversely, one would have to wonder why Saint Thomas holds so firmly to limiting the theological question to the field of *esse/ entia*. Be that as it may, the conceptual seriousness of this lexicon is attested by its consequence: the Dionysian nonbeings are no more (and, let us concede, no less) reducible to matter without form than the praise that they proffer—G~~o~~d as goodness—can be confused with the praise that beings proffer—G~~o~~d as Being itself. If with the Dionysian nonbeings and non-Being it were only a question of a lexical imprecision, Saint Thomas doubtless would have experienced neither such an interest nor such a difficulty in refuting the Dionysian primacy of the good over Being. Therefore, it is to an examination of this refutation that we now must commit the rigor of the debate.

On at least two occasions Saint Thomas encounters the Dionysian thesis of the primacy, among the divine names, of the good over the *ens,* first in the *Commentary on the Sentences* (I, d.8, q.1), and then in the *Summa Theologica* (I, q.5). The basic argumentation does not vary. Denys prefers the good because it carries beyond beings even to nonbeings. But this primacy over the *ens* comes only from the fact that the good "adds" the consideration of the cause, or rather takes "God" into view not only as efficient cause (which makes him a creator of beings) but as final cause, hence as indeed desirable also by what is not at all. The good therefore is limited to "adding"[61] the consideration of the final cause to that of the efficient cause, hence of the *ens.* This reasoning, obviously, proves nothing. First, it justifies neither the redistribution of the dilemma between the *ens* and the good according to the four Aristotelian "causes" nor the strange assimilation of the *ens* to efficiency, nor finally the untenable reduction of the *Aitia,* of the requisite of goodness, of the Dionysian beautiful and good, to the narrow final cause. But these insufficiencies matter little before an entirely different incoherence: if the consideration of finality is limited to a second, if not secondary, addition made to the *ens,* whose primacy would appear only in setting aside that addition, how is it to be understood that an addition might thus be added to a primacy? Either the good adds, and one must concede primacy to it; or it adds nothing, and one must establish positively the primacy of the *ens.* In short, if the *ens* arises first, this primacy cannot then be obtained by a subtraction.

Thus, Saint Thomas, constrained by the necessity of the thing itself, doubles the first—and feeble—argumentation by a positive and unconditioned justification of the primacy of the *ens* over the good. Why, indeed, does the *ens* retain its primacy—of which, in fact, it is robbed by consideration of the good finality? Under what relation does the *ens* overturn the unconditioned anteriority of goodness that even nonbeings praise? Because a new point of view enters into play. It is a point of view whose newness consists precisely in the fact that it designates a particular point starting from which one's view is engaged. The primacy of goodness depended on the praise of the Requisite by all the petitioners, even those who are not; whereby goodness transgressed Being by default—the default of the less than nothing—as also by excess—the hyperbole of the Requisite—according to a wonderful commerce of extremes, in defiance of ordinary Being as of all representation. For here, communion exceeds in charity what Being delimits as the common denominator, since no representation, finite by definition, could reach the steps of the Requisite or the abysses of its last condescensions. Thus, in order to establish—by restriction—a situation for the *ens* and for the community that it delineates, one is obliged to assure it a site, hence a point of view. In fact, Saint Thomas does not hesitate to establish the primacy of the *ens* by the primacy of a point of view that limits one's view to the measurements of the *ens;* the point of view: only a certain taking-into-view permits plotting the position of the *ens,* making the *ens* a solid point. One therefore will proceed in this way: "In the simple and absolute sense, the *ens* is anterior to the others [namely, transcendentals: good, one, true]. The reason for this is that the *ens* finds itself comprehended in their comprehension, and not reciprocally. For the first term that falls within the imagination of understanding is the *ens,* without which the understanding can apprehend nothing [*primum enim quod cadit in imaginatione intellectus est ens, sine quo nihil potest apprehendi ab intellectu*]." Or again: "Now the first thing conceived by the intellect is being [the *ens*]; because everything is knowable only inasmuch as it is in actuality. Hence being [the *ens*] is the proper object of the intellect, and is primarily intelligible [*primo in conceptione intellectus cadit, proprium objectum intellectus et sic* ... *primum intelligibile*]."[62] Here the point of departure, for Saint Thomas (and not for Duns Scotus alone) remains Avicenna: "being [the *ens*] is what is first conceived by the intellect, as Avicenna says."[63] The *ens* appears first, at least on condition that one takes the point of view of human understanding; the primacy of the *ens* depends on the primacy of a conception of the understanding and of the mind of man. The primacy of the *ens* has nothing absolute or unconditional about it; it relies on another primacy, which remains discreetly in the background. But it is this second primacy that one must question, since it alone gives its domination to the *ens,* to the detriment of the good (and of the Dionysian tradition).

In fact, to define the *ens* as an *objectum* of human understanding seems necessarily to imply interpreting it also starting from representation; indeed, Saint Thomas explicitly introduces the conception, the apprehension, and the imagination of understanding. Hence of man: the *ens* is presented as the first counterpart that man might apprehend as *his* object. As we intend to remain strictly theological in our remarks, we will not insist here on the difficulty and the importance of this submission of the *ens* to the essence and to the marvels of representation. But, theologically, a question immediately presents itself. If the *ens* is defined as the object first apprehended by the human mind, before every other specification, independent of every measure other than that of human understanding, how can the *ens* support the effort and the deviation of an analogy? From this position, must one not, on the contrary, draw the Scotist conclusion that the *ens,* result of a concept because first of a human (*in via*) apprehension, remains univocal for "God" as well as for all other beings; would the nomination of God as such consequently be the concern of an enterprise other than the discourse of the *ens?* The legendary opposition of the Thomistic school(s) and the Scotist school prohibits, of course, proceeding with such a question. But we would like to bring up an unavoidable strangeness: the Thomistic apprehension of

G~~o~~d as *ipsum esse,* hence his denomination starting from the *ens,* intervenes, in the order of reasons, *before* the doctrine of divine names, hence of analogy, is composed. Indeed, the endless difficulties raised by the formulation after the fact of a "Thomistic doctrine of analogy" interferes more than a little with this imbalance. At the risk of solidifying it, we will resume it thus: as, by definition and intention, every doctrine of divine names strives to "destruct" (in the Heideggerian sense) the idolatrous primacy of a human point of view supposed to be unavoidable in the principle of the nomination of G~~o~~d, as in addition the primacy of the *ens* over the other possible divine names rests on the primacy of human conception, Saint Thomas attempted—consciously or not, it matters little—to abstract the *ens* from the doctrine of divine names. In concrete terms, he inverted the primacy of goodness over Being that Denys acknowledged in his treatise on the *Divine Names.* From the point of view of the understanding apprehending an object, the *ens* becomes first. From the point of view of the Requisite that gives itself without limit, goodness remains first. One must choose: if theology proceeds by the apprehension of concepts, as a "science," then, for it also, the *ens* will be first, and man's point of view normative (at least according to the method; but method, in science, decides everything). If theology wills itself to be *theo*logical, it will submit all of its concepts, without excepting the *ens,* to a "destruction" by the doctrine of divine names, at the risk of having to renounce any status as a conceptual "science," in order, decidedly nonobjectivating, to praise by infinite petitions. Such a choice—by a formidable but exemplary ambiguity—Saint Thomas did not make, the Saint Thomas who pretended to maintain at once a doctrine of divine names and the primacy of the *ens* as first conception of the human understanding. For our purposes, the historically localizable heritage of this indecision matters little; all that counts is what provokes it: the claim that the *ens,* although defined starting from a human conception, should be valid as the first name of G~~o~~d. This claim does not easily escape the suspicion of idolatry, as soon as the *ens,* thus referred to G~~o~~d, is engendered not only *in conceptione intellectus* but also *in imaginatione intellectus*—in the imagination of the understanding, hence in the faculty of forming images, hence idols. For "the imagination forms for itself an [idol] of an absent thing, or even of something never seen [*vis imaginativa format sibi aliquod idolum rei absentis, vel etiam numquam visae*]."[64] If the imagination can produce the idol that takes the place of the absent, and if the *ens* falls largely in the conception of imagination, can one not hazard that, according to what Saint Thomas himself freely insinuates, the *ens,* related to "God" as his first name, indeed could determine him as the ultimate—idol?

The provocation of such a question has nothing gratuitous about it. For it is only after the great confrontation surrounding the *ens* and goodness and opposing Denys to Saint Thomas that the question (despite Duns Scotus) concerning Being is tied definitively to the question concerning the G~~o~~d of Jesus Christ. Henceforth theology will have to place the inclusion of "God" in *esse* at the center of its work, to the point of "comprehending" "God" in the object of metaphysics (Saurez).[65] The divine certainly did not await Saint Thomas to enter into metaphysics; but it is only with Saint Thomas that the G~~o~~d revealed in Jesus Christ under the name of charity finds himself summoned to enter the role of the divine of metaphysics, in assuming *esse/ens* as his proper name. Henceforth the necessary and sufficient conditions come together so that, with the destiny of the "God of the philosophers and the learned," the reception of the "God of Abraham, of Isaac and of Jacob" is also at stake. Descartes, deciding all of subsequent metaphysics, will determine that the one who remains for him the G~~o~~d of the Christians will be not only the idea of the infinite but also the *causa sui.* Thus the aporia of the *causa sui* will be able, through the intermediate stage of the "moral God," to engender a "death of God," where the metaphysical idol of "God" is positively accomplished, but where the idolatrous character of this idol is radically dissimulated. This dissimulation in fact is due to the inability of theological understanding, since the *ens/esse* prevails as divine name, to envisage a properly Christian name of the G~~o~~d who is revealed in Jesus Christ—a name anterior to the Being of beings (according to metaphysics), *hence* also to every thought of Being as such. For a single path can yet open: if "God is charity, *agapē*" (1 John 4:8), can *agapē* transgress Being? In other words, can it no longer appear as one of the "ways" of being (even if this being has the name *Dasein*)? Can it manifest itself without passing through Being, and, if it cannot determine Being as one of its—own—"ways," can it at least mark its distance from Being? For in order to free God from Being it does not suffice to invoke, by means of a highly suspect and insufficient return to . . . , another divine name, for example, goodness. One still must show concretely how the God who gives himself as *agapē* thus marks his divergence from Being, hence first from the interplay of beings as such.

4—The Indifference to Be

The liberation from Being does not at all mean abstracting from it, precisely because abstraction strictly renders possible one of the metaphysical modes of the Being of beings, the objective concept of *ens*. Nor does liberation from Being signify undoing oneself and stealing away from it, since this very evasion opens on nonbeing, hence remains within the dominion of the Being of beings. Finally, liberation from Being does not mean that one claims to criticize or revoke it—for that discourse still supposes a logos and a site from which to set it into operation, hence prerogatives of Being. Liberation from Being, but without abstraction, evasion, or revocation, might appear as mad as it does impossible—unless the words "liberation from Being" first be understood not as an emancipation with regard to Being (emancipation that confirms its author in the status of a being) but as freedom rendered to Being. To liberate Being so that, passing from a captive theft to free flight, it can liberate its play, liberate *itself*—like a player who finally lets his own moves occur instinctively with an unforeseeable and meticulous precision, in short, so that he can let himself go. However, in order for Being to liberate itself in this way, it undoubtedly must be capable of being envisaged; not to be envisaged starting from a being (privileged or not, it matters little *here*), hence always starting from, by, and for itself, in charge of the entire game through which the world renders beings worldly, but to envisage (the) Being (of beings) in some of its traits, so properly its own that it could not itself discern them in any invisible mirror, and which only a view instituted at and in a certain distance would be able to accord it. Would not liberating Being as such be like liberating oneself with respect to Being? In *one* sense, this indeed is the case: to envisage Being as it cannot envisage itself. What do we mean by this? Do we not risk mistaking the clatter of words for the rigor of concepts? What game are we playing, in the end? Answer: we are attempting to play at/upon Being according to another game than that of Being. Or again: we are attempting to make sport of Being by outwitting the rules it fixed for its own game. Or finally: to outwit Being, by making it play a game other than its own. Precisely, the game of Being (and thus of the Being of beings) is played according to ontological difference, thought or unthought as such, hence in the gap between beings and Being, or, at the very least, in the inclusion of beings within an ontology, indeed a science of the *on*. The *on,* taken as being, is expressed in this game only according to a difference that leads it back, as being, to the *on,* taken as Being; so that being only envisages Being, which, through it, always envisages itself. An interplay of ontological difference as fold [*pli*], but especially as withdrawal [*repli*] of Being/being into its invisible spectacle—idol again? If this is how the game is played, what would it imply to outwit it? Without any doubt, to play it *without* ontological difference. Such a game *without* ontological difference does not coincide, we should stress, with the metaphysical unthought of ontological difference; for to think within ontological difference without thinking that difference itself, following the example of metaphysics, obviously implies that one still thinks starting from it. Only in this way can one undertake to go from unthought ontological difference back to a differentiated thought of Being as such, since both lodge in the sole ontological difference. Here the case is quite different: to play on Being without ontological difference, in order to outwit it, requires dislodging it from ontological difference. Now, simply in order to outline this gesture, one especially must not continue to reside within ontological difference, even when con-[illegible]g it from oneself by the forgetful unthought. The game [illegible] outwitted only by finding another rule; merely to deny [illegible]t neither outwits nor liberates, but cancels the game. To play without (the rule of) ontological difference would imply that another rule can intervene in order to ensure the rules of the game, and, only in that way, to outwit it. To outwit, however, indicates more than to modify the rules of a game; to outwit even indicates to play against the quarterback, to turn back against him the play by which he attempted to play us. To outwit Being thus would require more than the revocation of ontological difference in favor of another difference.[66] Thus it is necessary that being play according to a rule such that its difference does not refer at all to Being; or even that being be disposed and interpreted according to such a difference that it no longer permits Being to recover *itself* in being or permits being to lead *itself* back to Being, so that the play of being can escape Being, which no longer would appear therein—not even under the figure of retreat or of the unthought. Through this difference that is indifferent to ontological difference, but above all not to being, one would have to turn the play of being with Being away from itself, so that (the) Being (of being) can appear with the features that it offers to no invisible mirror and hence which it itself would be incapable of seeing or telling. The other difference would distort this play of Being with being that ontological difference rendered reflexive and hence, in a sense, closed—in expectation of a release. Ontological difference leads—even in the case of the unthought—being back to Being, unfolds Being in being(s) in order to perfect the reflexive gaze of the one in the other, invisibly paired if not not visibly apparent: whereby, even and especially in its decided retreat, Being presents itself as the reserved idol, because it is reflexive of itself alone. On the screen of Being, through each being, Being is projected upon itself.[67] To distort one difference by another outwits (the) Being (of being) by resulting in a being that no longer refers to Being, in an obvious (though unthought) reflex, but to another instance, in relation to which another difference is freed, a difference more essential to being than ontological difference itself.

We have just traced an anticipatory draft, but only a draft, of the liberation of Being. To put the draft into operation concretely would require the intervention of an instance as much thinkable as foreign to ontological difference, thought or unthought. And no doubt we would think immediately of biblical revelation to play this role, for to "the wisdom that the Greeks seek" (hence to the always sought *on* of Aristotle)[68] it opposes the "wisdom of God" (1 Cor. 1:22, 1:24). But the opposition of the two wisdoms does not suffice to outwit the play of the Being of being, since—at least the evidence seems to be admitted everywhere without question—biblical revelation does not say a word about Being. Thus does one immediately rely upon this silence to limit the biblical word to a believing variant of being. But does this silence really elude every question? One must distinguish, in fact, between two extremely different points. Incontestably, biblical revelation is unaware of ontological difference, the science of Being/beings as such, and hence of the question of Being. But nothing is less accurate than to pretend that it does not speak a word on being, nonbeing, and beingness. We will now encounter three texts that concern three words about being, spoken in Greek and in conformity with at least the lexicon of the Greek philosophers. This homonymy (if not more) will allow us to measure concretely how a difference that is indifferent to ontological difference can, at the very least, attempt to outwit the play of being with Being. Before becoming indignant with this incongruous pretension, I hope the amazed reader will be patient for a while—in order simply to read.

The first text can be read in Romans 4:17; at issue is the faith of the first believer, Abraham; according to the Apostle Paul, he is made "the father of us all, as it is written, 'I have made you the father of many nations,' facing Him in whom he believed, the God who gives life to the dead and who calls the nonbeings as beings, *kalountos ta mē onta hōs onta.*"[69] If what is written remains written, one must understand what is thus said. The verse is immediately placed within faith, not only because Abraham believed but because from this paternal and originary faith come the one who writes and those who read him. In addition, faith recognizes that He in whom believers confide gives life to the dead themselves. Hence a first formula, strictly kerygmatic: we believe in the God who gives (back) life. But—and starting now the text amazes us—the kerygmatic statement is redoubled by a second formula, obviously constructed following its plan but with a new, even strange, lexicon. In it Paul speaks like the philosophers of a transition between *ta mē onta* and (*ta*) *onta,* the nonbeings and the beings. We might think, at first sight, of what Aristotle thematizes under the name of *metabolē kath'ousian,* that extreme form of change that leads from the nonextant [unfinished *ousia*] to the extant [finished *ousia*], or inversely; it is known that Aristotle doubts that such a change could ever really come about, since a "matter" always remains as a substratum.[70] How then, according to Paul, can such a radical transition be conceived? The response becomes possible only if we immediately correct the very formulation of this last question; for the transition, here, does not depend in any way on the conception of Paul—as if he could have had the least doctrinal knowledge of it—since it is a question of a discourse held about faith and on the basis of faith. Furthermore, if this transition can be conceived neither by Paul, by Abraham, nor by any man whomsoever, this results from another impossibility: this transition does not arise from the (*mē*) *onta* that it nevertheless affects most intimately. The *onta* do not dispose here of any "principle of change within themselves,"[71] of any intrinsic potentiality that would require or prepare its completion. The transition befalls them from the outside; the transition from nonbeing to being goes right through them, issuing from this side and proceeding beyond; the transition establishes them as *onta* by a wholly extrinsic establishment in the sense that, elsewhere, one speaks of extrinsic justification. Why an extrinsic transition from nonbeing to beings? If beings remain without reason or function in this transition, the text clearly gives the motive: this transition does not depend on (non-) beings but on Him who calls them. What does this call signify? Nonbeings are not (or no longer). This nothingness has its reason, which renders it just and impassable, death. The world leaves these men dead—nonbeings, then. In the world, there is no salvation at all for them. And the world no longer hails them, or names them, or calls them. The ontic difference between being and nonbeing admits no appeal; in the world, it acts irrevocably, without appeal. From elsewhere than the world, then, G~~o~~d himself lodges an appeal. He appeals to his own indifference against the difference between being and nonbeing. He appeals to his own call. And his call sets this indifference into play so that the call not only calls nonbeings to become beings (*hōs onta* here can can have this consecutive and/or final meaning), but he calls the nonbeings as if they were beings. The call does not take into consideration the difference between nonbeings and beings: the nonbeings are called inasmuch as they are not beings; the nonbeings appear, by virtue of the call, as if they were (and *hōs* also has this adverbial sense, *tanquam ea quae sunt,* says the Vulgate). The fundamental ontic difference between what is and what is not becomes indifferent—for everything becomes indifferent before the difference that G☒d marks with the world. This is an indifference of ontic difference and not, one should note, its destruction. For nonbeings are revealed as beings only by virtue of the call of God; the *as if,* if it does not at all weaken the power of their transition, irrevocably marks that this transition remains extrinsic to them, as much as the call that gives rise to it. This is an indifference to ontic difference that, furthermore, alone explains that the G☒d who calls should have considered the dead as *mē onta,* while in all rigor they are not nothing, but bodies without life, then cadavers without form, and finally biological materials destined to materialize new forms. But, from the point of view of Him who calls to faith and to charity, the ontic distinctions internal to death become indifferent and hence act *as if,* in death, absolute corruption were at stake.

Let us tie things together: the ontic difference between being and nonbeing indeed intervenes, located in the shadow of the kerygma; however, it no longer functions according to the norms of being but to those of operators (faith, call, as if) that, far from slipping into this ontic difference, make it appear indifferent, though leaving it intact. That ontic difference should thus be struck with indifference, as when a luminous contrast hitherto quite visible is effaced in a general bedazzlement, refers back to another difference, still anonymous, but already at work. Among the (non-) beings intervenes a difference that, making use of the being that it most certainly calls *as* such, diverts it from the ontic difference where beings and nonbeings are divided. We must still demarcate, with a firmer stroke, this other possible difference. And we must decide whether indifference to the difference between beings could affect ontological difference itself.

Along the path marked out by these questions, a second text awaits our reading. 1 Corinthians 1:28 is situated, we should note right away, in the same chapter that a few verses above (1:18–24) opposes to "the wisdom of the world" a "wisdom of God," and traces a difference between them so radical that it becomes a contradiction where each term can appear only as "foolishness" in the eyes of the other. One must attribute to this text an authority all the greater since Heidegger—hence with him the thought of Being—invokes it to determine theology in its relation with philosophy.[72] Let us cite it in its immediate context: "For consider your call, brethren, (*tēn klēsin humōn*), namely, that there are not [among you] many wise according to the flesh, nor many powerful, nor many well born. But God chose the foolish things of the world, God chose them to confound the wise, and the weak things of the world God chose to confound the strong, God chose the ignoble things of the world [*agenē, ignobilia* says the Vulgate] and the contemptible things, and also the non-beings, in order to annul the beings (*kai ta mē onta, hina ta onta katargēsē*)—in order that no flesh should glorify itself before God" (1 Cor. 1:26–29).[73]

What we have identified already as an indifference to the difference between beings and nonbeings is immediately recognizable: G̸o̸d chooses nonbeings in order to annul and abrogate beings. The indifference first manifests itself in that G̸o̸d can choose that which is not as if it were, whereas, if it is a question of that which, in fact, is not, there should be no choice. But for God, that which is nothing is as if it were. The indifference manifests itself in a second fashion: that which is can be, for God, as if it were not; the fact of being a being—and of remaining such, for it is not a question here of destruction, but of annulment[74]—in no way insures against the nothing: just as nonbeing, once chosen, is discovered as if it were, so being, once annulled, is discovered as if it were not. The *as if* plays from the nothing to being (the brethren) and from being to the nothing ("the world"). Thus, while Romans 4:17 indicated only a single form of indifference to ontic difference (of nonbeing to being), this text shows it at work simultaneously in two directions: from nonbeing to being, from being to nonbeing. The indifference thus establishes its indifference to the two possible transgressions of ontic difference (absolute generation, absolute corruption); it thus attests its coherence and its rigor.

Nevertheless, this first point settled, the very confirmation of the indifference to the difference between being and nonbeing causes a disquieting difficulty to appear suddenly; in playing so strongly with (non-) beings, and in too easily confusing the name and the thing, these two Pauline texts lose perhaps more than they gain; would their indifference to the difference between (non-) beings not simply betray the absence of rigorous thought, rhetorical excess, at the very least the unscrupulous distortion of the philosophical acceptation of the terms? It would betray a distortion, no doubt; but this distortion could result from neither chance nor passion but from a measured and coherent intention. The reversibility of *ta mē onta* and *ta onta* results from an "annulment" (1:28, *katargēsē*), not from a confusion or from a mistake. This annulment repeats another operation, carried out a few verses earlier in the same chapter: the "wisdom of God" (1:21), later designated "the wisdom come for us from God" (1:30), contradicts the "wisdom of the world" and drives it to distraction, "distracts" it (1:20), as a magnet distracts a compass, in depriving it of all reference to a fixed pole. But who exercises this now distracted wisdom? The response removes all ambiguity: alone and characteristically "the Greeks seek wisdom, *sophian zētousin*" (1:22); the distraction of the Greeks hence reflects on what their wisdom puts into play; but this wisdom, according to the most Greek among the Greeks who love wisdom (therefore the philosophers), is presented as a goal "always sought, *aei zētoumenon,* and always missed, the question, what then is being, *ti to on,* or, which is the same, what then is *ousia?*"[75] Nothing, consequently, is more coherent or more useful for the Pauline discourse than to verify the distraction not only of the philosophical "wisdom" of the Greeks, but even of the target at which it ceaselessly aims, as the needle of a compass does not cease to aim at a point that is quite unattainable: the love of wisdom (of the world) is distracted, because the sign that guides it, the *on,* first and primarily, is distracted. To be distracted: to become mad or to have a screw loose, to become loose as an idle wheel or a pulley becomes loose, having lost one's grip on reality, free from all actual hold on the axle: mad, unhinged, hence out of true.[76] Beings are distracted because, instead of marking direction or meaning, they become free of all direction or meaning, mad, alienated from and by a direction or meaning not only unknown, but above all, unenvisageable, unthinkable. The *on,* by definition, implies the fold of ontological difference, since it is implied or implicated in it; hence it is oriented according to Being (thought or not as such, what does it matter *here*. The *on* by definition and ontological difference is oriented to Being: it bends to Being in that it is unfolded according to the fold Being/beings. One orients oneself to Being as the needle orients itself to the north, for the Orient itself is found only if it does not lose the north, by relation to which it is defined; thus being spreads or is unfolded only by yielding to the fold of ontological difference that implies Being. To distract being hence would signify nothing less than driving it to distraction by rendering it free from Being, unhinging it from Being, dissociating it from Being. In other words; annulling the fold that bends being to Being, removing being from that through which it is, Being, spreading or unfolding being outside of its unique and universal meaning, that it *is.* To distract being would consist of defining it as such in a way that nonetheless never approaches it through what it is, to wit, precisely that it is and is only that—that which is, without any other specification; to approach being as such, ignoring in it that which lays it out as such—Being. The distraction of the "wisdom of the world" (philosophy) by the "wisdom of God" is accomplished in a distortion of the fold of being/Being that determines being without recourse to Being: indifference to ontic difference, but also to ontological difference.

Let us see, then, how the Pauline text outwits Being by setting being in motion as if it were not bent to the fold of Being. For if Paul merits being called a "terrifying forger" one must take this in a sense more radical than Nietzsche himself intended, in the sense, very precisely extra-moral, of a certain distortion of being.[77]

What is designated *here* by nonbeings, *ta mē onta?* Obviously, paradoxically but incontestably, it is a question of what common sense would name beings, or "things": it is a question of men, Christians, in Corinth, who are there—very much there, as their confusions and quarrels prove. Nevertheless, Paul names them nonbeings. Thus, must one conclude that for Paul nonbeing does not mean nonbeing, that nonbeing does not designate that which is not, and that it is attributed independently of deployment in and according to Being? Let us verify before explaining. In order to grasp Paul's intention, let us first note the construction of the text. At the start, we have the "brethren" (1 Cor. 1:26), at the end, "the nonbeings" (1 Cor. 1:28); it is a question of the same, who at the beginning are and, at the end, are no longer (even though in fact they still are). What happens between these two moments? This: if one approaches and interprets the brethren not as what they are in themselves—namely, beings, as everything and anything—but as what, in fact, they are "according to the flesh" (1 Cor. 1:26), in other words, in the eyes of the "world" (1 Cor. 1:27, 1:28), then they are undone, defeated. This defeat deepens in two moments: in the first, the brethren remain human though not very gifted: neither wise, nor powerful, nor of good birth; in short, they are "no big deal" (1 Cor. 1:26). In a second moment they are undone infinitely more, for their insufficiencies in the eyes of the "world" not only render them weak, mad, contemptible, and ignoble but go so far as to deny them humanity: the attributes turn from masculine plural to neuter plural; "the world" takes them, as it takes slaves, for impure and simple "things"; it clearly does not recognize them as brethren, or even humans, but only as "less than nothing"; less than nothing, below the threshold of recognition, where alterity appears other because it still presents a minimum of recognizable reality. This less than nothing, this degree less than zero, to which "the world" no longer even gives a name, because in it the world sees nothing proper and nothing common (with itself), Paul names, *in the name of the "world,"* nonbeings, *ta mē onta* (neuter!). This name beneath every name arises at the end of a reduction operated by "the world." In the name of what does "the world" take for a nonbeing that which, at the least, is a pure being? In order to respond, one must take a step back and ask oneself in the name of what Paul can recognize as "brethren" that (neuter!) which the "world" looks upon as less than nothing; the response is found at the beginning of the text: "Consider your call, brethren" (1 Cor 1:26); Paul does not say: "consider yourselves," for in considering themselves only under their own gaze (literally *blepete,* "look!"), in an elementary cogito, they would see themselves as the world sees them—as "less than nothing." Paul asks them on the contrary to look at what they are not or, better, at what does not depend on them or on their brute beingness or on the "world", namely, "their call," *their* call; not the call that is theirs, but the call addressed to them (*tēn klēsin humōn,* 1 Cor. 1:26). Which call is thus thrown at them? We have encountered this call already in Romans 4:17; it is a question of the call of the G~~o~~d who gives life and "calls nonbeings as [if they were] beings, *ta mē onta hōs onta.*" Through the call of G~~o~~d, the "less than nothing" appear, not in their own eyes or in the eyes of the "world," as beings; but, inversely, wisdom against wisdom, folly against folly, as nonbeings. Hence a second thing is evident: the decision on beingness depends neither on the categories of a philosophical discourse nor on Being deploying itself in ontological difference, but on instances separated by the limit between "the world" and the "call" of the G~~o~~d who gives life. And curiously, for an informed reading at least, the nonbeingness of that which nevertheless is results from the "world," whereas G~~o~~d outside-the-world prompts the beingness of nonbeings. In this case, how are we to conceive that "the world" goes so far as to refuse beingness to humans who in themselves are? For, in sound logic, "the world," following its wisdom which leads to philosophy, would have to know what being is and recognize beings everywhere where what is is. Why, according to Paul at least, does it go back upon its own logic, why does it distort the first correctly conceptual usage of the terms *ta onta/ta mē onta?* Response: because "the world," in its funding, does not belong to the domain of ontological difference or of the fold Being/being; in its funding, it is founded on itself, on its "works," and wants thus "to glorify itself before God" (1 Cor. 1:29). The "world" by itself distorts the usage of *ta onta/ta mē onta* in naming "less than nothing" not the nothing that absolutely is not but that on which it cannot found itself in order to glorify itself before G~~o~~d; and thus in naming *ta onta* what at that point is and "is important" enough that it can found itself in it as upon its appropriate fund, to glorify itself before G~~o~~d. The distortion of beingness therefore is not due to Paul; Paul limits himself to bringing to light a distortion that is characteristic of the "world," which, in correctly philosophical discourse, dissimulates its funding; now the foundation of the discourse of the "world" does not consist in the calm management of beingness but in the acquisition of funds against G~~o~~d. Before the difference between beings, before the conjunction of being to Being, before the fold of ontological difference, the "world" holds the discourse of the acquisition of funds—to glorify oneself before God. And moreover, in extreme cases, before Christians chosen among the people of little means, for example, the "world" spontaneously admits the distortion of its own language. Under the invisible light that dazzles it from outside of the "world," the "world" is distracted to the point of itself leading being astray outside of the path of Being, to the point of outwitting the Being in beings, of disarticulating ontological difference. The "world," under the light of G~~o~~d, is revealed as a forger of itself. It acknowledges that its funding does not lie in ontological difference, but in the pretension to "glorify itself before God."

Thus to look on the brethren as nonbeings proves that the world in its funding does not at all belong to the domain of ontological difference. In that event, what does G~~o~~d answer? He answers that salvation does not come "from works [*ouk ex ergōn*], so that no one should be glorified" by himself (Eph. 2:10); for "my glorification I have in Christ" (Rom. 15:17), "your glorification, brothers, I have in Christ" (1 Cor. 15:31), in short, "may he who is glorified be glorified in the Lord" (1 Cor. 1:31). The debate between beings and nonbeings is played out in complete indifference to the ontic and ontological differences only because here the contradiction of glorifications alone makes a difference. Everything—even and especially the difference (non-) being/Being—founders in indifference before the differing of glories, or rather of the two sources of glory and of glorification: the funding of the "world" or the call of Christ.

Only this differing allows the transition from being to nonbeing; for the "world," not what is, but what permits founding appears as a being; and not that which is not, but that which does not offer any funding disappears as a nonbeing. For Christ, that which is does not appear as a being, but rather that which believes in the call, and that which is not does not disappear as a nonbeing, but rather that which believes itself able to found itself on its own funding. Thus, because it is not a question here of any beingness thought on the basis of Being, the inversion by G~~o~~d of the "world" does not imply, now, any ontic destruction; G~~o~~d does not destroy, he abrogates (*katargēsē*) the judgment of the world: to abrogate, to look upon a decree or law as null and void, to look upon it as nothing without even having to refute it. A line, along which the "world" divides into beings and nonbeings that on which it wants to found itself, crosses another line, along which the call reestablishes beings and nonbeings in the measure of their faith. The crossing of these two lines decidedly distorts the play of being by withdrawing it from Being, by undoing being from the rule of Being. This crossing traces a cross over ontological difference, a cross that abolishes it without deconstructing it, exceeds it without overcoming it, annuls it without annihilating it, distorts it without contesting its right. In the same way that a window opens the view to an immense space that it nevertheless measures by a crossbar, this crossing opens ontological difference to a differing that renders it indifferent only by excess and that places it in reserve only in that it preserves it from an entirely different dilemma.

We now see, then, how being and nonbeing can be divided according to something other than Being. But this something, although working under various names (call, glorification, "world," G~~o~~d), remains to be discovered—if it can be done. Henceforth we ask, at what game does being play when it outwits the difference that inscribes it in Being? This question leads us to a third text, that of the parable of the prodigal son, in Luke 15:12–32. This text ineluctably demands our attention, since it offers the only usage in all of the New Testament of the philosophical term par excellence, *ousia* (Luke 15:12–13): "A man had two sons. And the younger of the two said to his father: 'Father, give me the share of *ousia* that is coming to me,' [*to epiballon meros tēs ousias, portionem substantiae quae me contingit*]. And the father shared his goods [*ton bion, substantium*] between them. And, without waiting many days, gathering everything, the youngest of the sons left for a great region [*eis khōran makran*], and he dissipated his goods in the life of a libertine, [*dieskorpisen tēn ousian autou, dissipavit substantiam suam*]" (Luke 15:11–13). In view of this usage, a prelimiinary question becomes unavoidable: *ousia* undoubtedly appears on two occasions (translated by *substantia,* which also appears to transpose *ton bion*), but, can one thus legitimately establish the least comparison between this use, obviously nonphilosophical, and the conceptual use of *ousia* in philosophy? Can one approach *ousia* here as if it were a question of the concept chosen by Aristotle to delimit the inquiry concerning *to on?* Can one proceed as if the New Testament, after having employed *to on,* also made use of *ousia,* in repeating, according to a divergence as intriguing as this similitude of sequences, the Aristotelian relation between *on* and *ousia?* Certainly not in the strict sense. But *ousia* also admits, first, of a prephilosophical acceptation that shares with its properly philosophical turn the indication of a present disposability: *ousia* indicates that which, here, and now, remains to be useful for . . . , in short, disposable goods; this trait common to the two acceptations of *ousia,* which Heidegger underlined in his course at Marburg,[78] has to do with the disposability of a "possession" (*Besitz*) which thus assures a "power" (*Vermögen*). The translation of the text by Luther indeed insists on this and renders *to epiballon meros tēs ousias* by "*das Teil Güter, das mir gehört*, the share of the [disposable] good that belongs to me." Doubtless it is not at all a question here of *ousia* as the definition of a specific being, according to the categories, in kind and species, as opposed to the attributes; but, as this *ousia* of the philosophers is deployed always again according to disposable possession—each thing "posseses some stability of *ousia,*" says Plato[79]—in this precise relation, the *ousia* of the prodigal son can resonate legitimately, to our ears at least, with the echo of the *ousia* of the philosophers; our reading, in its conclusions, will call for nothing more than this weak interpretation of *ousia:* the goods disposable for possession and power. In fact, here, with regard to *ousia,* only possession is at stake; the parable concerns only this point—the entrance of *ousia* into the logic of possession, or more exactly of possession as the mode par excellence of the placement of goods at one's disposal. Let there be goods, the *ousia* common to the father and the two sons, goods in the sense that one "has some property," some "landed property."[80] The son, in the role of heir, although the younger, already had the use and enjoyment of them: son of the master, heir by right, he was able to look on these goods as his own; or rather, this enjoyment did not strictly coincide with possession, nor this usage with disposability: between one and the other term intervened an irreducible authority, the father. Not that the father, abusive and stingy, would disinherit his sons (proof being that as soon as the share is asked for, he gives it with neither delay nor discussion). The father gave, and immediately gives what one asks of him, the share of the *ousia;* the younger son therefore does not suffer from not having the enjoyment of the *ousia,* but from owing it to a tacit and imprescriptible gift from his father. Therefore he asks not so much for his share of *ousia*—since he has always enjoyed that—but not to have to owe that share of *ousia* to a gift; he demands less the *ousia* than "the share of the *ousia* that is coming to him" as out and out property—not the *ousia* but possession of the *ousia.* Ultimately one even would have to say that he asks that one deprive him of something he already has: he has the enjoyment of the *ousia* as given, he asks for the *ousia* without the concession, the *ousia* less the gift, the *ousia* without concession—without having to concede that it comes to him by a gracious concession.[81] The son requests that he no longer have to request, or rather, that he no longer have to receive the *ousia.* He asks that one grant that he no longer have to receive any gift—precisely, no longer have to receive the *ousia* as a gift: He asks to possess it, dispose of it, enjoy it without passing through the gift and the reception of the gift. The son wants to owe nothing to his father, and above all not to owe him a gift; he asks to have a father no longer—the *ousia* without the father or the gift. In the *ousia* thus possessed, a censure excludes the gift from which the *ousia* issues. The *ousia* becomes the full possession of the son only to the extent that it is fully dispossessed of the father: dispossession of the father, annulment of the gift, this is what the possession of *ousia* implies. Hence an immediate consequence: in being dispossessed of the father, the possession that censures the gift integrates within itself, indissolubly, the waste of the gift; possessed without gift, possession cannot but continue to dispossess itself. Henceforth orphan of the paternal gift, *ousia* finds itself possessed in the mode of dissipation—with a view to an expenditure: possessed by the son inasmuch as dispossessed of the paternal gift, it no longer "holds" in him. Landed property, now without ground, becomes liquid money, which, by definition, seeps and trickles between the fingers. If the son dissipates his goods in a life of dissipation (Luke 15:13, *dieskorpisen*),[82] the reason is not the sudden immorality of an heir seized by debauchery. The reason for the concrete dissipation of *ousia* is found in a first and fundamental dissipation: the transformation of the *ousia* into liquid (money), which itself results from the abandonment of the paternal gift as place, meaning, and legitimacy of the enjoyment of the *ousia*. From gift received, *ousia* becomes property appropriated without the gift—abandoned by the gift, because first abandoning the gift—to be lost as dispersed liquid. Famine (Luke 15:15) symbolically marks this dispersed dissipation—dispersed in a great "region," or rather *khōra,* an empty and undetermined space, where meaning, even more than food, has disappeared. In fact, it is not the abandoned *ousia* alone that is lost: the son had gambled his filiation for it; he had broken his filiation in order to obtain the *ousia* as a possession; he had exchanged, as the other his birthright for some lentils, his filiation for the possessed *ousia;* now, he has dissipated the *ousia* and no longer has filiation. The abandonment starves him, but above all makes a "hireling" of him, less well fed than "swine" (Luke 15:15); abandonment deprives him of *ousia,* filiation and even humanity. Thus he no longer even hopes for filiation, but only for the food of swine or, at best, the treatment of a hireling; when he goes back to his father, he no longer even has the idea of asking him for a filiation of which the very notion doubtless escapes him (but, previously, had he glimpsed it? Surely not): "I am not worthy of the name of your son" (Luke 15:19, 15:21). Abandonment is played out in this way. Finally, the moment of pardon comes; the father recognizes his son from afar, embraces him, and takes him in; what does the father say, give and forgive? No doubt he returns humanity (in washing, clothing), but above all he returns filiation: "because here is my son who had died and who lives anew" (Luke 15:24); the father gives back to the son his filiation; with the ring and the fatted calf, he gives him what the son did not even think to ask for, the paternal gift of filiation to the son. In what does this gift consist? Here, the jealous lack of intelligence of the elder son—who understands the paternal gift as little as does his younger brother—enlightens us.

Becoming indignant for not benefiting from as much generosity as does his younger brother, and deploring not having anything "of my own" (Luke 15:29) to have a party with "my" (15:29) friends, the elder brother thus tardily admits sharing the initial aim of his sibling: to consider the paternal goods only as a concession awaiting full possession. His father's response to him, in fact, is addressed also to the younger son and provides as a conclusion that which, when forgotten, had served to open the parable: "You, son, you are always with me, and all that is mine is yours also" (Luke 15:31). The father does not see the *ousia* as the sons see it. In it the latter read, according to desire, the object of a possession without concession which abandons every trace of a paternal gift. The father sees in it the gift ceaselessly re-given at a new cost (eventually in forgiveness). Or rather, the father does not see the *ousia,* and indeed the term appears only in the speech of the sons; the father does not allow his gaze to freeze on a transitory term, an idol if it did not fade entirely in the exchange of which it constitutes only the medium, the sign, even the residue. The father is not fixed on the *ousia* because with his gaze he transpierces all that is not inscribed in the rigor of a gift, giving, received, given: goods, common by definition and circulation, are presented as the indifferent stakes of those who, through them, give themselves to each other, in a circulation that is more essential than what it exchanges. The *ousia* is valuable to him only as the currency in an exchange of which it can mark, at the very best, but a moment, an exchange whose solemnity of infinite generosity most often is masked by the title of property. Under the idolatrously charged gaze of the sons, currency obfuscates exchange; to the profoundly iconic gaze of the father, *ousia* never stops the aim of the exchange or circulation of the gift. All that is mine is also yours; in other words: nothing becomes *ousia* (as request for possession without gift) amid "that which" is woven by the invisible tissue of aims that are themselves exchanged in the glances that they cast and return to each other without loss, end, or weariness; as a sign of the gifts, the "that which" has neither the occasion nor the temptation to make a possession of itself, *ousia* separated, delimited, and given to the possession of a solitary individual. *Ousia* is dispossessed of itself in the infinite exchange of possessives (yours, mine), so poorly named by grammar, since here they indicate only perfect dispossession. *Ousia* appears as such only to the gaze that abandons the admirable exchange of aims enough to freeze on one point that, thus fixed, is forged into an idol. On the contrary, *ousia* dissipates the marvels of the idol in itself as soon as the communion of aims that intersect through it displace the *ousia* in such elusive movements that, instead of stopping the gaze, it refers the gaze to the infinity of other gazes that envisage it. Thus, *ousia* is inscribed in the play of donation, abandon, and pardon that make of it the currency of an entirely *other* exchange than of beings. But, precisely, have we not just seen these beings themselves taken up, displaced, and distorted according to a rigor other than the logic of Being/beings? Would one have to conclude that *ousia,* just as much as *ta (mē-) onta,* finds itself taken up in a game radically foreign to Being? No doubt. And from now on one can delimit even more closely the game that, indifferent to ontological difference, thus causes being to elude Being: it is called the gift. The gift that gave rise to the operations of preceding readings—call, give life, as if, father, and so on—*gives* Being/beings. And moreover, when Paul addresses himself to the Athenians, Greeks par excellence, he not only finally announces of God that "in him we live, and move, and have our being" (Acts 17:28), but above all he first specifies that this, God "gives" us (17:25). Paul does not maintain that we are by, because of, or after G~~o~~d who would himself also be a being; he inscribes us, inasmuch as we are, living in the mode of *phusis* (that which "we move" indicates), within G~~o~~d; G~~o~~d comprehends our Being of beings, in the sense that the exterior exceeds the interior, and also that the understanding is not confused with the understood—in short, that the comprehending diverges from the comprehended. This divergence does not have the function of establishing any inferiority whatsoever, but of clearing the space, precisely the distance, where the gift is spread out. Would Being/beings befall us as a gift? No. It affects us as a gift, which can as well be refused so as to deliver only a gift abandoned to itself, dissipated outside of its originary giving.[83] As to specifying how distance determines Being/beings without however affecting it intrinsically, that would demand another whole study, whose difficulty stops us.

It is important to point out here this unique attainment: biblical revelation offers, in some rare texts, the emergence of a certain indifference of being to Being; being thus makes sport of Being only in outwitting ontological difference; it outwits it only inasmuch as it is first distorted by another instance, the gift. The gift crosses Being/being: it meets it, strikes it out with a mark, finally opens it, as a window casement opens, on an instance that remains unspeakable according to the language of Being—supposing that another language might be conceived. To open Being/being to the instance of a gift implies then, at the least, that the gift may decide Being/being. In other words, the gift is not at all laid out according to Being/being, but Being/being is given according to the gift. *The gift delivers Being/being.* It delivers it in the sense first that the gift gives Being/being and puts it into play, opens it to its sending, as in order to launch it into its destiny. The gift delivers also in that it liberates being from Being or, put another way, Being/being from ontological difference, in rendering being free from Being, in distorting being out of its subjection to Being, in short in undoing the jointing of Being/being: the fold undoes its unfolding, being plays freely, unhinged, out of true with Being as a free wheel turns madly around its axle; Being/being is distracted by the gift that precedes it and that abandons ontological difference to it only in that it first annuls it. The gift liberates Being/being through the very indifference by which it affects it.

The gift, in liberating Being/being, in liberating being from Being, is itself finally liberated from ontological difference—not only the sending, not only the distortion, but the freeing of the first instance, charity. For the gift itself is liberated only in its exertion starting from and in the name of that which, greater than it, comes behind it, that which gives and expresses itself as gift, charity itself. Charity delivers Being/being.

5—The Inessential Name Thus First

It would remain only to go back to our initial question, if, however, a very pertinent objection did not stand out. We have just pointed out the excellence of the gift as if, necessarily, it went beyond Being/being, delivered and distorted it. But, on the contrary, must we not envisage the hypothesis that the gift does not strictly deploy Being/being as such? Or even more: that far from taking up the play between Being and being from a phantasmagorical "elsewhere," the gift does not rather deliver this play as such? In short: the gift still would belong to Being/being, precisely in that the gift would release its very opening. No one more than Heidegger allowed the thinking of the coincidence of the gift with Being/being, by taking literally the German *es gibt,* wherein we recognize the French *il y a,* there is: superposing one and the other, we would understand the fact that there should be (of course: being) as this fact that *it gives, ça donne.* Being itself is delivered in the mode of giving—from one end to the other along the path of his thought, from *Sein und Zeit* to *Zeit und Sein,* from 1927 to 1962, Heidegger did not cease to meditate on this equivalence.[84] Do we not delude ourselves, then, by claiming to discover in the gift an instance anterior to Being/being that distorts the ontological difference of Being/being? Does not that which we apprehend as "otherwise than being" constitute precisely its most adequate and most secret thought? Indisputably—unless "gift" and "giving" can and must be understood in different ways, unless "gift" and "giving" are not determined here, always, despite the appearances, starting from Being/being. In fact, the gift can be understood in two so radically different ways that it will suffice to outline them here. On the one hand there is the sense of the gift that leads, in the *there is,* to the accentuating of the *it gives* starting from the giving itself, thus starting from giving insofar as it does not cease to give itself; in this case, the *it* that is supposed to give does not provide—any more than does the impersonal *il* on the threshold of the *il y a*—any privileged support. For it could appear, if thought began with it, only as a sort of being; with regard to "the enigmatic It [*ça/il*]" one would end up seeking what "indeterminate power" it masks; and one would miss precisely the whole stake of the gift, by a gross ontic and even causal regression. We therefore must leave the giver in suspension, even the very idea that a giver is necessary to the *it gives,* in order to interrogate the *it* solely "in light of the kind of giving that belongs to it: giving (*Geben*) as destiny, giving as a clearing porrection, *das Geben als Geschick, das Geben als lichtendes Reichen.*"[85] The gift is conceived as giving, and not first starting from any giver whatsoever; the giving in its turn is understood as the destinal sending. What destinal sending? The clarification of a "porrection," of a *Reichen;* porrection by what authority? Of the clarification rendered possible by the clearing. What clearing? "The *giving* in the 'there is' [*it gives*] manifested itself as the clearing porrection of the four-dimensional region, *des vierdimensionalen Bereichs.*"[86] The dominion (*Reichen*), which unfolds its clearing, unfolds it as the four-dimensional, as the Fourfold. The Fourfold joins the divinities and the mortals, as well as the sky and the earth. The giving (which seizes the giver, *es/ça*/it) gives through a giver no more than the Fourfold admits of transgression outside of Being/being. The giving, in a sense, has the function of instituting a deal [*une donne*] (*Geschick*), only in dispensing it of every anterior and exterior "principle"; in porrection, the giving permits that "it gives" according to the Fourfold—in the sense that, when the painter looks at his canvas to see "what it gives" [*ce que ça donne*], he does not seek in it, obviously, any giver, or the motive, or himself; he seeks to see what the canvas itself "gives"; it does not even give itself, moreover, since the canvases that present themselves do not all "give" something, namely, themselves. If from a canvas it "gives something," it gives only the canvas, which results from the gift, far from provoking it; the canvas itself is discovered in the mode of the giving: it "gives," in the sense that a sound, a voice, a color gives—it appears. Or rather, it disappears as a canvas, and, in its place and spot, "it" appears as a (first) visible. In the Fourfold, the giving—"it gives," with neither giver nor given, in a pure *giving.* The gift here is of a piece with the *Fourfold* and the *Ereignis:* the gift arises from the appropriation of Time to Being, hence also of being to Being—gift as appropriation, without any distance.

On the other hand, the gift can be understood starting from giving—at least, as it is accomplished by the giver. The gift must be understood according to giving, but giving [*donation*] must not be understood as a pure and simple *giving* [*donner*]. Giving must be understood by reference to the giver. Between the gift given and the giver giving, giving does not open the (quadri-) dimension of appropriation, but preserves distance. Distance: the gap that separates definitively only as much as it unifies, since what distance gives consists in the gap itself.[87] The giving traverses distance by not ceasing to send the given back to a giver, who, the first, dispenses the given as such—a sending destined to a sending back. Distance lays out the intimate gap between the giver and the gift, so that the self-withdrawal of the giver in the gift may be read on the gift, in the very fact that it refers back absolutely to the giver. Distance opens the intangible gap wherein circulate the two terms that accomplish giving in inverse directions. The giver is read on the gift, to the extent that the gift repeats the giving of the initial sending by the giving of the final sending back. The gift gives the giver to be seen, in repeating the giving backward. Sending which sends itself back, sending back which sends—it is a ceaseless play of giving, where the terms are united all the more in that they are never confused. For distance, in which they are exchanged, also constitutes that which they exchange. Distance can be exchanged only in being traversed. This other model of the gift, since it unites only to the extent that it distinguishes, can, precisely, distort Being/being by disappropriating in it what the *Ereignis* appropriates; being remains in its appropriation to Being—how would it get rid of it?—but distance includes it in another apparatus, in another circulation, in another giving. Beings, hence Being/being, hence also *ousia,* over and above what is given to them by the pure and simple *giving* of the *Ereignis,* discover themselves taken up again, as unbeknown to them and from the point of view of another aim. Here one could object: does this inclusion of Being/being in distance, supposing that it should have some legitimacy (but we agree that it does have to do with a violence), offer the least possibility? Are we not condemned to regressing to the point where the other term of distance will appear, if not as a cause, at least as a being, which, in the capacity of "creator," would give Being/being? What is to be gained by such a crudeness, which believes itself apologetic while actually foundering in nonthought? But this objection comes up, in its turn, only to the extent that it does not take the trouble to think distance. Distance implies an irreducible gap, specifically, disappropriation. By definition, it totally separates the terms that, precisely for this reason, can play through it their sending and return. If therefore, with the *ousia* of the prodigal son, nothing less than Being/being enters into distance and giving, the other term, "enigmatic," will remain so forever—even more than according to Heidegger. Doubtless it will not be named "Being," since Being is of a kind with being by virtue of ontological difference appropriated to itself through the *Ereignis.* Doubtless it will not be recognized in any being (and especially not a being "par excellence"), since being belongs to this side of distance. Doubtless we will name it G~~o~~d, but in crossing G~~o~~d with the cross that reveals him only in the disappearance of his death and resurrection. For the other term of distance, G~~o~~d, strictly does not have to be, nor therefore to receive the name of a being, whatever it may be. *G~~o~~d gives.* The giving, in allowing to be divined how "it gives," a giving, offers the only accessible trace of He who gives. Being/being, like everything, can, if it is viewed as a giving, give therein the trace of another gift to be divined. All that matters here is the gift model that one accepts—appropriation or distance. In the first, naturally, the instance of G~~o~~d could not intervene, since the *giving* is included in the Fourfold. In the second—but what then authorizes reducing it immediately to an ontic regression?—the known instance, here Being/being (of whatever mode that this knowledge may be), can by rights enter in distance with an instance that must remain unthinkable in order precisely to exercise the gift: we say, G~~o~~d who crosses Being/being only in submitting the first to the cross by which the hyperbolic *agapē* "which surpasses all knowledge" (Eph. 3:19) makes the sign of the cross. In the distance, only *agapē* can put every thing on earth, in heaven, and in hell, in giving, because *agapē* alone, by definition, is not known, is not—but gives (itself). At the heart of *agapē,* following its flux as one follows a current that is too violent to go back up, too profound for one to know its source or valley, everything flows along the giving, and, by the wake traced in the water, but without grasping anything of it, everything indicates the direction and meaning of distance. Even, eventually, Being/being—like the rest.

Hence it follows that G~~o~~d is expressed neither as a being nor as Being, nor by an essence. We have learned again to be amazed that metaphysics should have been able, starting with Descartes, to think G~~o~~d on the basis of causality (efficient moreover) and to impose *causa sui* upon him as a first name. We are in the process of discovering, as much through Denys the Mystic as through Nietzsche, that it is not self-evident that an *ousia* or that a concept should be able to determine in what way this might be G~~o~~d. It remains to be glimpsed, if not with Heidegger, at least in reading him, and, if really necessary, against him, that G~~o~~d does not depend on [*relève de*] Being/being, and even that Being/being depends on distance. *Relève:*[88] neither abolition, nor continuation, but a resumption that surpasses and maintains. In other words, among the divine names, none exhausts G~~o~~d or offers the grasp or hold of a comprehension of him. The divine names have strictly no other function than to manifest this impossibility. More positively, they function to manifest the distance that separates (and hence unites) all the names of G~~o~~d—all, for in distance all can merit the qualifier divine. Here, predication must yield to praise—which, itself also, maintains a discourse. We questioned our silence on G~~o~~d. We asked our silence if it acceded to a dignity great enough to be able to claim to concern, with neither blasphemy nor ridicule, something like G~~o~~d. This journey, at once long and summary, which led us to the point of glimpsing the amplitude of what distance places in giving, allows us to outline a response. Every silence that remains inscribed in banality, in metaphysics, and even in Being/being, indeed, in a theology forgetful of the divine names, offers only mute idols. To remain silent does not suffice in order to escape idolatry, since, preeminently, the characteristic of the idol is to remain silent, and hence to let men remain silent when they no longer have anything to say—not even blasphemies. The silence that is suitable to the G~~o~~d who reveals himself as agape in Christ consists in remaining silent through and for agape: to conceive that if G~~o~~d gives, to say G~~o~~d requires receiving the gift and—since the gift occurs only in distance—returning it. To return the gift, to play redundantly the unthinkable donation, this is not said, but done. Love is not spoken, in the end, it is made. Only then can discourse be reborn, but as an enjoyment, a jubilation, a praise. More modestly, the silence suitable to G~~o~~d requires knowing how to remain silent, not out of agnosticism (the polite surname of impossible atheism) or out of humiliation, but simply out of respect. Despite oneself, one must recognize that, if we do not love agape enough to praise it, we must at least preserve this impotence as the trace of a possibility. We must guard our silence like a treasure, still held in the gangue that obfuscates its splendor, but nonetheless protects its future brilliance. This silence, and no other, knows where it is, whom it silences, and why it must, for yet a time, preserve a mute decency—to free itself from idolatry. If we succeeded in glimpsing only the outline of that by which agape exceeds everything (and Being/being), then our silence could let us become, somewhat, "messengers . . . announcing the divine silence."[89]

4

THE REVERSE OF VANITY

1—Suspension

The crossing of Being: up to this point, we only glimpse G~~o~~d who may accomplish it. And hence, because G~~o~~d alone could accomplish it, and because at best, we can glimpse G~~o~~d only in the intermittent half-times of our idolatries, in the meantimes of our mirror games, in the margins of the solar bedazzlement in which our gazes culminate, we perceive this crossing only from time to time. For that which crosses Being, eventually, has the name *agapē*. *Agapē* surpasses all knowledge, with a hyperbole that defines it and, indissolubly, prohibits access to it. The crossing of Being is played in our horizon, first because Being alone opens the space where beings appear, and then because *agapē* does not belong to us in itself. We fall—in the capacity of beings—under the government of Being. We do not accede—in the capacity of "sinners"—to *agapē*. The crossing of Being therefore exceeds and escapes us on two accounts. From the point of view of philosophy, we hold the value of beings, which the opening of Being governs in their deployment; a fortiori, if we admit and recognize ourselves in the site of *Dasein* which ontological difference thoroughly and most intimately determines, we are exhausted in and by the privileged claim that Being addresses to us. Thus from the point of view of theology, we must recognize that the condition that is as much finite as it is "sinful" situates us at an infinite distance from *agapē:* a gap which sin can accentuate only inasmuch as, to begin with, it is inscribed in the constitutive distance of the creator, inconceivable to the creature, which is itself, and in all senses, conceived. From this point on, a simple situation may be established. In rough outline, without entering into detail, it could be described in this way: finitude, ontic and above all ontologically determined, discovers (itself in) the openness of Being, which does not cease to bring about being's possibility, to the point of being given in forgetfulness itself; nothing human breaks forth otherwise than in the openness of Being. This inalienable site governs every possible world. Theology would add, it governs every world as created; in short, the finitude according to which, essentially, being is deployed in and for Being, coincides with the field of the created; creation indicates not only being but even Being, since Being is only at play in the measure of finitude. In finitude (understood then as creation), the crossing of Being would not have any meaning, or the least possibility of finding itself actually thought, hence accomplished. On the contrary, from the radically other—other to the point of strangeness—point of view of G̸o̸d, *agapē* would find itself granted the power to cross Being; let us understand Being/being playing in finitude in *Dasein,* itself overinterpreted as *ens creatum.* Of this crossing we would know nothing, in whatever sense this nothing should be expressed, since finitude, as well as the status of creature and the ignorance of *agapē* implied by the condition of sinner forbid us access to it. The crossing of Being could be admitted on condition that it remain totally empty and senseless from the point of view as much of philosophy as of the (sinful) "economy" of the creature. It would be the concern of the radically unthinkable, which, beyond even divine names, is deployed secretly in a silence whose very vacuity remains horrifying to us.

In this simple situation, a violence most certainly reverses the Heideggerian topography: the gap between creature and creator is no longer inscribed in the sole ontic region; on the contrary, all of ontological difference would find itself reinscribed in the field of creation: the *creatum,* while remaining neutral, would go beyond the strict domain of the *ens* (*creatum*) to comprehend as well, though in a different capacity, Being taken as *"neutrale tantum."*[1] But this reversal still maintains the option, for us decisive, of the Heideggerian topography: from the point of view of a thought actually thinking, here and now, nothing would be unveiled that is not deployed as a being according to the openness arranged by Being, the unique and invisible screen where the aim stops its gaze—discovering in it, in this very stop, a being; so that "God" himself, if he must be, should be—a being. Whereby, though in a different way, access to the icon, which envisages our very aim from its infinite gaze, is still closed: the icon of *agapē* would remain for us inaccessible, even if it no longer necessarily follows that its possibility may be envisaged outside of Being/being. But of what importance is a possibility that, by rights, would appear to us to be decidedly impossible? In other words, if the crossing of Being and the distraction of ontological difference could be conceived only from the point of view of G~~o~~d as *agapē,* the analytic of man as *Dasein* would remain, *for us,* impassable, ontological difference, *for us,* unavoidable—hence the screen of Being would be insuperable.

One therefore must attempt—and it is indeed a question of an attempt whose success is not prejudged—to accede, from the very point of view of our situation defined by finitude, to the crossing of Being. Hypothetically, this attempt would consist of investing an interspace, a space undetermined because belonging to the domain neither of the idol nor at the same time of the icon. Indeed, more than of space, one must speak here of attitude (in the Husserlian sense of the term)—of an attitude characterized neither by the idolatrous gaze nor by the iconic face. Let us specify. In this attitude, it is a question of challenging what the screen of Being can affirm of idols (beings) by lending them its own idolatry (as screen), hence of distracting ontological difference. But this attitude could not, and even should not, for all that, reach the icon; for the icon begins to play, we have verified, only at the moment when *agapē* envisages our gaze; henceforth, our gaze alone cannot pretend to the icon except by deceiving itself again, since in no way does it depend on our gaze that a face envisages it, that it is envisaged by the distance that *agapē* dispenses and traverses. From *our* real point of view, the *agapē* that envisages remains unenvisageable (since, precisely, the icon intervenes only when it takes the initiative to envisage us and consists only in such an inversion of the gaze). We are looking for an attitude where the gaze no longer would freeze in a first (and last) visible, though not yet find itself envisaged by the invisible, whose initiative still escapes it; in a word, we are looking for an attitude where the gaze no longer would see any idol, though still not pretending to the impossible *agapē;* a gaze, therefore, that would see nothing that it does not immediately transpierce, and that nothing would come to envisage; a gaze, in the end, that would see nothing and that would not discover itself seen—a gaze that sees nothing, but that nothing loves, with neither idol nor *agapē*.

The analysis of such an attitude presents a prejudicial difficulty: can it ever be realized in fact? We could doubt this fact, if literary fiction had not described this type to us with more truth than factuality suggests. From among the numerous examples available, let us take M. Teste as sketched by Valéry. A witness of himself, Teste in fact cannot attest any idol, or be attested by any *agapē*. No idol holds up under his gaze, "somewhat larger than all that is visible."[2] This gaze always looks beyond what it looks at, it always goes beyond its spectacle, as if ahead of the visible because more fundamentally ahead of itself. The "frightening purity"[3] of its aim always notes a fringe of free light between the visible spectacle and the horizon which is always still open, never cloudy; the horizon always feels like an indraft [*appel d'air*] that, come from elsewhere, appeals against the threatening idolatry of the visible, and, in a puff of wind, arouses the aim toward a new visible, infinitely. This gaze never sees what other gazes, in its place, would see to the point of freezing: instead of seeing the visible, it immediately spots another part that is not filled, in the *visable* horizon, by the spectacle. It sees what is not presented as visible, the empty space between the *visable* and the visible; this gaze strictly forms an empty space before itself and around the visible; it makes an empty space of the visible and, transpiercing it or bypassing it, makes the invisible; it makes the invisible, as one makes a vacuum; this gaze, by dint of always aiming farther than its visible, always aiming "farther than the end of its nose," takes a journey to the end of the day. Nothing—no visible—stops it, just as nothing stops an armored column that "makes a breakthrough," as nothing stops a half-back who "makes an opening," as nothing stops the gaze in a flat landscape or an equally flat, fashionable salon. If nothing stops this gaze, however, one must not infer that it neither encounters nor sees anything; on the contrary, precisely because nothing stops it, it can, by that very fact, see and traverse everything with the eye of the proprietor. Nothing stops it, precisely because it reduces to nothingness everything offered to its sight: "The object his eyes fix upon may be the very object that his mind means to reduce to nothing."[4] Teste's gaze puts to the test what it beholds as one holds an enemy to the ground, in order to destroy him. The gaze hammers objects, not as a sculptor who disengages the apt figure from them, but as a mad person who disfigures a statue for fear of having to venerate it—or even as a thinker who philosophizes "with a hammer" in order to destroy the oldest idols. For this "stranger's way of looking at things, the eye of a man who *does not recognize,* who is beyond this world, the eye as frontier between being and non-being—belongs to the thinker."[5] Pensively, Teste destroys every spectacle with a pure and simple glance; or rather, in transpiercing every visible being with his gaze, he does not annihilate it so much as he disqualifies its pretension to offer the idol, which precisely would have fixed this gaze. No violence, no refutation, no speech even, but only the advance of the gaze, as if nothing *were.* And, in fact, immediately, nothing any longer is—nothing, at least in the sense of an idol, since everything remains exactly as before. Teste detests: to detest in the sense of an oath in reverse (*detestari*), to repulse by an oath; he abjures the world, presents himself as witness (*testis*) for the prosecution's charge against it, or rather as a witness who discharges it from all idolatrous dignity; a witness who dismantles all its dignity, visibility, splendor; a witness who deprives it, so to speak, of the right to testify for itself, who interdicts and disqualifies it. The detestation that Teste exercises deprives the world of all confidence—the world no longer merits confidence and, in return, it loses all confidence in itself. In the light of this idoloclastic gaze, the world becomes the indiscernible and translucent shadow of itself.

Hence the question: what then, from now on, will this gaze be able to attest? That one should have to pose this question is indicated by the fact that Teste now finds himself, as we saw, "beyond this world between being and non-being." He finds himself on the border between worldly being and that which, in fact, goes beyond it, since he transpierces the figure in which being culminates, the idol that captivates sight. Outside of the idol's regime, where are we to situate the gaze that Teste bears? Undoubtedly, one cannot hold it back in any idol whatsoever, since even self-idolatry—"I made an idol of my mind"[6]—reinforces the question, far from dispelling it. If my mind merits becoming an unimpeachable center, it has this privilege because of its irrepressible acuteness that detests the world; but how could the principle of such a dazzling disaster itself become that which it renders impossible—an idol? As much as self-idolatry seemed to be the rule of the idolatrous gaze,[7] so it appears from now on untenable to a gaze defined by its power to transpierce every idol. Thus the alternative no longer consists in deciding between an external idol and self-idolatry, but between the icon par excellence and self-hate: "Will he find life or death at the extremity of his expectant wishes?—Will this be God or some terrifying sensation of encountering, in the depths of thought, only the pale radiance of his own and miserable matter?" In other words, can Teste prevent the hatred of the idol, destroyed because seen—"I despise what I know—what I can do"—from flowing back on the gaze itself, which thus, in order not to fall away, would have to be destroyed by a hatred where it only appraises itself? "With no trouble at all I found within me all that was needed to hate myself," "I am not stupid because every time I think I am stupid, I deny myself—kill myself."[8] That which permits Teste's gaze to transgress everything visible without ever fixing on it as on an idol—detestation—also prohibits him from ever encountering in the world a gaze other than his own, in order to envisage it. As nothing holds under Teste's gaze, nothing holds up this gaze either. To hold up the gaze: to resist it, most certainly, but also, in resisting it, to balance the first pressure by another, equal pressure, so that the shared tension should save one and the other gaze from collapse. No face comes to envisage Teste, hence to hold up his gaze. By dint of having eyes a little too wide, Teste no longer sees anything, if not the impossibility of ever being able to stop his gaze. Like Oedipus, who Hölderlin assures us had one eye *too many,* Teste sees that by dint of lucidity (bringing to light) he destroys every visible, to the point that nothing will fix his gaze, that is, nothing that might come from the visible or that might occur in it. The radicality of the detestation of idols puts into question the possibility of an icon, whose gaze would be able to spare Teste from drowning in his own obviousness. Each idol that collapses marks the necessity of an icon, but also the impossibility of ever seeing it—at least from this point of view. That is, from this unstable gaze, which sees too much to be envisaged, suspended between the still falling twilight of the last idols and the ever-deferred dawn of an icon, a gaze too fixed not to occasion the suspicion of its death.

This tension, which indeed seems to go as far as contradiction, nevertheless does not indicate any existential impossibility. Teste imaginatively manifests a situation that is both possible and actual every day: our own. For we can go beyond the idols, without however receiving the icon that envisages us. Teste brings this situation of intolerable suspension to its most perfect version; thus he shows us only the rigor of our own situation. And indeed, *this* writing, taken literally, is inscribed in this untenable but trampled interspace: we, or rather I, do not cease to work up momentum in order *not* to fix myself on a given idol, and, the more this momentum leads me where I want, the more enigmatic to me becomes the invisible appearance of a gaze that envisages me—the icon. Since the opening of *this* writing, I stand in the position of Teste, and my readers (*you,* reading here, now) as well. We must ask, less of Teste, therefore, than of ourselves, how we manage in this way to maintain a gaze that does not see and does not let itself be seen, neither idolatrous nor iconic; in short, of what use, finally, is this gaze? In other words, when we see like Teste, with one eye too many, we undoubtedly see nothing (as regards the idol), and we let ourselves be envisaged by nothing (as regards the icon); but this nothing, once again, does not mean nothing. What then is effected in this gaze that is blinded by its very lucidity? This gaze is practiced in the carrying out of boredom. Boredom defines an attitude and a manner of looking that are perfectly definable, first by contraposition with other modes of the gaze, and then as such.

2—Boredom

The gaze of boredom, although disqualifying the idols, nevertheless cannot be confused with annihilation, nihilism, or anxiety. Let us indicate these three distinctions. (*a*) The gaze of boredom does not annihilate, or destroy, or even deny. On the contrary, the movement of destroying, precisely because it is a movement, implies a nonindifference that boredom characteristically places in parentheses. Boredom does not have any interest in whatsoever may *be,* and hence has no more negative interest than positive: it never destroys, but always turns away; more exactly, its sole quasi destruction ends with the dismissal implied by the mere fact that its gaze turns away; even less, boredom does not have to turn its gaze away in order to dismiss the thing from all (eventually idolatrous) dignity. This gaze, on the contrary, in positing itself, turns dignity far away from its spectacle, by immediately spotting the halo of invisibility that begins to appear (aureole and inverted glory) around the visible. By not paying attention at the very moment when it sets itself on the visible, the gaze abolishes the visible, dismisses it from any pretension to erect itself as first visible (idol), annuls it without having to annihilate it. (*b*) The gaze of boredom cannot be confused with a nihilistic attitude either. Nihilism begins with the devaluation of the highest values; this devaluation itself follows from the discovery that every value, even positive, loses its dignity simply because it receives such dignity from a foreign evaluation, that of the will (to power); thereby nihilism, as much passive as active, assigns to every being a new way of Being—evaluation by the *Wille zur Macht.* Moreover, only this nihilistic foundation of the beingness of being allows one to understand how nihilism itself completes (and hence continues as much as it kills) metaphysics. Nihilism fundamentally implies the impartial instance of the *Wille zur Macht,* for lack of which, obviously, passive nihilism could not lead to active nihilism any more than the fable of the "true world" could be abolished in the final (and inaugural!) indistinction between the "true" world and the "apparent" world. Nihilism disengages the *Wille zur Macht* as the essence (founder without foundation) of being. But boredom in no way founds being, not even in disputing, in its own favor, its foundation; for the gaze of boredom, in disqualifying the idols of the visible, does not establish itself as ultimate idol; it lost this naïveté long ago—in hating itself, to the point, eventually, of killing itself. Boredom renounces, without any tragedy, without any "merit" or "courage," the very intention of any idolatry whatsoever. Any fulfillment of the gaze by the visible repulses it; its "frightening purity" would be disgusted with it, if the chance—no: the danger, the temptation—happened to present itself. That the gaze of boredom does not concern nihilism, or exercise itself therein, is confirmed by the gap between Teste and reactive thought. Reactive thought hates itself, and it hates that which is not at all hateful, only in order to discipline itself, to straighten itself, and finally to be set straight again—in short, paradoxically but inexorably, in order to affirm (itself); and this, because precisely, at bottom, it remains *Wille zur Macht,* in search of affirmation. Teste, on the contrary, does not react any more than he acts, does not deny any more than he affirms. He detaches everything from the idol's dignity, he detaches himself, with neither asceticism nor effort, from his own affirmation, as from a last impurity, an impurity of the gaze, as one speaks of an impurity in a stone, which in this sense becomes truly precious only by subtraction. The gaze of boredom neither denies nor affirms; it abandons, so far as to abandon itself, with neither love nor hate, through pure indifference. (*c*) Finally, boredom must not be confused with anxiety. If by anxiety one understands the "fundamental mood" thematized by Heidegger,[9] one must read in it the phenomenological operation that accomplishes a reduction of being in its entirety, at the end of which there remains, as a threatening obsession, in face of and around *Dasein,* only the Nothingness/Nothing; the repulsion [*renvoi*] of beings indicates and denounces as well the Nothingness/Nothing, which, more intimately than their individual essences, assures them in presence, hence the beingness of being which, for that very reason, is not given in the manner of being. Repulsion (*Abweisung*) and gesture (*Verweisung*)[10] allow *Dasein* silently to hear the claim that Being addresses to it: that *Dasein* should be made if not "shepherd of Being," at least "sentinel of Nothingness/Nothing." Anxiety holds its place as *fundamental* mood only from the claim which it thus experiences on the part of Nothingness/Nothing as Being. Anxiety inaugurates a complex process, of which the claim of Being (*Anspruch des Seins*) constitutes the summit and unique stake. The retreat of beings counts only to the exact degree that it disengages the horizon where Being advances, under the species of Nothingness/Nothing. Here, that which opposes anxiety to boredom clearly appears; certainly, one and the other share the frightened retreat, but without ontic annihilation, of beings; however, in this desert, a voice still cries out an appeal for anxiety—the claim that Being silently utters. Boredom, on the contrary, can hear nothing here, not even the Nothingness/Nothing. For boredom, at least understood in its essential acceptation, remains deaf, even to what it hears. If there is no greater deafness than in the one who does not want to hear, then no deaf person hears less than boredom. What it hears it gives no attention to, no intention, no retention. Its characteristic function indeed consists in provoking indifference to every provocation, especially to a strong provocation, especially to an essential invocation. Boredom suspends the claim, and above all that of Being, because it has no function or definition other than this very suspension. We must take another step. Anxiety, strictly philosophical in this, repeats in its own way the amazement (*thaumazein*) that opens the way for the thought (metaphysical or not, it matters little here) of the Being of being; this goes to show that the *Anspruch des Seins,* the claim that Being makes heard through its "voice," causes it to experience "the marvel of all marvels: *that* what-is is."[11] Amazement, stupor, bedazzlement, which alone allow the silent "voice" of Being to make itself heard, have to do with the fact that being is (given): the pure *dass/that* of being mobilizes *Dasein* to the point of putting, through it, thought into movement. But boredom does not hear anything, does not want to hear anything, any more than its gaze can, or wants to, let itself be filled by a first visible, radiating with the dignity of an insurmountable idol. Before the fact that being is, boredom does not budge, does not see, does not respond. Boredom does not suffer any exception to its crepuscular gaze, and the being purely there forms no exception. No idol before boredom, not even the insurpassable spectacle of a given being. But, as nothing more essential than given being[12] (*dass:* Nothingness/Nothing, Being) can ever appear, boredom will never manifest itself more absolutely than in its uninterest for the given being. Boredom, which lends no interest to given being, is accomplished absolutely—absolutely, which means in absolving itself from every tie and every limit. Boredom dissolves, in the end, given being itself, and undoes itself from that which gives given being: Being, which here sets in motion ontological difference, in the open.

In comparing boredom with anxiety, we have not simply added a third negative point to two others. We have secured the most decisive gesture of boredom—to distract, this time negatively, ontological difference. As such, boredom becomes disinterested in everything. It interests itself in nothing. Before whatever may *be,* hence before everything to the extent that everything, at least, *is,* boredom is not interested: *mihi non interest,* that does not concern me, nor is it for me, I am not at stake in that which, here, is. Boredom withdraws from every interest that would make it enter among (*inter*) beings (*inter-est*). It disengages itself from them, leaves its place among them empty, *is* not among them for anybody or for any being. Boredom withdraws from being and from its stakes, as one withdraws from an affair, as one withdraws funds from a bank, as one gets out of a scrape. Henceforth free from everything, even and first from given being, absolute boredom deploys its indifference. Strictly, henceforth, nothing any longer makes a difference, including ontological difference. Even viewed according to the marvel *that* it is, being does not make the difference, for the Being that speaks in it no longer manages "to make itself interesting." Instead of anxiety provoking difference, because the claim of Being that speaks ontological difference interests it, boredom sees no difference in it. The indifference to a particular possible idol in a particular visible being is enlarged to the dimension of a world: it exerts itself on the fact *that* being is given, hence on nothing less than ontological difference which, in this way, is at play.

The gaze of boredom is not the concern, therefore, of a common existential analysis. It constitutes a "fundamental determination," as does anxiety, but in a totally inverted sense: instead of characterizing man as *Dasein* starting from ontological difference, it disqualifies ontological difference (by excess, not ignorance), and hence displaces man—at least in part—outside of his status as *Dasein*. Man, provided that he see with the absolute gaze of boredom, overflows *Dasein* as he disinterests himself in ontological difference. This indifference, absolute though tangential, distracts ontological difference. Most certainly not in deploying *agape*—which Teste, more than any other, knows to be inaccessible at the very moment when he most perfectly mimes it[13]—but by a sort of retreat and default, which, paradoxically, the gaze's advance and excess of lucidity assure. Beyond the idol (even the ultimate idol that Being/being gives), short of every icon where *agape* would envisage us—so wavers, decided but in suspension, the gaze of boredom.

3—Vanity of Vanities

What does this gaze see? It sees nothing, since it disqualifies the pretension of everything visible to constitute itself as an idol. It sees all, since its disqualification is addressed to all that is, whatever that might be. It sees all and nothing, all *as* nothing, all that is *as if* it were not. Under the indifference of boredom's gaze, the ontic difference between being and nonbeing becomes indifferent, because first ontological difference became so—*that* being is. Boredom does not impose annihilation on what it sees, but rather undifferentiation between the status of being and nonbeing. The suspension of boredom's gaze tears its spectacle from Being. This tearing away can be expressed with the word "vanity." Boredom's gaze strikes being in general with vanity. Just as anxiety, in dismissing being in general, designates Nothingness/Nothing as Being, so boredom brings on being in general the vanity that renders it indifferent to ontological difference. Boredom, in disengaging itself from ontological difference, undoes being from its very beingness, abolishes the very name of being.

Now, such vanity, which undoes being under the gaze that boredom places between idol and icon, is offered textually for our meditation in the inaugural phrase of one of the books in the Old Testament, the Qoheleth (or Ecclesiastes). This text belongs, we should immediately note, to the wisdom writings, as do Job, the Proverbs, and the Book of Wisdom—with, however, the notable difference that it is also one of the five "scrolls" (*megilloth*) that were proclaimed publicly for the five great Jewish holidays; it shares this high dignity with the Book of Ruth, the Song of Songs, Lamentations, and the Book of Esther, which all mark a great joy or a great suffering experienced by Israel along its indissolubly historical and spiritual itinerary. Hence, despite its strangeness, one cannot look upon the Qoheleth as marginal or of lesser authority. Now, this text reveals to us the sentence that, no doubt, best sustains the moment reached by our meditation: "Vanity of vanities," says the Qoheleth. "Vanity of vanities, and all [is] vanity! What advantageous difference for man in all the labor by which he labors under the sun?" (Eccles. 1:2–3).[14]

We must still read. We are looking for an understanding of vanity, of which we still know nothing, if not that it would result from the gaze of boredom. In what sense can we presume that what appears here, under the still undetermined name of "vanity," corresponds correctly to what the gaze of boredom provokes—the distraction of ontological difference that allows the marvel *"that* being is" to appear? Let us proceed with remarks at first external to "vanity" itself.

a) What the vanity in question touches has no limit: vanity affects "all"; in other words, nothing escapes it, as another verse soon will say: "nothing new under the sun" (Eccles. 1:9); one must note here the curious construction, rare according to the exegetes,[15] which would have to be translated literally by, "Nothing—all new, under the sun," in other words, by taking into account the strange juxtaposition of contraries, "nothing new in all the new"; therefore all the new—and it does not cease to arise in the course of the days and years—in fact, does not offer any novelty. The totality of things thus must be understood not only in space but—especially—in time. Indeed, it is a question of all, in a summation that is empirically impossible but actual to the eyes of a certain consciousness; we say, to the eyes of the gaze of boredom; strictly, to the gaze of, or with regard to, boredom. This gathering of "all," beyond the powers of clear and common consciousness, finds confirmation in the very formula "vanity of vanities" that precisely introduces the "all" ("all [is] vanity"); juxtaposition here indicates the superlative that the Greek and the Latin, for example, formulate by a suffix, for which the Hebrew knows no equivalent and which it replaces by repetition; thus in the "song of songs," which of course must be understood as "the song par excellence." This remark, rather banal philologically, nevertheless offers more than a little for consideration: if the totality is struck with vanity, vanity itself must reach a maximal intensity; or rather, in order that the "all" should fall under its power, vanity must become absolute, without limit or reserve, superlative. Hence a comparison, hardly avoidable: boredom can bring vanity on the totality, just as anxiety gave rise to "beings as a whole."[16] This comparison, however, immediately leads to a new question. Can the totality that boredom strikes with vanity be confused with being in totality, in short, with the totality of being?

b) Hence a second remark: despite the necessity in which translations find themselves constrained to use the copula *is,* the Qoheleth, itself, does not use it: "all-vanity." Without entering a complex, ambiguous, and too crowded discussion, we note that, literally, the Hebrew offers no strict equivalent of "to be," and from this we will draw only one modest conclusion: that which boredom strikes with vanity is not expressed as a being. This is not to say, to be sure, that it is not, since Qoheleth will review life, death, knowledge, love, power, goods, evils, etc.—in short, all that is—without exception. But, if he evokes these, he in no way evokes them as beings; indeed, he would not manage to envisage the totality of them if he undertook their empirical summation as positive beings. He can escape indefinite enumeration only from a point of view other than universal and positive presence, here and now. The totality appears, in fact, both as such but also as vain, only because it first appears as creation: "creation was subjected to vanity [*mataiotēti*]" says Paul (Rom. 8:20). Insofar as it is created, the whole is disengaged as an absolute whole; not as being, but as created, the world appears as a whole. In fact, two totalities (or totalizations) enter into competition, the one that interprets the world as being in its difference from Being, and the other that approaches the world as vain in its status of creation. Creation undoubtedly does not coincide entirely with vanity; but undoubtedly also, the totality could not appear as vain if the point of view—still enigmatic—that designates it as creation did not arise. What common terrain reunites them, then, at least in part? Vanity marks the world with indifference; but, in the world, the difference seems large between living and no longer living, enjoying and suffering, having and not having, knowing and erring, even (despite the lexicon, here faltering, of the Hebrew) being and not being; the difference does not at all seem to be an appearance, but a reality, *the* reality. Vanity can suspend this difference, to which nobody in the world can remain reasonably indifferent, only from a point of view that is mad or exterior to the world. Moreover, from the point of view of the world, this exteriority very precisely seems to be foolishness. Such an exteriority is marked by the concept of creation. One should not be surprised if this concept does not arise in the Qoheleth, and if we must borrow it from a text in the New Testament: the limit concept, the concept of the limit, creation can become intelligible only to the strict degree that a thought approaches it, keeps close to it, that above all an act manifests it by transgressing it; creation becomes possible, in a strict sense, only through incarnation, as much as the first Adam can be seen only in the brilliance cast on him by the second Adam. In the lack of this advent, thought is restricted to walking toward the limit, without, for that very reason, being able to name it. Along this path, the Qoheleth marks a decisive step—acceding to creation through consideration of the vanity by which the world is marked on the basis of a yet obscure fire lighted outside of the world. The black light of vanity already testifies to the fact that another sun can light the totality; that this other sun should render any novelty in this world unthinkable attests already that this world admits an outside.

c) The other sun strikes the totality, seen as creation and not as being, with indifference. Now a third remark can confirm. The maxim we are analyzing continues with a second verse: "What advantageous difference for man in all the labor by which he labors under the sun?" The question bears on a difference; no doubt the term here utilized (root *ytr*) designates the surplus, the profit between an investment or a labor and a result, and the question could be understood as: "What is there to be gained?"[17] But through the honestly self-interested triviality of the expression, we accede directly to what seemed to us the stake of vanity: the putting into question of interest properly defines boredom and hence constitutes a necessary moment in the setting into operation of vanity. Under the black sun of vanity, nothing matters: the labor of man no longer makes any difference; or rather, the difference that men's work gains among things with interest in view no longer holds from the point of view that throws light on these same things as vain creatures; interest itself in no way interests man; he no longer feels interested in interest, since vanity renders indifferent every difference peculiar to the world and internal to it.

The text that we are reading now offers a construction that is less obscure, though surprising, since it expresses an operation of thought according to the reverse order of its real moments. We first bring up the boredom (fundamental mood) that suspends the interest in interest by indifference (1.3); then we notice that boredom trains itself on a totality that is non-ontic but in a state of creation (1.2); finally, we accede to the vanity whose superlative redoubling extends the domain to the dimensions of a world (beginning 1:2). Having begun at the end, we gave ourselves the means to conclude by and with the beginning. Hence to ask: when vanity strikes, what does it accomplish, *in fact?*

At last, vanity. What does it signify? By what blow does it strike? Boredom, we posited above, does not annihilate or reduce to nothingness that which it nevertheless strikes with vanity. Does it not seem, though, that Qoheleth looks on things as vain precisely because they disappear? But exactly, he looks on them as vain before they disappear. We should even underline here that which separates Qoheleth from Job; Job appeals to G~~o~~d only after having lost his goods and for having lost them (unjustly); he bemoans having lost them as goods, and suffers for having lost a complete terrestrial happiness; he does not contest the goodness of this happiness, but the injustice that deprives him of it; before suffering from an injustice, he suffers from a lost good. Qoheleth declares, on the contrary, the vanity, not at all of what he would have lost or desired in vain, but of what he possesses; for he has it all, in well-accounted and known goods, as much for the spirit ("I have a considerable sum of wisdom"; Eccles. 1:16), as for matter ("I satisfied all the desires of my eyes, I refused my heart no pleasure"; Eccles. 2:10); that which he strikes with vanity consists in the very thing that he has, hence in goods that he has enjoyed and that he will continue to enjoy. He does not deplore their absence, but he strikes them with vanity in their very presence; vanity aims at goods to the very extent that they remain present and possessed in full enjoyment. One undoubtedly would have to say that vanity can annihilate whatsoever may *be,* precisely because it aims at the presence of things; it strikes them in their presence, face to face, and could not train itself on absent or annihilated goods. The gaze of boredom strikes with vanity presence as such, in the tranquil strength of its permanent display. Whereas Job acts, suffers, and speaks in (the) difference (between that which is and that which is not, between the just and unjust), Qoheleth thinks in the platitude, in an infinitely more disquieting sense, of perfect and serene possession, which, in one silent, invisible, and imperceptible blow, collapses into complete vanity—by a collapse that leaves it in place, as if nothing *were* the matter. For nothing changed, nothing took place, not even that nothing about which one says after a bout of anxiety, "it was nothing." Not even the nothing, strictly nothing whatever. One need not be overly struck by the blow that strikes with vanity, since it makes nothing out of nothing. To be sure, it does not introduce the nothing, since it suspends the difference between being and the nothing,—or, what amounts to the same thing, manifests the equivalence between present being (the presence of being) and the nothing. Vanity renders ontological difference indifferent. It therefore goes beyond the nothing as much as beyond being. It does not annihilate, nor does it have to do with the nothing, no more than with present being. We now can note that, in fact, the term we traditionally render by "vanity," the Hebrew *hebhel,* cannot be translated by "nothingness"[18] but suggests the image of steam, a condensation, a breath of air. A mist, as long as it remains immobile in the atmosphere, remains under the gaze like a genuine spectacle; in the same capacity as an edifice, an animal, or a tree, it occupies the horizon, even eventually investing it to the point of closing it; it presents itself to the gaze as a reality—that it *is.* But this reality, without destruction or annihilation, can nevertheless disappear in a light breeze. Disappear? In truth the word is not suitable, since that which constitutes the mist will not suffer any destruction: the droplets in suspension will remain in the air or reside in another state. Hence no reality disappears, but only a certain aspect of the reality: the cohesion, the consistency, the opaque compactness, which, with minuscule droplets and minute particles, erected an enclosure of space. Condensation, mist, steam disappear—without destruction—as soon as another wind, stronger and more violent, picks up. One breath yields to another; breath, *ruah,* hence spirit. A breath dissipates when the spirit breathes. The spirit undoes every reality in suspension, dissipates every suspension that appeared, before it and by rights, as a reality. "Vanity" therefore can define whatsoever may *be* only inasmuch as all that is can dissipate, like a mist, under a powerful breath. But, precisely, can everything thus dissipate, and what spirit can breathe in this way? The Psalmist had announced already that "Man like a breath [*hebhel*], his days, like a shadow that dissipates" (Ps. 144:4). Under the force of an overly violent spirit the days of man dissipate, just as the blade of grass flies away, as does the tree, and even the abode, if the wind become a storm. One therefore must admit that the more violently the spirit breathes, the more being becomes the shadow of itself, flies away, and dissipates its permanent subsistence. Before the violence of the spirit that breathes, man, hence also all of his works, can, without dying or being annihilated, simply no longer hold—man, puffed up by the breath of the spirit, lets himself be carried away, as if he had no weight (*kabhod,* "glory"). Man does not weigh a lot: under the breath of the spirit, he flies to pieces, dissipates, is undone. What the Psalmist proclaims: "Nothing but a breath [*hebhel*], *all* men who stand, nothing but a shadow, the human who walks, nothing but a breath [*hebhel*], the riches that he heaps up, and he does not know who will gather them. . . . Nothing but a breath [*hebhel*], *all* humans" (Psalms, 39:6–7, 12). All, here again, becomes or can become a puffed-up breath, without any weight: the works of man (his labor), as man himself, dissipate like a "light air, a vapor" (Saint Jerome).[19] Man does not hold under the wind, man does not hold the spirit; his presence floats, in suspension, in the flux that comes to him from elsewhere: "You are in fact a breath, which appears for a little while, and then disappears" (James 4:14).[20] Man appears and disappears, enters into presence or exits from it, to the rhythm of a wind or breathing that stirs him up or sets him down, allows him to remain or carries him away; his "vanity" does not stem from such an alternation (in which it is only a question of the simple contingency of the finite); nor does it stem from the radical exteriority of the breathing that provokes the alternation (in which it could only be a question of a domination); it stems from the fact that absolutely external alternation neither annihilates nor destroys but simply disperses, loosens, undoes. The spirit does and undoes, man finds himself carried away by the breath of his own defeat; or, if he remain, he knows that he owes this to a calm that has come, itself, from elsewhere, and which is therefore no less foreign.

4—As If

Striking with vanity therefore amounts to placing in suspension, to leaving the case (of all) in suspension. Not that the spirit drops everything, since on the contrary it carries everything away and lets everything rest. But suspension itself marks everything with the indication of caducity—all becomes caduke.[21] Not that all disappears or falls, but all *can* fall and disappear; this great propensity cannot be summarized in a final and irremediable moment; it saturates each instant and each fiber of permanence in presence; the possibility of falling penetrates the caduke itself, even and especially when it does not fall; it appears caduke precisely because it does not fall in that instant, while it could and will have to. Its present permanence is saturated with its abolition: not falling, in fact, reveals itself in order to manifest—as much as being able (and having) to fall—the suspension: the thing resists its disappearance only in order better to indicate that the very possibility of disappearing defines it; the fact of residing does not contradict the possibility of disappearance, but only its actuality; thus caducity is posted on the face of that which is—for the moment—and indicates by its suspension that which remains—for a time. That which remains immediately becomes that which does not remain, that which holds coincides with that which is undone, all or nothing, without any difference. This indifference, by the indication of an "as if, *hōs*,"[22] places the two faces of suspension in strict equivalence: "I tell you, brothers: the moment [*kairos*] is limited; it remains therefore [*to loipon*] that those who have wives should be *as if* they had no wives, that those who cry [should be] *as if* they were not crying, that those who rejoice [should be] *as if* they were not rejoicing, that those who have commerce should be *as if* they did not possess, and that those who make use of the world should be *as if* they did not make use of it. For the figure of this world is passing away" (1 Cor. 7:29–31). That which is, having become caduke because struck by vanity, is as if it were not: not that it is not or no longer, but because it appears indifferent to being or not being; to be or not to be, that is *not* the question; to be or not to be, there is no choice, precisely because between the two terms vanity undoes the difference. The "figure of the world" passes away neither simply nor to begin with because its final destruction approaches; for, in addition to the fact that this final point is comcompleted less as an annihilation than as a radical modification (1 Cor. 15:52), it can occur only inasmuch as, first, the "world" assumes a new figure that might admit and receive a completion. What figure? We have encountered it already: it makes of the world a "creation," it sees the world not as the assured subsistence of a (self) presence that is saturated (with itself), but as a suspension, suspended by that which goes beyond—outside of space as outside of time—the world.

For vanity only strikes the "figure of the world" when the latter compares itself to a pole that transports it outside of itself, unseats, and disables it. "We too can very easily indicate in themselves the sky, the earth, the sea, and all things contained in this small circle; but, once compared to God, they are as nothing [*sed ad Deum comparata esse pro nihilo*] . . . vanity of vanities, all: vanity" (Saint Jerome).[23] For, continues Jerome, a small light shining in the night indeed reveals therein all possible and real visibility; no one would doubt that it gives us *the* light. Nevertheless, it lights absolutely only until the sunrise, whose brilliance renders the first luminous source strictly invisible. The sun does not extinguish the lantern, does not hide it or swallow it up; it simply annuls it: rising from elsewhere, it relieves the first light of its function, not through a struggle between the light and the darkness, but through a slow subversion of light by light. The first light disappears without being destroyed, without the night triumphing, without even being extinguished: it does not even disappear—it suffers vanity. Thus the world suffers vanity only by comparison with another sun, "the black sun of melancholy" (G. de Nerval), which lights it up and invades it from an absolutely extrawordly Orient and which, at the very moment of rising over the world, remains no less extraterritorial, by an inadmissible and unthinkable privilege. Over the world rises a gaze that comes to it from elsewhere because it allows the exterior of the world to appear; the world, in its own eyes, recognizes no exterior, limits, or caducity; its exterior appears only if the obverse is turned over, in order to present the reverse, only if the world finds itself turned toward the exterior. What, then, would turn it thus? Only the gaze that strikes it with vanity, for this gaze sets itself on the world as a stranger: a stranger's gaze, which renders the world strange, deranged, a stranger to itself. The world no longer exceeds this gaze of boredom (no longer surpasses it, no longer exasperates it); on the contrary, henceforth it can exceed the world—take it to its breaking point and go beyond it. The gaze of boredom thus exceeds the world only by taking it into view from another pole—G~~o~~d; vanity strikes the world as soon as the world finds itself taken into view—envisaged—by another gaze than its own, under the gaze, impracticable to man, of G~~o~~d. Between this gaze and the world, distance is established, a gap that unites as much as it separates, a gap whose first term cannot but comprehend the incomprehensibility of the second, a gap, therefore, that offers itself less to be conceived or reduced than to be traversed and inhabited. Thus when Qoheleth fixes a gaze of boredom over "all," to discover therein a world struck by vanity, he sees from the point of view, not of the world, but of the exteriority of the world—between world and G~~o~~d. He sees the world not, to be sure, as G~~o~~d sees it, but as seen by G~~o~~d—as bathed in another light, transfixed by exteriority, suspended by another breath. In short, the world in distance.

The observation that vanity strikes the world only at its entrance into distance permits of conceiving three corollaries. (*a*) If vanity puts the status of the world into question, by subjecting it to a gaze that comes from elsewhere, the placement in suspension cannot touch only some beings (as a destruction or contingency); by definition it strikes all the world, the world as a whole, the whole of the world. We can even specify: all that which challenges the exteriority of another gaze exceeding the world at once recognizes this gaze (in admitting distance, if only to deny it) and does not recognize it (in refusing to efface itself before this gaze); closing oneself off to distance, without being able to draw away from it, is what characterizes the idol, which can only be spotted the moment when, already, another gaze confounds it, simply because it transpierces it. Vanity first becomes the vanity of the idol, and of the first of idols—that is, thought, which refuses to glorify: the world, under certain conditions, could glimpse its exterior (invisible distance, to be traversed), but if it does not accomplish this excess where it is itself exceeded, its thoughts vanish immediately, because of their own vanity. Saint Paul formulates this precisely: "The invisible things of God, since [and by the fact of] the creation of the world, can, starting from on high, be seen in the mode of spirit, in the works [as works done], and also the eternal power and divinity of God; such that they, men, cannot plead their cause, since having known God, they did not glorify him as

God, nor did they render him thanks, on the contrary [and consequently] they went up in smoke by their thoughts, and their unintelligent heart was darkened. Pretending to be wise, they becamefools—were distracted" (Rom. 1:20–22). What we translate by "went up into smoke," the Latin *evanuerunt* chosen by Saint Jerome, exactly renders *hebhel:* to fly off and dissipate like smoke or steam under an overly strong breath of spirit; the original Greek, *emataiōthēsan,* itself corresponds directly to the other equivalent of *hebhel* from the biblical Greek (in the Septuagint), *mataios;* therefore one also could translate, without contradiction, by "were struck with vanity, and with caduke insignificance." The distraction of men therefore comes from a situation that is as untenable as it is common: their thoughts are viewed by the invisible gaze of G☒d, who sees them as creatures, and offers himself to be recognized as creator—to be glorified *as* G☒d. Instead of responding to this silent injunction by "making use of the world *as* not making use of it," men deny, by thoughts that are idolatrous and bent back upon themselves as invisible mirrors, the distance where the world is set in motion as creation. Creation, not recognized as such, immediately finds itself struck with vanity, and thoughts, with distraction. This status—distance known and not recognized, suspension—marks with caducity, hence with idolatry, everything and anything: "thoughts" (Eph. 4:17–18), "pursuits, *zētēseis*" (Titus 3:9), the "thoughts of the wise" (1 Cor. 3:20), and even "religion" understood as *pietas* (James 1:26). Vanity strikes all—the world—as soon as thoughts are distracted by not recognizing distance as such. Distraction consists, in a sense, not in the alienation, but in the refusal of the other: the world is alienated from its exterior, it is alienated from distance. It suffers from vanity because it pretends to solitude.

(*b*) The fact that vanity strikes the world only at its entrance into distance implies that the world by itself cannot—except in recognizing distance as such (in glorifying G☒d as G☒d)—glimpse its own vanity. "That something so obvious as the vanity of the world should be so little recognized that people find it odd and surprising to be told that it is foolish to seek greatness; that is most remarkable" (Pascal).[24] But not at all! If vanity strikes the world only in distance, it reaches it only from the sole point of view that, by definition, the world cannot, as world, produce or even suspect. By definition, the arrogant closure of the world on itself closes to it access not only to distance but to the very suspicion of its own vanity. So that to perceive, even by a very vague suspicion, "the black sun of melancholy" that dazzles the light of the world, already constitutes a transgression of the world, a sketch of an excess, the outline of distance. Hence a question: in reading the Qoheleth we thought that we were confronting the difficulty of simply conceiving vanity—that the world in its entirety would become caduke under another gaze. But the stakes of the Qoheleth, and of the theoretical moment that it designates, could go further: since vanity already implies glimpsing distance through one of its poles, vanity permits access to it. One indication immediately confirms it; the crucial sentence, "Vanity of vanities. All-vanity," which marks the world with caducity, inverts and duplicates the word of the creator pronounced over creation at the opening of time: "and God saw that it [was] beautiful and good."[25] The same distance designates the same world as vain or as "beautiful and good," according to whether the gaze perceives the distance through one pole or the other: from the world, on the fringe that opens it to the excess of a distance, the totality appears to be struck by vanity; from the inaccessible point of view of G~~o~~d, at the extremes of distance, the same world can receive the blessing that characterizes it in its just dignity.

(*c*) Such an ambivalence permits one to specify the situation from which Qoheleth speaks, and where he introduces us: he sees the world suspended by the breath of vanity only insofar as he himself is situated in an untenable suspension. The world, if it *is,* and if a gaze of boredom apprehends it, suffers vanity, because the gaze of boredom accedes to distance without genuinely traversing it; but only Qoheleth—we, therefore—experiences boredom, because he experiences distance only in the degree of his own inadequacy. For another gaze, which would be able to traverse distance—the gaze of G~~o~~d—boredom no longer arises; the gaze that can love strikes no longer with vanity, but prompts "goodness." Vanity disqualifies the world only for the gaze that accedes to distance through boredom, without charity; vanity arises from a gaze that exceeds Being/being without yet acceding to charity, a gaze that discovers the world as being beyond Being/being without seeing it loved—by G̶o̶d. The gaze of Qoheleth—ours—enters into distance without traversing it, strikes the world with vanity without covering it with charity. Vanity comes from the boredom of man, not from the boredom of G̶o̶d; for G̶o̶d loves, and from the gaze of charity comes the "goodness" of the gazed at. Boredom designates the suspension only of the human gaze, beyond Being/being, but short of charity, just as vanity disqualifies the world in its being in the absence of its requalification through charity. Qoheleth trains over the world a gaze that is more than human but not yet divine. He enters at the site where charity becomes the requisite of that which is, and where that which is is exceeded, without however being oriented in charity. The empty bed of an absent love, the world is presented as deserted to the gaze of boredom, whose impotence to attain charity can pour out onto the world only vanity—the reverse of charity. This site, between Being and charity, is called melancholy.

5—Melancholia

Melancholy, or rather *Melancholia,* if we stick to the title of a famous engraving by Dürer.[26] Let us look at it. Let us look at it, since it looks, and even consists only in a look. Heavy, sitting down, his head weighing on his left hand, a man gazes. Not a man, but an angel, as his wings indicate; a man nevertheless, as other characteristics demand: human finitude is betrayed by the silver, which swells a purse at his belt, by the crown of leaves that circles his forehead, as a poet's, and by the time shown by the hourglass situated directly above his thoughtful and frozen head. Neither angel nor man—can one imagine it? Undoubtedly, if, bearing in mind the figure of Teste, we envisage the possibility, here exemplified, of a gaze, between idol and icon, that looks at everything without seeing anything, perceives everything without recognizing itself in anything, or recognizing anything other than its own absence. For, under the gaze of melancholy, what presents itself as a spectacle? All the visible: Dürer displays in the horizon the splendor of a landscape composed of water, mountain, city, and forest. An animated being complements these inanimate beings: here a magnificent dog, dozing in the foreground. These spectacles do not, however, captivate the gaze of melancholy, which, visibly, does not stop in them as at its first visible. But Dürer, himself, suggests more to be seen: all the art of men is presented to the gaze, with the various tools of the carpenter, of the mason, of the peasant (the millstone), and so on; and more yet, justice, time, numerals, geometrical figures, even—according to the compass held by the right hand—intelligible measure and order. The gaze of melancholy no longer stops at them, or aims at them. Finally there remains, beyond the sensible, beyond the arts and sciences—in short, beyond the domain of the finite, that which incites transgression of the finite: the small but central figure of an angel (this one genuine), situated just between the summit of the compass and the thrust of a ladder that is lost in the sky; ladder, angel: undoubtedly a climactic angel, at the foot of the ladder which orders the degrees of things and of the world, as far as to promise (if not to permit) their transgression. Would the gaze of melancholy fix itself on the angelic ladder, on the climactic angel? Even that does not suffice to hold it back. What does this gaze look at instead, this gaze whose insistent heaviness hollows the engraving as by an imperious and crushing center of gravity? For this gaze gazes—but without gazing at things, animals, or the arts; nor does it transgress the visible and rational spectacle in the direction of the heavens. Where, then, is its aim set? Can one imagine that it gazes beyond the engraving, for example, on the very spectator of this engraving? Obviously not. But, by this new question, we approach the right answer: the gaze of melancholy, not setting itself on any of the beings seated in the frame of the engraving, therefore exits from it; but in what direction? Neither at the upper part (the heavens, the angels, the divine), nor at the foreground (us, the onlookers), but at the left side of the engraving. Now, on this left side opens the azimuth where, from another point of view, the flight lines [*lignes de fuite*] of diverse figures converge *outside* of the engraving. Which is confirmed by the rainbow: the part that is truncated by the frame of the engraving invites a continuation strictly out of frame. The engraving, by its very organization, refers outside of itself—toward a vanishing point that it does not grasp. And melancholy gazes at nothing other than this absent vanishing point [*point de fuite*]—absence of an escape, flight from any flight. It strikes with vanity the beings that encumber and overwhelm it, by simply gazing at the vanishing point—a strange instance that constitutes the visibility of melancholy without itself ever appearing and that, here, escapes the visible a second time in being situated outside of the engraving, whose frame Dürer solidly and intentionally fixes. Of the beings here present—in fact, their totality and all their degrees—melancholy disturbs neither the order nor the substance nor the essence; it touches nothing in them; better, it is in no way interested in them, since it does not stop in them. Its gaze merely transpierces them toward this point totally exterior to them but that governs their visible representation and nevertheless misses them doubly: a vanishing point that is not a being, and that, in addition, here escapes the frame of the engraving. The gaze of melancholy sees beings in the way in which they are not: by the escape of their vanishing point, they appear to it as not being. They appear to it, despite the heavy calm by which the engraving is framed, as seized by vanity: which the clearing of the upper left corner of the engraving designates precisely not as a void, and which exceeds this void itself, the flight from flight. The engraving flees through the imperceptible flight of its beings toward their vanishing point. The world leaks vanity through all its beings. The world leaks vanity, as being exudes boredom.[27] Melancholy, black sun: but if Dürer allows a sun still clear as the day to rise, does he not make a bat unfurl the banderole on which *Melencolia* is inscribed? Half-bird of night, for a gaze half-angelic, and black.

Melancholy strikes with vanity, and progresses to the degree that the gaze perverts what it sees. What, then, could limit the advance of melancholy? If melancholy relays the distraction of *ousia* by *agapē,* we can presume that the vanity it imparts also maintains a privileged relation with that same *agapē.*

A first confirmation of this comes from the texts of the New Testament. In them, vanity often recognizes *agapē* as its contrary: "The goal of this injunction is the *agapē* that is born of a pure heart, of a good conscience and of a sincere faith—by having deviated from this goal, some have strayed into vain language, *eis mataiologian*—a distracted *logos*" (1 Tim. 1:5–6). When *agape* alone does not preside over the *logos,* the latter is distracted, struck with vanity. If vanity is opposed also to G☒d himself (Acts 14: 15), or to the risen Christ (1 Cor. 15:17), one must see in this the confirmation of their common identification as *agapē* (following 1 John 4: 8, 16). Hence one understands that vanity may also agree with idolatry: one and the other in fact admit an identical contrary, G☒d as *agapē.*

Another indication comes to corroborate this: while he studies spiritual sorrow, which is saddened not before an evil, but precisely before a good whose accomplishment is prohibited (*taedium operandi*), Saint Thomas speaks of *accidia,* echoing the *akēdia* of the desert Fathers; now he lends it some characteristics of vanity by finally opposing it to charity: "the sorrow whereby one is displeased at the spiritual good which is in each act of virtue, belongs, not to any special vice, but to every vice, but sorrow in the Divine good about which charity rejoices [*de quo charitas gaudet*], belongs to a special vice, which is called sloth [*accidia*]."[28] Sadness, which refuses a good that is not only spiritual, but strictly divine, needs nothing less than charity to contradict it. The supernatural boredom that turns the spiritual away from the good hence takes it away from charity, which alone, in return, can restore it to its good—itself.

It finally becomes possible to introduce an ultimate, more common confirmation of the relation of vanity to *agapē.* Sometimes we in fact experience vanity growing in direct proportion to love. Let us take the hypothesis—less unrealistic than it appears—of a love that is reciprocal as much as it is extreme: I love and discover myself loved in return, in both cases with all the suitable excess. Two poles are defined, in a relation that polarizes not only the partners but their whole environment; at the extreme limit, the polarization would define a world where each term would be determined, not for and by itself, but by its relation to the two poles, and to the attraction that their mutual draw exercises on the world. Such a situation admits at least two variations.

First variation: if what I love is lacking, for me who loves, if therefore reciprocal polarization is suspended, even for an instant, even if for an innocuous motive, nothing less than the entire world is immediately and completely struck with vanity; the disconnection of the polarizing relation suspends not only its two terms but also and especially all the other terms. The suspension of love also affects that which love itself does not affect, at least for the one who loves. The one who loves sees the world only through the absence of what he loves, and this absence, for him boundless, flows back on the entire world; if a single person is lacking, all will fall back into vanity. For the world, as opposed to the one loved, has not disappeared; it remains present, here and now; in no way does the disappearance of the loved one make the world disappear; but this disappearance nevertheless strikes the appearance of the world with vanity. What marvel can still be found in the fact that being in general (the world) is—when what one loves is no more, and when this itself could not be expressed by the name being? The disappearance of what one loves shatters a double certainty: that the world is offers no marvel in itself, and that the loved one is not to be loved insofar as he or she is. The proof is that the world, which is, does not become more lovable for that reason—on the contrary. And the loved one, who is no longer, does not become less lovable for that reason—on the contrary. That which is, if it does not receive love, is as if it were not, while that which is not, if love polarizes it, is as if it were: the indifference to determination according to ontological difference reappears as the responsibility of love, as before it was the responsibility of the divine *agapē*. In this situation, where vanity strikes the world as such because one of its poles of polarization is lacking, there is nothing more reasonable than the insanity of sacrificing all that is (being in its totality) for that which is not (the absent loved one); the insanity in fact stems from the ontological illusion that it would be a question of sacrificing being for nonbeing, whereas, for the one who loves, it is only a question of exchanging that which knows nothing about love for that which loves and is loved. To give the world which is, empty of love, for that which is not but belongs to the domain of love—there is nothing more reasonable and even advantageous. And no doubt Pascal's wager would have to be understood in this way—on the basis of the heterogeneity of the third order to the first two. This first variation is nevertheless open to an objection: vanity strikes that which is only inasmuch as the loved one, the other pole, is not; it would suffice that it be, in order that all being should be separated from vanity; and hence, vanity flows forth not so much for lack of the love of the loved one than, more simply, for lack of its presence here and now; vanity, in fact, is amenable to the beingness of beings, not to love.

Let us go back, then, in order to test the objection, to the second variation. What becomes of the world, if the polarization between those who love (one another) reaches its perfect and constant reciprocity? According to the objection, vanity struck the world only because of the absence of the loved being: vanity resulted from an ontic absence. Here, there is no ontic absence: the two poles of love are, here and now. What happens with regard to the rest of the world? In fact, it still and equally suffers the blow of vanity: in itself, simply because it *is,* it suffers from vanity. No doubt a particular beautiful landscape supports by its peculiar charm a particular moment of love, as do the particular brilliance of a picture, a particular moment of music, a particular elegance of dress or dwelling; but these marvels only frame: if no love had by chance turned them into a momentary resting place, their gathered splendors never would have been able to produce the least movement of love. Apparently, their intrinsic beauty separates them from vanity; in fact, they escape it only in the strict sense that the love they dress condescends to be clothed by them—once, out of pure benevolence. Venice becomes beautiful only because one loves there, and not the inverse, despite appearances; indeed, Clichy, ever since Miller, certainly equals Venice; the beauty of the stones and of the sites still belongs to the domain of truth, hence of beingness—before love, it receives the dull blow of vanity, or escapes it only by pure grace of association. Love strikes the world with vanity in all indifference to its virtues—it is an extrinsic vanity; in the same way, it touches certain beings with a grace just as extrinsic, according to which it associates with its incommensurable action the most trivial of beings: the cobblestone that one passes, a child's sleigh, an invented proper name, the being matters little, provided that it stem from a love to which, in any case, it will remain foreign. Vanity covers as much what love includes in its exclusionary logic as what is excluded by this same love. The difference does not at all pass between beings and nonbeings, or even between those who indeed wish to join the polarization of love, and the others; it passes between love itself and the world—being—by itself. Vanity, which follows and redoubles love as its shadow, has no other function, as long as *agapē* has not recapitulated everything under a single authority, than to mark this indifferent difference.

Only love does not have to be. And G~~o~~d loves without being.

5

OF THE EUCHARISTIC SITE OF THEOLOGY

Theology can reach its authentically *theo*-logical status only if it does not cease to break with all theo*logy.* Or yet, if it claims to speak of God, or rather of that G⊗d who strikes out and crosses out every divine idol, sensible or conceptual, if therefore it claims to speak of G⊗d, in such a way that this *of* is understood as much as the origin of the discourse as its objective (I do not say *object,* since G⊗d can never serve as an object, especially not for theology, except in distinguished blasphemy), following the axiom that only "God can well speak of God";[1] and if finally this strictly inconceivable G⊗d, simultaneously speaking and spoken, gives himself as the Word, as the Word given even in the silent immediacy of abandoned flesh—then there is nothing more suitable than that this theology should expose its logic to the repercussions, within it, of the *theos.*

1—Let It Be Said . . .

What, in fact, does theology—Christian theology—say? For in the end, what distinguishes Christian theology from every other does not stem from a singularity of meaning (as decisive as one would like) but from what, precisely, authorizes this eminent singularity, namely, the very position given to meaning, to its statement, and to its referent. Christian theology speaks of Christ. But Christ calls himself the Word. He does not speak words inspired by God concerning God, but he abolishes in himself the gap between the speaker who states (prophet or scribe) and the sign (speech or text); he abolishes this first gap only in abolishing a second, more fundamental gap, in us, men: the gap between the sign and the referent. In short, Christ does not say the word, he says *himself* the Word. He says *himself*—the Word! Word, because he is said and proffered through and through. As in him coincide—or rather commune—the sign, the locutor, and the referent that elsewhere the human experience of language irremediably dissociates, he merits, contrary to our shattered, inspiring or devalued words, to be said, with a capital, the Word. To say that he says himself the Word already betrays that we stutter: for this "he says himself" already means to say—the Word. He says himself, and nothing else, for nothing else remains to be said outside of this saying of the said, saying of the said said par excellence, since it is proffered by the said-saying. In short the *dict* of the Said. He is said and all is said: all is accomplished in this word that performs, in speaking, the statement that "the Word pitched its tent among us" (John 1:14), because he has nothing to do, here, other than to say [himself]. That he simply should say [himself], and all is accomplished. That he should say [himself], and all is said. He only has to say [himself] in order to do. Better, he does not even have anything to say in order to say everything, since he incarnates the dict in saying it: no sooner said than done. And hence the Word, the Said, finally says nothing; he lets people speak, he lets people talk, "Jesus gave him no answer" (John 19:19 = Luke 23:9). And so he does by letting be said, and so he says by letting be done. So be it: "He says: all is finished" (John 19:30). The Word does not say [itself] as Word, or better: says [itself]—Word!—only by letting be said: which one can understand in a double sense. The Word, as Said of God, no man can hear or understand adequately, so that the more men hear him speak their own words, the less their understanding grasps what the said words nevertheless say as clear as day. In return, men cannot render to the

Word the homage of an adequate denomination; if they can—by exceptional grace—sometimes confess him as "Son of God," they do not manage (nor ever will manage) to say him as he says himself. The Word is not said in any tongue, since he transgresses language itself, seeing that, Word in flesh and bone, he is given as indissolubly speaker, sign, and referent. The referent, which here becomes locutor, even if he speaks our words, is not said in them according to our manner of speaking. He proffers himself in them, but not because he says them; he proffers himself in them because he exposes himself in them; and exposes himself less as one exposes an opinion than as one exposes oneself to a danger: he exposes himself by incarnating himself. Thus speaking our words, the Word redoubles his incarnation, or rather accomplishes it absolutely, since language constitutes us more carnally than our flesh. Such an incarnation in our words can be undertaken only by the Word, who comes to us before our words. We, who on the contrary occur only in the words, we cannot freely carry out this incarnation. Incarnate in our words, the Word acquires in them a new unspeakableness, since he can be spoken in them only by the movement of incarnation that is, so to speak, anterior to the words, which he speaks and which he lets speak him. Any speech that speaks only from this side of language hence cannot reach the referent, which, alone and in lordly manner, comes nevertheless, in language, to meet us. Before our words, the Word lets people talk, thus manifesting that he cannot be spoken in them, but that, by the lordly freedom of this redoubled incarnation, he gives himself in them to be spoken. What is unheard of in the Word stems from the fact that he only says [himself] unspeakably (gap Word/words), but that in this very unspeakableness he is said nevertheless perfectly (the gap traversed by redoubled incarnation). The Word says [himself] absolutely though unspeakably, unless he is only absolved from unspeakableness in traversing it by a perfect incarnation. He is unspeakable, not simply like an overly high note that no throat can sing, by default of speech: it is not only a question of speech, but especially of the sign and meaning. He is unspeakable also, but not only, like the untenable thought of the abyss, where Zarathustra founders, because it opens to the terror of an unfurling of divinity: for it is not a question here first of a thought, but of a referent, in flesh and bone, of the Word whose incarnation occupies and transgresses at once the order of speech and of meaning. No human tongue can say the Said of G~~o~~d. For to say it, one must speak as He alone speaks, with *exousia* (Mark 1:22, etc.), with that sovereign freedom, whose (super-) natural ascendancy impresses all as an omnipotence so great that it only has to speak in order to be admitted. The Word says itself, it therefore becomes unspeakable to us; labile inhabitant of our babble, it inhabits our babble nevertheless as referent. The Word, as Son, receives from the Father the mandate and the injunction (*entolē*) to say; but, when he becomes the locutor, this message already coincides otherwise (or precisely: not otherwise) with that message which the paternal illocution eternally realizes in him as Word; such that he can legitimately transfer, in the very act of his statement—the incarnation—not only the message spoken by him, but the speaker who, with and before him, speaks it, him, the unspeakable Said, as such—*Verbum Dei*. When he speaks the words of the Father, he lets himself be spoken by the Father as his Word. Thus *the Word is said as it is given:* starting from the Father and in return to the Father. This very transference designates the Spirit. Or rather the Spirit takes the turn to speak in order to designate this transference of the speaker (Jesus) in the sign (the text of the divine will) as that of which the Spirit trinitarily offers the referent—"A voice came from heaven; I glorified you and I will glorify you" (John 12:28), the voice where Spirit speaks (at the baptism; Matt. 3:16), in the name of the Father (transfiguration, Mark 9:7) who speaks the Son as such. In other words: I hold this one as my preferred son in whom I proffer myself, the proffered that, of all the proffered, I prefer because he prefers to proffer me, rather than himself. Preferred, proffered: the Word, beloved Son. The Word lets himself be said by the Father—in the Spirit that consists, in a sense, only in this—exactly as he lets his will do the will of the Father. Thus appears the Said of the Father: the Word seems to be the Said, when he appears as the Son of the Father. Said of the Father: the Word proffered by the breath of the paternal voice, breath, Spirit. Upon the Cross, the Father expires as much as the Word—since they expire the same Spirit. The Trinity respires from being able to breathe among us.

Of such a Word, of such a *logos,* a discourse becomes legitimate, hence possible, only if it receives and maintains the repercussion of that which it claims to reach. To justify its Christianity, a theology must be conceived as a *logos* of the *Logos,* a word of the Word, a said of the Said—where, to be sure, every doctrine of language, every theory of discourse, every scientific epistemology, must let itself be regulated by the event of its redoubling in a capital, intimate, and anterior instance. It is not simply a question of making a concession, for example, of admitting that, given the event of Christ, certain conditions of linguistics, of hermeneutics, and of the methods of human sciences have to undergo a few modifications, even exceptions. For here, the Word arises short of the field of possible objects for given methods: one can well attempt (in fact though, one cannot) to do "theologies" of labor, of nonviolence, of progress, of the middle class, of the young, and so on, where only the complement of the noun changes; but one could not do a "theology of the Word," because if a *logos* pretends to precede the *Logos,* this *logos* blasphemes the Word (of) G⊗d. Only the Said that lets itself be said by the Father can assure the pertinence of our *logos* concerning him, in teaching it also to let itself be said—said by the Word made flesh, unspeakable and silent. Theology: most certainly a human *logos* where man does not master language but must let himself be governed by it (Heidegger); but above all, the only *logos* of men that lets itself be said—remaining human *logos* more than ever—by the *Logos.* To do theology is not to speak the language of gods or of "God," but to let the Word speak us (or make us speak) in the way that it speaks of and to G⊗d: "Receive the spirit of filiation, in which we cry, 'Abba, Father' " (Rom. 8:15), "You then, pray thus: Our Father who art in heaven . . ." (Matt. 6:9).[2] Theology: a *logos* that assures its pertinence concerning G⊗d to the strict degree that it lets the *Logos* be said in itself, *Logos* itself understood (strictly: heard) as he who alone can let himself be said perfectly by the Father: for in order to say G⊗d one first must let oneself be said by him to the point that, by this docile abandon, G⊗d speaks in our speech, just as in the words of the Word sounded the unspeakable Word of his Father. It is not a question, for the "theologian," of reaching that which his discourse speaks (well or poorly—what does it finally matter, for what norm in this world would decide?) of G~~o~~d, but of abandoning his discourse and every linguistic initiative to the Word, in order to let himself be said by the Word, as the Word lets himself be said by the Father—him, and in him, us also. In short, our language will be able to speak of G~~o~~d only to the degree that G~~o~~d, in his Word, will speak our language and teach us in the end to speak it as he speaks it—divinely, which means to say in all abandon. In short, it is a question of learning to speak our language with the accents—with the accent of the Word speaking it. For the Word, by speaking our words, which he says word-for-word, without changing anything of them (not an *iōta* Matt. 5:18), takes us at our word, literally: since he speaks what we speak, but with an entirely different accent, he promises us the challenge, and gives us the means to take it up—to speak our word-for-word with his accent, the accent of a G~~o~~d. The theologian lets himself say (or be said by) the Word, or rather lets the Word let him speak human language in the way that G~~o~~d speaks it in his Word.

2—The Foreclosed Event

This position secured, it becomes possible to intervene in the debate that defines, if not theology, at least the function of the theologian. On what does Christian theology bear? On the event of the death and resurrection of Jesus, the Christ. How does this event, separated from us by the course of time and documentary distance, occur to us? It occurs to us through a word spoken by a man, *fides ex auditu.*[3] What does this word say? Inevitably, it transmits a text: that of the originary kerygma, in stating it or by allusion, or else by deploying its dimensions following the complete New Testament. In any case, the announcement makes use of a text in order to tell an event. The word does not transmit the text, but rather, through the text, the event. The text does not at all coincide with the event; at best, it consigns the traces of it, as the veil of Veronica retains the features of Christ: by rapid imposition of the event that transpires. The evangelical texts fix literarily the effects of meaning and of memory on the witnesses of an unimaginable, unheard of, unforeseeable, and in a sense invisible irruption. The Christic event left its traces on some texts, as a nuclear explosion leaves burns and shadows on the walls: an unbearable radiation.[4] Hence the text does not coincide with the event or permit going back to it, since it results from it. The shadow fixed by the flash of lightning does not reproduce the lightning, unless negatively. The text assures us a negative of the event that alone constitutes the original. One also can understand this gap as from the sign to the referent. This gap finds confirmation *a contrario* in two contradictory impasses of hermeneutics.

Either, in "scientific" exegesis, one attempts to read the text on the basis of itself, as if it meant nothing more than what it obviously says (historical meaning); the frequent triviality of the result ensues from the breakdown of every event other than the text, which, bearing only on itself, must support itself. In this case, the only event still possible will consist in the simple encounter of the text by its reader. Hence the temptation to master the text scientifically, to prohibit in it all utterance of the event, of the Said.

Or else again, as the text remains so radically nonfactual that no salvation can occur in it, one will be tempted to assign it another event, no longer anterior to the text, as beyond, hence inaccessible, but subsequent, as short of it, still to come in the future of the reader himself. The sign does not at all forget its referent, it waits for it, tends toward it, announces it. This "prophetic" (in the common sense) treatment of the text would not undertake its hermeneutic by the utopia of an event to come ("liberation," "hope," "kingdom of the Spirit," etc.) if it were not first conscious that the text *does not* make an event. The false event testifies at least to the absence of the authentic, hence of its function.

Consequently, by thus hollowing out the gap between the text and the event, the sign and the referent, does one not destroy the possibility in general of all authentically theological discourse? Literature, as regards the referent, either dispenses with it (Emma Bovary, Werther, Swann "do not exist") or rediscovers it in each of its readers (Emma Bovary "is me," Werther "is not me," etc.), which amounts to the same thing. In any case, literature dispenses with having recourse to an event in order to find its referent in that event. History, as regards the referent, publishes an abolished text, or rather publishes the text of an abolished referent at which one aims to the very extent that it remains forever abolished, undone. As to poetry, it alone provokes, if not produces, its referent by a pure and simple text: the very emotion that the letter causes in us; immanent, this referent, in a sense, does not constitute one.[5]

Theology alone remains; it claims to tell the only living one; it therefore must open up access to the referent; but this referent consists in the past death and resurrection of Jesus, the Christ; the Easter that was—it is said—actual as an event of history, by the very fact of this undone fact, is accomplished, hidden away, and foreclosed in it; the text carries the trace of a foreclosed event but no longer opens any access to it. The confinement of its text protects this finite event, inaccessible referent. Would we be deprived of the event by the very sign that refers to it? Would the theological discourse culminate in the repetition of the irrefutable? Let us not dissolve too easily, by whatever clever move, this closure which closes theological discourse, but also meaning upon itself. For whereas, no doubt, every other discourse can adapt to the closure of meaning whence the referent is exiled, the theological discourse, which proceeds from an event and only announces the indefinite repetition of it, alone cannot do so.[6] But, such access to the finished event, such aim and vision of the referent—how are we to recognize in them more than pious wishes? But a wish that remains "pious" rightly has nothing pious about it—only that which would accomplish its duty with respect to the divine would become pious—it founders in sterility, at the level of blasphemy.

But this impasse, in which the supposedly theological discourse is implicated, results from what that discourse wants to reproduce, concerning the *Logos* come into our words—a linguistic device that the *Logos* overturns to the benefit of another device, this time theological, one that is in effect explicitly in the episode told about the disciples at Emmaus (Luke 24:13–49). The Paschal event is accomplished, the Paschal accomplishment has occurred (Luke 24:18, *ta genomena* = John 19:28, *hoti ēdē panta tetelestai*). For the disciples, as for us, it no longer belongs to the present. Once things have happened, there remain only words: for us, there remains the text of the New Testament, just as for the disciples there remained only the rumor, or already the chronicle, of the putting to death (Luke 24:17, *hoi logoi hous antiballete pros allēlous*). In both cases, the event referred to is lacking. We cannot lead the biblical text back as far as that at which it nevertheless aims, precisely because no hermeneutic could ever bring to light anything other than a meaning, whereas we desire the referent in its very advent. When the disciples interpret what is said of the event, their correct interpretation can reach only one meaning—the meaning of an elapsed event, whose visible contemporaneousness does not even become envisageable to them: "their eyes were kept from recognizing him" (Luke 24:16). It happens—a new event, which coins the Paschal event—that the referent in person redoubles, completes, and disqualifies the hermeneutic that we can carry out from this side of the text, through another hermeneutic that, so to speak, bypasses its text from beyond and passes on this side. The referent itself is interpreted in it as referring only to itself: "and Jesus himself (*autos*) approached and went with them . . . and he himself (*autos*) said to them: O unintelligent men and slow of heart to believe all that the prophets said! Did not the Christ have to suffer all these things to enter into his glory? And beginning with Moses and all the prophets, he carried out the hermeneutic at length, in all the Scriptures, of what concerned him (*diermēneusen . . . ta peri heautou*)" (Luke 24:15, 25–27). It is a decisive moment: the Paschal event can be read in a text (Old Testament, first chronicles of the apostles) only if the text itself receives an adequate interpretation. But what human thought will be able adequately to refer a (human) text to an unthinkable event? Who thereby would not become "unintelligent"? "Only" (Luke 24:18) he who "does not know" what all know—and, in fact, he does not know what the spectators know, nor as they know; this "he learned from what he suffered" (Hebrews 5:7); he knows it in fact and in body, not by sight and hearsay. He can aim at the referent since he assures it; he whom no text can speak, because he remains outside the text, the referent (unspeakable Word), transgresses the text to interpret it to us, as an interpreter authorized by his full authority *(exousia):* less explaining the text than explaining himself with it, explaining himself through it, he goes right through it, sometimes locutor, sometimes referent, saying and said; in short, strictly, he is told in it.

Hence a first principle for the *theo*logian: to be sure, he proceeds to a hermeneutic of the biblical text that does not aim at the text but, through the text, at the event, the referent. The text does not offer the original of faith, because it does not constitute its origin. Only the Word can give an authorized interpretation of the words (written or spoken) "concerning him." Hence the human *theo*logian begins to merit his name only if he imitates "the theologian superior to him, our Savior,"[7] in transgressing the text by the text, as far as to the Word. Otherwise, the text becomes an obstacle to the comprehension of the Word: just as the Old Testament for the disciples, so, for us, the New. In developing a letter indefinitely commented on by itself, the text silences the Word—kills it. It is the masters *ès-verba,* the scribes of the self-sufficient text, who condemn the Word—for all time. "Some cause trouble as if we were introducing a foreign God added by a fraud of writing (*pareggrapton*) and battle excessively over the letter; may they know, may they 'fear there where there is no place to fear' (Psalms 14:5), because their love of the letter is but the mask of their impiety."[8] They refuse the divinity of the Spirit, which, proclaiming alone the divinity of the Word, assures the transgression of the text. Such transgression, which the Verb carries out in person at Emmaus, offers nevertheless the unique possibility not of a spiritual reading but of any reading of the Scriptures whatsoever, indeed of the sole access to an originary word: "The veil is lifted [namely from the prophecies], as soon as you move forward to the Lord; thus is nonwisdom (*insapientia*) lifted, when you move forward to the Lord, and what was water becomes wine. Do you read the books of the prophets without hearing Christ? What could be more insipid, more extravagant? But if you hear Christ in them, not only do you savor what you read, but you are elated by it, lifting your spirit out of your body, 'forgetting what is behind you, no longer to strain but toward what is before' (Philippians 3:13)."[9] Even and especially in the hermeneutic of the biblical text, one must rely "less on the literality of the letter, than on the powers of the Lord and his justice alone."[10] We should be understood: it is precisely not a matter here of any praise of fundamentalism (which sticks to the letter) or of a falsely "spiritual" fantasy, but of this principle: the text results, in our words that consign it, from the primordial event of the Word among us; the simple comprehension of the text—the function of the theologian—requires infinitely more than its reading, as informed as one would like; it requires access to the Word through the text. To read the text from the point of view of its writing: from the point of view of the Word. This requirement, as untenable as it may appear (and remains), cannot be avoided. The proof is that as long as the Word does not come in person to interpret to the disciples the texts of the prophets and even the chronicle of the things seen (*logoi,* Luke 24:17) at Jerusalem, this double text remains unintelligible—strictly, they comprehend nothing of it (*anoetoi,* Luke 24:25), they do not see what is evident (Luke 24:17). *The theologian must go beyond the text to the Word, interpreting it from the point of view of the Word.*

3—The Eucharistic Hermeneutic

But, one will object, does this principle not lead at all to a delirious presumption, strictly to a delirium of interpretation, which asks a man to take the place and position of the Word himself? Do we not even open the field to all the rationalist interpretations of Scripture, made in the name of the Word himself reduced to our rationality? There is more: in supposing that the Word in person should carry out for us *hic et nunc* the hermeneutic of the words, we behave exactly as the disciples from Emmaus. Even *after* the self-referential hermeneutic of the texts by the Word, we remain equally blind, unintelligent. That this absolute hermeneutic should be realized or not, that we should be on the path toward Emmaus or on the way to the end of the second millennium, this finally matters little: no hermeneutic could open our eyes to see the exegete of the Father (John 1:18). This objection leads to a remark: curiously, the account of Luke 24, which expressly informs that Christ "carried out the hermeneutic" of the text, does not recount the argument to us, or a fortiori the developments of that argument. Oversight? This hypothesis, passably common, does not hold, since the whole account aims at a hermeneutic that may render the Word visible in the biblical text. How is this to be understood? An absolute hermeneutic is announced, and not only does it reveal nothing, but it shines by its absence; barely named, it disappears to the benefit of the eucharistic moment (Luke 24:28–33). Does not such an abrupt transition from the hermeneutic to the Eucharist admit the impossibility of the former? No doubt, but only if, following a serious prejudice of reading, one distinguishes here, as between two acts of Christ, between the hermeneutic and the Eucharist. Otherwise, another hypothesis would present itself: the hermeneutic lesson appears truncated, even absent, only if one takes it to be different from the Eucharistic celebration where recognition takes place; for immediately after the breaking of the bread, not only did the disciples "recognize him" and at last "their eyes were opened" (Luke 24:31), but above all the hermeneutic went through the text as far as the referent: "and they said to one another, 'did not our hearts burn within us, when he was speaking along the way, when he opened to us [allowed us to communicate with] the text of the Scriptures?' " (Luke 24:32). The Eucharist accomplishes, as its central moment, the hermeneutic (it occurs at 24:30, halfway between the two mentions of the Scriptures, 24:27 and 24:32). It alone allows the text to pass to its referent, recognized as the nontextual Word of the words. Why? We know why: because the Word interprets in person. Yes, but where? Not first at the point where the Word speaks of the Scriptures, about the text (24:27–28), but at the point where he proffers the unspeakable speech, absolutely filial to the Father—"taking bread, he gave thanks . . ." (24:30). The Word intervenes in person in the Eucharist (in person, because only then does he manifest and perform his filiation) to accomplish in this way the hermeneutic. The Eucharist alone completes the hermeneutic; the hermeneutic culminates in the Eucharist; the one assures the other its condition of possibility: the intervention in person of the referent of the text as center of its meaning, of the Word, outside of the words, to reappropriate them to himself as "what concerns him, *ta peri heautou*" (24:27). If the Word intervenes in person only at the eucharistic moment, *the hermeneutic (hence fundamental theology) will take place, will have its place, only in the Eucharist.* The first principle (the *theo*logian must pass through the text as far as the Word, by interpreting it from the point of view of the Word) here finds its support and the norm that spares it delirium: the theologian secures the place of his hermeneutic—the one that passes through the text toward the Word-referent on the basis of the Word-interpreter—only in the Eucharist, where the Word in person, silently, speaks and blesses, speaks to the extent that he blesses.

One even must specify: the theologian finds his place in the Eucharist because the Eucharist itself offers itself as the place for a hermeneutic. Offers itself as place: at the very moment of his recognition by the disciples, the Word in flesh disappears: "for it is to your advantage that I go away" (John 16:7). For what? So that the Word recognized in spirit, recognized by and according to the Spirit, should become the site where those might dwell who live according to this Spirit, his own received from the Father. In fact, the Word, at the eucharistic moment, does not disappear so much as the disciples, who eating his body and drinking his blood, discover themselves assimilated to the one whom they assimilate and recognize inwardly; the Word does not disappear to their sight so much as they themselves disappear as blinded individuals, literally stray on paths that lead nowhere.[11] They enter into the place of the Word, and now, like him, they go up to Jerusalem (Luke 24:33 = Matthew 16:4). This place—in Christ in the Word—is opened for an absolute hermeneutic, a *theo*logy. For the two disciples go back up to Jerusalem only to say the eucharistic hermeneutic that they have just experienced, and to sanction it: "they themselves recounted [did the exegesis, *exegounto*] the things that happened on the way and how he was recognized by them in the breaking of the bread" (Luke 24:34). To say the eucharistic hermeneutic, to repeat it for the first time, as one tries a new art, a new thought, a new mode of the real, hence to perform it, this draws, so to speak, an immediate (and in a sense supererogatory) confirmation: "While they said these things, he himself stood among them" (Luke 24:37) to give the Spirit, and to be repeated as absolute Word: "It is me," but also "I am me, *ego eimi autos*" (Luke 24:38–39). The circle is closed: the hermeneutic presupposes that the disciples occupy the eucharistic site of the Word, but their hermeneutic, in return, passes through every text and all speech, toward, again, the absolute referent ("I am," Luke 24:39 = John 8:24 and 58 = Exodus 3:14). The Christian assembly that celebrates the Eucharist unceasingly reproduces this hermeneutic site of theology. First the text: the prophets, the law, the writings, all of the Old Testament (as in Luke 24:27), then the *logia* of the Christ (as in Luke 24:17: *logoi* displayed in 24:18–24, through a sort of hypothetical kerygma, hypothecated by death). It is read before the assembly that, theological in negative, asks that a hermeneutic allow it to comprehend not words, but the Word. Then the hermeneutic: the priest who presides over the Eucharist begins by "carrying out the hermeneutic" (as in Luke 24:27) of the texts, without the community yet distinguishing in him the Word in person (like the disciples); the hermeneutic that the homily verbally executes—henceforth the literary mode par excellence of the *theo*logical discourse—must be accomplished in the eucharistic rite where the Word, visibly absent, makes himself recognized in the breaking of the bread, characterizes the priest as his *person,* and assimilates to himself those who assimilate him. Finally the community: it hears the text, verbally passes through it in the direction of the referent Word, because the carnal Word comes to the community, and the community into him. The community therefore interprets the text in view of its referent only to the strict degree that it lets itself be called together and assimilated, hence converted and interpreted by the Word, sacramentally and therefore actually acting in the community. Hermeneutic of the text by the community, to be sure, thanks to the service of the theologian, but on condition that the community itself be interpreted by the Word and assimilated to the place where *theo*logical interpretation can be exercised, thanks to the liturgical service of the theologian par excellence, the bishop.

4—Whereof We Speak

This compound device, which we could develop and confirm in a number of results, directly has at least four consequences. Two concern the theologian, two others theology. If, first, theology as *theo*logy attempts the hermeneutic of the words in view, hence also, from the point of view of the Word, if the Eucharist offers the only correct hermeneutic site where the Word can be said in person in the blessing, if finally only the celebrant receives authority to go beyond the words as far as the Word, because he alone finds himself invested by the *persona Christi,* then one must conclude that *only the bishop merits, in the full sense, the title of theologian.* This proposition may appear paradoxical, but at the risk of simplifying, we must insist on it: the teaching of the Word characterizes the apostles (hence also those who follow in their place) as does the presiding of the Eucharist; the close tie between the two functions clearly marks that it is in fact a question of the same. Without the presiding of the Eucharist, the hermeneutic does not attain the theological site: the Word in person. No doubt the function of the *theo*logical hermeneutic can be delegated, but in the same way that the bishop delegates to the simple priest the function of presiding over the Eucharist. And just as a priest who breaks his communion with the bishop can no longer enter into ecclesiatical communion, so a teacher who speaks without, even against, the Symbol of the apostles, without, even against, his bishop, absolutely can no longer carry on his discourse in an authentically *theo*logical site. From this perspective, one cannot avoid considering every attempt to constitute theology as a science to be at least very problematic; beyond the fact that the status of science makes of theology a theo*logy,* beyond the fact that demonstrative rigor doubtless has hardly more pertinence here than in philosophy, this epistemological mutation prompts, or requires, the loosening of the tie of delegation between the bishop, theologian par excellence, and his teaching adjunct, who, always and naturally brought to postulate his independence, henceforth finds a possible justification for this illusion: for to detach oneself from the bishop does not offer to "theological science" an "object" that is finally neutral, but does away with the eucharistic site of the hermeneutic; henceforth, instead of interpreting the text in view and from the point of view of the Word, hence in service of the community, the theo*logian* will have only one alternative: either to renounce aiming at the referent (positivistic "scientific" exegesis) without admitting any spiritual meaning, and the text has no referent—it says nothing—or else to produce by himself, hence ideologically, a new site of interpretation, in view of a new referent. In one case, breaking with the bishop, the theo*logian* no longer serves the community in any way, and he abandons it to the hunger dodging of the "pastoral"; in the other, manipulating the bishop as he does the community, the theo*logian* turns them away from the eucharistic site.[12] For a few years we have seen these two attitudes and experienced their common impasse. The rectification of theological discourse can only result from a restoration of the tie of delegation from the bishop to the teacher, who—learned person and hermeneut—constitutes only one particular case of charismas which are worth nothing unless related to charity and the edification of community (1 Cor. 14, passim). The theological teacher is not justified unless he serves charity. Otherwise, he brings death. But, the more the teacher inscribes himself in the eucharistic rite opened by the bishop, the more he can become a *theo*logian.

Hence, second, an inverse requirement: if the theologian cannot or must not want to reach a "scientific" status, he can only become holy himself. Holiness existentially redoubles the institutional requirement of a tie to the bishop: it is a question, in both cases, of the same access to the eucharistic site of the *theo*logical hermeneutic. Let us not fool ourselves here: the requirement of holiness is not the concern of pious edification any more than the requirement of an episcopal delegation imposes a limit on the freedom to think. Something entirely different is at stake: to satisfy the conditions of possibility of a *theo*logical discourse, namely, of a discourse that does not contradict, in its formal definition, that which it claims to reach. As the teacher becomes a *theo*logian by aiming in the text at the referent, he must have an anticipated understanding of the referent, for lack of which he will not be able to spot its effects of meaning in the text. There are many exegetes or theo*logians* who commit massive misinterpretations of texts (biblical or patristic), not for want of knowledge, but out of ignorance of what is in question, of the thing itself. He who never knew passion can with precision analyze a scene from Racine or Stendhal; he cannot understand it from the point of view of its author—a fortiori the Song of Songs or even Hosea (of which many commentators seem to lack even an historical sense). He who never heard an orchestra sound can indeed decipher a musical score, he cannot hear or understand it as the musician composed it, in listening to it silently—a fortiori the Psalms or the Gospels (concerning which many commentators sometimes seem to omit that they were always destined for prayer). He who claims to go beyond the text as far as the Word must therefore know whereof he speaks: to know, by experience, charity, in short, "to have learned from what he suffered" (Heb. 5:8) like Christ; thus, according to Denys the Mystic, the divine Hierotheus: "either he received them from the holy theologians, or he considered them at the end of a scientific investigation of the *logia* [texts of Scripture] at the price of long training and exercise, or finally he had been initiated into them by a more divine inspiration—he did not learn things of God other than through what he suffered, and by this mystical compassion toward them, he was led to the perfection of mystical union and faith, which, if one might say, are not taught."[13] To go through the text of the *logia* in order, through passion, to receive the lesson of charity (in the sense that *to receive a good lesson* indicates that one suffered a good thrashing), here is the qualification, extrascientific but essential, that makes the *theo*logian: the referent is not taught, since it is encountered by mystical union. And yet, one must speak *of* him. With this mystical experience, the morality or private virtues of the theologian are not first at stake, but above all his competence acquired in the matter of charity, in short of knowing the Word nonverbally, in flesh and Eucharist. *Only the saintly person knows whereof he speaks in theology, only he that a bishop delegates knows wherefrom he speaks.*[14]

the rest, it is but a question of vision, of intelligence, of and of talent—as elsewhere, quite simply.

5—The Delay to Interpretation

For theology also, two consequences become unavoidable. The first: *theo*logy, eucharistic or impossible, is practiced by traversing the gap from the text (signs) to the referent, from the words to the Word. In this gap, the unspeakable Word saturates each of the signs of its text with the absolute: the absolute of the referent reflects, so to speak, on the most trivial of signs—each of which takes on a spiritual meaning. The text, where the Word's effect of meaning is fixed in verbal signs, consigns the incommensurability of the Word: the Scriptures thus exceed the limits of the world (John 19:30, 21:35). The text escapes the ownership of its literary producers in order to be inspired, so to speak, by the Word: or rather, it assumes the "objective" imprint of it in the same way that the disciples receive, from the Word, an "objective" figure: apostleship. For the text also becomes apostolic—sent by another than itself to go where it did not want to go. Hence a sort of infinite text is composed (the closure of the sacred canon indicating precisely the infinite surplus of meaning). It offers, potentially, an infinite reserve of meaning (as one speaks of "the reserved Eucharist"), hence demands an infinity of interpretations, which, each one, leads a fragment of the text back to the Word, in taking the point of view of the Word; hence it implies an infinity of eucharistic hermeneutics. Theology can progress in this way to infinity, on the condition that the Word and its text appear as given once and for all: the historically indefinite unfolding of eucharistic hermeneutics implies, impassable and unique, the transtextual revelation of the Word. Indeed, in what does the production of a new theology consist? In a new way of leading certain words from the Scriptures back to the Word, an interpretation rendered possible, more even than by the talent of a mind, by the labor of the Spirit that arranges a eucharistic community in such a way that it reproduces a given disposition of the Word-referent, and is identified with the Word, interpreted according to this relation. Coinciding with this new persona, the community (hence also the theologian who doubles in it for the bishop) realizes a new dimension of the original event, thus accomplishing a new hermeneutic of some words, signaling a "new" theology. This endless fecundity depends on the power of the Spirit that gives rise to the eucharistic attitudes (therefore, there can be no "progress" of *theo*logy without a deepening of the eucharistic gesture, which is confirmed by the facts). A theology is celebrated before it is written—because "before all things, and particularly before theology, one must begin by prayer."[15] In order to give an (infinite) hermeneutic of the (finite) text in view of the (infinite) Word, an infinity of situations are mobilized from the point of view of the Word, hence an infinity of Eucharists, celebrated by an infinity of different communities, each of which leads a fragment of the words back to the Word, to the exact degree that each one repeats and welcomes eucharistically the Word in person. The multiplicity of theologies—if these indeed eucharistically merit *theo*logical status—ensues as necessarily from the unspeakable infinity of the Word as does the infinity of Eucharists. And the theologies contradict one another as little as do the Eucharists—and all as much, if both lose their site. In short, *the "progress" of theology works only to overcome the irreducible delay of the eucharistic interpretation of the text in relation to the manifestation of the Word.* And despite all our "realizations," no theology will ever be able to attain the first Parousia by an adequate extension of the text to the referent; for that, nothing less than a second Parousia of the Word would be necessary. In this way the indefiniteness of our new interpretations (theologies) also (and especially?) indicates our impotence to enter into an authentically eucharistic—eschatalogical—site. Theo*logical* chatter, like liturgical *bricolage,* often testifies less to creativity than to impotence in performing the original repetition—that is, the reintegration in the center, the "recapitulation in the unique master, the Christ" (Eph. 1:10). Nevertheless, time dispenses with patience, so that our Eucharist may interpret without interruption or delay the words in view and on the basis of the Word—until he returns.

Hence an ultimate consequence. The theological function

does not constitute, in the Church, an exception to the initial deal of its foundation: "There has been given to me *all exousia* in heaven and on earth. Go teaching *all* the nations . . . , teach them to keep *all* that I have commanded you; and here it is that I, I am with you *all* the days until the end of time" (Matt. 28:18–20). All is given to the Church (space: the nations; time: the days) so that the Church may return it (keep the commandments) to the Word, because he already received all (*exousia*) from the Father; in theology it is not a question, any more than elsewhere, of working to a completion yet to come: completion, for the Church, is accomplished definitively at Easter, hence at the origin (*tetelestai,* John 19:28 = 13:1). Accomplishment occurs at the origin and moreover alone renders it possible, fertile, pregnant with a future. To speak of progress, of research, of discovery in theology, either means nothing precise or betrays a radical ignorance of the eucharistic status of theo*logy,* or else finally must be understood in a roundabout way: not that theo*logy* progresses in producing a new text, like every other discourse, but in the sense that *theo*logy progresses eucharistically in a community, which accomplishes its own extension, through the text, to the Word. In short, *theology cannot aim at any other progress than its own conversion to the Word,* the theologian again becoming bishop or else one of the poor believers, in the common Eucharist. Once all is given, it remains to say it, in the expectation that the Said itself should come again to say it. Thus understood, *theo*logical progress would indicate less an undetermined, ambiguous, and sterile groping, than the absolutely infinite unfolding of possibilities already realized in the Word but not yet in us and our words; in short, the infinite freedom of the Word in our words, and reciprocally. We are infinitely free in theology: we find all already given, gained, available. It only remains to understand, to say, and to celebrate. So much freedom frightens us, deservedly.

Hors-Texte

6

THE PRESENT AND THE GIFT

To explain the Eucharist—a multiform, inevitable, and instructive naïveté. In another sense, a decisive moment of theological thought.

Inevitable, since the sacrament that completes what all the others aim at, in corporally assimilating us to Christ, the sacrament that brings the logic of the incarnation to its most obviously paradoxical term, the sacrament that visibly gathers men to "form the Church," becomes like the obligatory site where every somewhat consistent theological attempt must come in the end to be tested. For the moment, we will retain in this summons only the challenge thrown out to every theology by the most concrete and least intelligible mystery of faith in Christian life. The Eucharist thus becomes the test of every theological systematization, because, in gathering all, it poses the greatest challenge to thought.

Naïveté above all. Why? What indeed does it mean here "to explain"? Undoubtedly something like giving the reason for a mystery of charity on the basis of a preliminary group of reasons, supposed in their turn to be founded in reason, hence on reason itself. Explanation, even theological, always seems to end up in a "eucharistic physics" (we will see that it matters little if for *physics* one substitutes, e.g., *semiotics*), that is, by an attempt to reabsorb the eucharistic mystery of charity in a rational conceptual system. In the case of failure, such an effort appears either useless (if it limits itself, through theological concern, to recognizing a pure and simple "miracle" in the succession of physical or linguistic events) or else insufficient (if it imputes its conceptual insufficiency to a mystery that it has not even approached, by an infracritical and terroristic subjectivism). But in case of apparent success, this effort is open no less—and here the essential appears—to two other suspicions: does one not contradict oneself by seeking, in principle to reinforce credibility, to frame and then to reabsorb the liturgical fact and the mystery of charity in a system (physical, semiotic, etc.), at the risk, here again, of attaining only a conceptual idol? Do transubstantiation, transfinalization, and transsignification allow one to reach the Eucharist? Or do they substitute themselves for it? Above all, what relevance are we to acknowledge in the enterprise that, in order "to explain," would attempt, voluntarily or not, to consider as self-evident the equivalence between the gift that Christ makes of his body and a conceptually retraced transmutation? A gift, and this one above all, does not require first that one explain it, but indeed that one receive it. Does not the haste to explain disclose an inability to receive and hence the loss of a primordial theological reflex?

Instructive nevertheless. For the inevitable naïveté does not suffice to disqualify every effort of meditation on the eucharistic presence. On the contrary, it incites one to consider thoroughly the conditions in which this effort will not remain vain. If "explanation"[1] there must be, we will understand it in the sense of delinquents or, if one prefers, in the sense that Jacob had, at the ford Jabbok, an "explanation" with the angel: in such an "explanation," it is a question not so much of speaking as of struggling; each adversary demands of the other, first, avowal or "blessing," hence recognition. Here, explanation would have to admit reciprocity: it is a question less of knowing whether a particular explanation can account for the eucharistic presence than of seeing whether the theoretical apparatus will let itself be criticized by that of which it is a question, to reach the dignity of what is at stake. Language, if properly theological, must therefore let itself be taken up again on the basis of the epistemological, or rather mystical, demands of that to which it pertains (and which has precisely nothing like an *object,* theology having none of the characteristics of scientificity, and especially not its objectivity).[2] This rule is valid in all matters and all manners—for the mystery of G~~o~~d, to be sure, but even for the paradoxical figures of his advent in Christ or finally in the eucharistic Christ. In a sense, the eucharistic presence of Christ constitutes the case par excellence where this demand becomes unavoidable: in the two other cases, in fact, a theology that transgresses it condemns itself to idolatry or to heresy but can conceal the one and attempt to exculpate itself from the other; on the contrary, before the eucharistic presence, the sanction cannot be avoided: if theological language refuses "explanation," then that to which it pertains—eucharistic presence—is dissolved. The Eucharist requires of whoever approaches it a radical conceptual self-critique and charges him with renewing his norms of thought. We will attempt to show this with regard to one precise and fundamental case: the application to the Eucharist of the concept of "presence."

1—One or the Other Idolatry

Let us take a look, then, at the usual and ceaselessly repeated critique of the theology of transubstantiation. It is most often reproached, among other things, for using concepts—substance, accidents, species, transubstantiation—stemming from a historically defined metaphysics, that of Aristotle (to which one boldly likens Thomistic theology). But the "good news of Jesus Christ" exceeds every metaphysic. Therefore, becoming conscious of the historical relativity of a eucharistic theology of transubstantiation, one would have to renounce it (while saluting it from a distance as "legitimate in its time") and attempt to "invent" a new eucharistic theology, founded on a more modern philosophical thought. This critique, one must recall, relies on summary or inexact reflections. For in the end, *substantia* is introduced in eucharistic theology independently of the reading of Aristotle;[3] *transsubstantiatio* is validated by the Council of Trent only as an equivalent of the *conversio,* that is to say of the *metabolē* of the Greek Fathers;[4] rather than the Thomistic explanation (which, of course, modifies Aristotle quite a bit, since it inverts his terms, going so far as to speak of a permanence of accidents and of a substitution of substances) acting as the foundation of the dogmatic texts, the latter precede the former (*transsubstantiare* appears as early as 1202, and *transsubstantiatio* as early as 1215)[5] or correct it (substituting species for accidents, during the Council of Trent, etc.). The equivalence of the Tridentine doctrine with Thomistic theology therefore is not self-evident.[6] As to recognizing the essential of Aristotle's metaphysics in the latter, one needs as little philosophical as theological sense to try to do so.

All the same, the critique will not yield. It can now only generalize an objection, which it cannot assure in detail. One can say: even if the theology of transubstantiation is not reducible to a particular theme imported from a particular metaphysic, in any case, it exposes itself to an otherwise serious danger. Indeed, the transposition of one substance into another (that of the bread and that of the body of Christ) leads one to recognize the traits of a person under the appearances (species) of a substance; the substantial presence therefore fixes and freezes the person in an available, permanent, handy, and delimited thing. Hence the imposture of an idolatry that imagines itself to honor "God" when it heaps praises on his pathetic "canned" substitute (the reservation of the Eucharist), exhibited as an attraction (display of the Holy Sacrament), brandished like a banner (processions), and so on. In this sense, profanation would increase with the bustle of a too obviously "political" worship: political in the profound sense that the community would seek to place "God" at its disposition like a thing, its thing, to reassure its identity and strengthen its determination in that thing. Of this "God" made thing, one would expect precisely nothing but *real* presence: presence reduced to the dimensions of a thing, a thing that is as much disposed to "honor by its presence" the liturgies where the community celebrates its own power, as emptied of all significance capable of contesting, in the name of G~~o~~d, the collective self-satisfaction.[7] Real presence: "God" made thing, a hostage without significance, powerful because mute, tutelary because without titularity, a thing "*denuded of all signification except that of presence,*" (Mallarmé).[8]

He who pretends to go beyond a metaphysic must produce thereby another *thought.* And he who pretends to go beyond all metaphysics most often risks taking up again, without being conscious of it, its basic characteristic. Here exactly, it would be a matter of going beyond, with real presence, the idolatrous reduction of "God" to a mute thing, a vainly impotent presence. This operation is usually effected by mobilizing the explanatory models of transignification. But these remain neutral: they can perfectly be integrated within the perspective of transubstantiation, which ballasts them, so to speak, with reality, while they themselves give to it all of the "existential" dimension required by the mystery of charity.[9] These models, therefore, taken in their legitimate usage, constitute no break with the preceding model—on the contrary. What decision or anterior condition will therefore render them polemical? The true debate obviously bears on the determination of new meanings and goals, or, more exactly, on the instance that determines them. Either it is still Christ, the priest *in persona Christi,*[10] who gives to the community the new meanings and goals of the bread and wine, precisely because the community does not produce them, does not have them at its disposal, or perform them; then this gift will be welcomed as such by a community that, receiving it, will find itself nourished and brought together by it. Or else, on the contrary, it comes back to the community, on the basis of the meanings and goals ("evangelical values," "human values," etc.) whose experiences ("struggles," "progressions," "searches," etc.) enriched it, to establish the liturgical novelty of the bread and of the wine. Among these meanings and goals, "God" will recognize his own! But He will be content with recognizing them therein, far from taking the initiative "from above" to consecrate (Himself) in a thing distinct from the community. Bread and wine will become the mediations less of the presence of G~~o~~d in the community than of the becoming aware, of "God" and of itself, by a community that *"seeks the face, the face of the Lord."* And precisely at the moment of receiving the sacrament, the community still seeks it, and has found nothing more of it than what its collective consciousness, at a given moment in its "progression," had been able to secure.[11] Presence is no longer measured by the excessiveness of an irreducibly other gift, as far as assuming the corporally distinct appearance of an irreducible thing. No doubt there remains an irreducible presence of Christ, but it is displaced from the thing to the community: "One must pass from Jesus present in the host to Jesus present to a people whose eucharistic action manifests reality under the sacramental form."

> The heart of this mystery is that communion with God passes by way of the communion of men among themselves. It is for this reason that the sign of communion with God is the sharing between men. . . . It must not be forgotten that the Eucharist is before all else a meal, the sharing of which is the sign of the communion of those who participate in it. And the community of those who share it is in its turn the sign of communion with God. It is like a ricochet: there is a reality which is the sign of something that, in its turn, is the sign of something else.[12]

We immediately note an essential point. Even if the theology of transubstantiation has lost its legitimacy and, with it, real presence, the very notion of presence remains. It is simply displaced from the eucharistic "thing" (real presence) to the community; or, more exactly, the present consciousness of the collective self is substituted for the concentration of the present of "God" under the species of a thing.

In addition, this substitution does not mark an equivalence of presence or in presence so much as it accentuates the role of the present as the unique horizon for the eucharistic gift. Presence, which no thing here comes to render real, no longer remains distinct from the collective consciousness, but strictly coincides with it, hence as long as, in that consciousness, presence endures. Or even: presence is valid only in the present, and in the present of the community consciousness. Presence—ceasing to rely on a *res*—henceforth depends entirely on the consciousness of it possessed, here and now, by that community communion. This is why all sensible mediation disappears: the bread and wine serve as a simple perceptible medium for a wholly intellectual or representational process—the collective awareness of the community by itself. The concern for the "concrete" leads, as often, to a gnostic intellectualism that in fact disqualifies every liturgy. The consecrating prayer (the canon) becomes, in the extreme, as useless as its performance by the substitute of Christ (the priest). A gesture or a gaze, provided that it permit the community awareness, suffices.[13] The immediate consciousness of the collective self hence produces the first appearance of the presence of "God" to the community. The (human and representational) present commands the future of divine presence. In the same way, presence disappears as soon as the consciousness of the collective self defines itself: the insistence with which one recalls that the sacred species only constitute finally, some "leftovers," that the eucharistic reservation has little or no theological justification, even that one can throw out or burn[14] the consecrated bread, and so forth, obviously testifies that no thing suffices to maintain presence, once conscious attention has disappeared. The immediate consciousness of the collective self hence prompts the end of the presence of "God" to the community. The (human and representational) present determines the relegation of divine presence to the past.

2—Consciousness and the Immediate

A double dependency henceforth affects the eucharistic presence. Because the gift of "God" in it depends on human consciousness, and because the latter thinks time on the basis of the present, the gift of "God" still depends on the present of consciousness—on attention. Eucharistic presence is measured by what the attention of the human community presently accords to it. It is a question of a perfect inversion (perversion?) of perpetual adoration. Far, indeed, from the eucharistic presence ceaselessly provoking the attention of men who fall ecstatically outside of the disposability of the present moment, to exceed themselves in the past and the future, and to weave, without end or beginning, a perpetuity of attention to the eucharistic gift where the presence of the Alpha and of the Omega shines—here, on the contrary, present consciousness believes itself to govern all eucharistic presence offered to the community. The intermittencies of attention provoke the interim of presence. Adoration henceforth becomes as impossible as perpetuity: everyone knows that a group cannot concentrate its attention for a long time, all the more in that here no exterior object captivates or provokes the attention. It is not a question of adoring itself perpetually, but of becoming conscious of itself ("elevating the level of group consciousness"). But, said Descartes, the cogito endures only from moment to moment, and one need not consecrate to it more than a couple of hours a year. For the collective cogito, the case will be the same: no perpetuity, but coming to consciousness according to needs and occasions. The attention of human and collective consciousness measures the eucharistic presence on the basis of the present that, here and now, dominates, organizes, and defines the common conception of time.

Having thus defined, in its characteristic traits, the conception that pretended to reject a—supposed—idolatry in the theology of transubstantiation, we can turn back on it the question that it itself posed. Is the danger of an idolatrous approach to eucharistic presence now averted? Obviously, far from disappearing, idolatry here knows its triumph, and all the more that it divides into two.

The idolatry for which one accused, wrongly, the theology of transubstantiation bore upon the reification of eucharistic presence: in it God would become an idol, in the strict sense of a material, inert, and available representation. For the moment, let us not criticize this summary criticism. Let us remark simply that the thing has at least an immense advantage over immediate consciousness of (and as) presence: it *ex*ists, in other words, poses itself outside of the intermittencies of attention, and mediates the relation of consciousness to presence. In becoming conscious of the thing where eucharistic presence is embodied, the believing community does not become conscious of itself, but of another, of the Other par excellence. It thus avoids—even at the risk of an eventual material idolatry—the supreme as well as subtly dissimulated idolatry, the spiritual idolatry where consciousness becomes to itself the idol of Christ. In fact, community consciousness, if it "realizes" what animates it, becomes the only veritable "real" presence, without any thing any longer having to mediate its relation to the eucharistic presence. Then consciousness claims to be immediately the presence of Christ: the idol no longer stems from any representation whatsoever, but from the representational consciousness of self. Thus any gap between self-consciousness and the consciousness/knowledge of Christ among us, between revelation and manifestation, is abolished. The absence of a represented object hence does not eliminate idolatry but establishes the coming to immediate consciousness of eucharistic presence as the insurmountable idol.

Hegel saw precisely in this eucharistic consciousness without real mediation the great superiority of Lutheranism over Catholicism. Hence nothing better than his reproach can allow us to understand, *a contrario,* how real presence (guaranteed by a thing independent of consciousness) alone avoids the highest idolatry: "And yet in Catholicism this spirit of all truth [that is to say, God] is in actuality set in rigid opposition to the self-conscious spirit. And, first of all, God is in the 'host' presented to religious adoration as an *external thing.* (In the Lutheran Church, on the contrary, the host as such is not at first consecrated, but in the moment *of enjoyment,* i.e. in the annihilation of its externality, and in the act of *faith,* i.e. in the free self-certain spirit: only then is it consecrated and exalted to be present God.)"[15] What the consecrated host imposes, or rather permits, is the irreducible exteriority of the present that Christ makes us of himself in this thing that to him becomes sacramental body. That this exteriority, far from forbidding intimacy, renders it possible in sparing it from foundering in idolatry, can be misunderstood only by those who do not want to open themselves to *distance.* Only distance, in maintaining a distinct separation of terms (of persons), renders communion possible, and immediately mediates the relation. Here again, between the idol and distance, one must choose.

3—Metaphysical or Christic Temporality

But idolatry, here, is not exhausted with this first inadequacy. Indeed, the reduction of the eucharistic presence to the im-

mediate consciousness that the (community) consciousness has of it plays its reductionist function only as long as consciousness itself is grasped as a self-presence of thought. Or better, as a thought in the present, which measures the future and the past of presence—and of eucharistic presence in particular—starting from the present time, from time as present. Eucharistic presence is valid here only as long as the present of consciousness measures it and imparts the present to it starting from the consciousness of the present. But, to think time starting from the present constitutes the function, stake, and characteristic not of a specific metaphysic, but of metaphysics as a whole, from Aristotle to Hegel (and Nietzsche)—if at least one admits the initial thought of Heidegger, hence first if one accedes to it. According to *Sein und Zeit,* in fact, metaphysics deploys an "ordinary conception of time," whose inaugurally Aristotelian formulation is found again, term for term, in Hegel.[16] Time is deployed in Hegel in favor and on the basis of the present, itself understood as the *here and now* by which consciousness assures itself, or rather whereby consciousness assures itself of being. For, through metaphysics, being is deployed in its Being only as long as its handy and assured availability endures. The presence available in the present—as the *here and now*—guarantees the permanence where spirit maintains a hold on being. The present not only determines the only visible, assured, measurable mode of time but also thereby delivers to the disposition of consciousness each being that can become an object to it. The present assures an objective possession of that which *is* (in the) present. This ontological overdetermination of a primacy of the present leads to a double reduction of the future and of the past: the past finishes and the future begins as soon as the present begins or finishes. Their respective temporalities count only negatively, as a double nonpresent, even a double nontime. Above all, this negative definition prohibits them from producing the available and assured hold over being that only the present confers. It appears that eucharistic presence never finds itself so much submitted to metaphysics as in the conception that criticizes the theology of transubstantiation as metaphysical: in this conception the primacy of the present (as the *here and now* of an

ontic disposability) and that of the human consciousness of time act in the open and in full. The norms that metaphysics imposes on every being, starting from its conception of time, thus exert themselves even on the eucharistic presence, without exception or compromise. Idolatry finds its metaphysical completion in the very enterprise that claimed to criticize an apparently metaphysical eucharistic theology. Which proves, once again, that to surpass metaphysics, it does not suffice, even in theology, to forget or to ignore it.

It therefore remains to attempt to think eucharistic presence without yielding to idolatry—whether it be that, supposed, of the transubstantial thing, that, obvious, of (collective) self-consciousness, or that, metaphysical, of the "ordinary conception of time." Is it a question, for all that, of resuming the slogan of a "theology without metaphysics"? Obviously not, for the overcoming of metaphysics—besides that far from implying the least scorn for conceptual thought, it redoubles the demand for it—is not the concern of theology, but only of philosophical thought, on condition that it accede to the nonmetaphysical essence of metaphysics. Our task here remains theological. It amounts to a precise question: can the eucharistic presence of Christ as consecrated bread and wine determine, starting from itself and itself alone, the conditions of its reality, the dimensions of its temporality and the dispositions of its approach?[17] Does eucharistic presence suffice for its own comprehension? And, first, of what presence is it a question? Not first of a privileged temporalization of time (the *here and now* of the present) but *of the present, that is to say of the gift.* Eucharistic presence must be understood starting most certainly from the present, but the present must be understood first as a gift that is given. One must measure the dimensions of eucharistic presence against the fullness of this gift. The principal weakness of reductionist interpretations stems precisely from their exclusively anthropological, hence metaphysical, treatment of the Eucharist. They never undertake to think presence starting from the gift that, theologically, constitutes presence in the present. For the dimensions of the gift can be determined, at least in outline, according to a strictly theological approach. The rigor of the gift must order the dimensions of the temporality where the present is made gift. Now it happens that the eucharistic gift, which Christ makes of himself under the species of the consecrated Bread and Wine, includes the fundamental terms of a temporality of the gift. This temporality is in no way added here by the artifice of an indiscreetly apologetic zeal. It springs from the most concrete analyses that exegesis can give us. The present of the eucharistic gift is not at all temporalized starting from the *here and now* but as memorial (temporalization starting from the past), then as eschatological announcement (temporalization starting from the future), and finally, and only finally, as dailyness and viaticum (temporalization starting from the present). As opposed to the metaphysical concept of time, the present here does not order the analysis of temporality as a whole, but results from it. This reversal, which remains for us to retrace, implies that we will understand the eucharistic presence less in the way of an available permanence than as a new sort of advent.

4—The Memorial

Temporalization starting from the past: the Christian Eucharist takes the memorial up again from the Jewish blessing, not, to be sure, in order to recall to the subjective memory of the community a past fact that would be defined by its nonpresence, by the cessation of the presence concerning it.[18] It is not at all a question of commemorating a dead person to spare him the second death of oblivion. In this case, the past still remains radically thought in view of the present (to maintain a second-order presence, immortality in the memory of men: idolatry through the collective consciousness), and starting from it (as a nonpresence in the *here and now*). It is a question of making an appeal, in the name of a past event, to G̶o̶d, in order that he recall an engagement (a covenant) that determines the instant presently given to the believing community. Whether it be a question of the crossing of the Red Sea or of the conquest of the Promised Land, "the memorial of the Messiah, son of David your servant, and the memorial of your people,"[19] the event remains less a past fact than a pledge given in the past in order, today still, to appeal to a future—an advent, that of the Messiah—that does not cease to govern *this* today from beginning to end. The Christian Eucharist does not recall to memory the death and the resurrection of Christ—would we be "Christians" if we had forgotten them?—it relies on an event whose past reality has not disappeared in our day (the Ascension belongs intrinsically to the death and resurrection), in order to ask with insistence—eschatological impatience—that Christ return, hence also that his presence govern the future as much as it is rooted in the past. Thus far from the past being defined as a nonpresent, or as an accomplished actuality, it orders through its irreducibly anterior and definitively accomplished "deal"[20] a today that, without it, would remain insignificant, indifferent, in a word null and void—unreal. The memorial makes of the past a decisive reality for the present, because "if Christ is not risen, our faith is vain, and you are still presently (*eti*) in your sins. . . . For if it is only for this life [present, *tautē*] that we hope in Christ, we are the most miserable men of all" (1 Cor. 15:17–18). The present no longer opposes its clear and conscious self-sufficiency to an immemorial past. On the contrary, the memorial, because a real and past event, renders this day tenable. The past determines the reality of the present—better, the present is understood as a today to which alone the memorial, as an actual pledge, gives meaning and reality.

5—Epektasis

Immediately, one sees how the temporalization of the today, by its past, intimately refers to an even more essential temporalization—by the future. For the memorial itself is valid only as a support in order that prayer may implore of the Father the innovation and completion of an eschatological advent. The memorial aims at the Parousia: "You shall do this in memory of me" (Luke 22:17), "until he comes" (1 Cor. 11:26). Moreover, this is a question not only of a future period that will be unveiled in waiting for Christ to come (again), but indeed—as the exegetes agree—of a call that asks for and, in a sense, hastens the return of Christ: "so that he return," one almost would have to translate.[21] The presence to come does not define the horizon of a simple possibility, tangential utopia or historical term, as if it were a question of a simple nonpresence that it would remain to bring, finally, to presence. On the contrary, the future determines the reality of the present in the very mode of the advent. The eucharistic gift relies, so to speak, on the tension that raises it since and for the future. The future *as future,* governs, runs through, and polarizes the eucharistic gift, thus "straining [*epekteinomenos*] toward that which is coming to it" (Phil. 3:13). The pledge, which the memorial sets into operation, now anticipates the future, so that the present itself occurs entirely as this anticipation concretely lived. The eschatological *epektasis* that temporalizes the eucharistic present through the future is expressed in many ways in the Christian tradition. We will say that the Eucharist constitutes the first fragment of the new creation, the pledge (*pignus*) that Christ gives us through his resurrected body, sacramentally present.[22] We will even say that the Eucharist, body of the Living par excellence, leads to eternal life, since it "is the remedy of immortality, the antidote that saves us from dying, makes us live in the Christ Jesus in all."[23] We might also say that, in the Eucharist, we find ourselves figured. It is generally and quite naturally supposed that the Eucharist lacks something to manifest the corporal presence of Christ, that the evidence is concealed to avid or curious gaze; it envisages, hopes for, or imagines "eucharistic miracles"; in fact, by itself, the absolute gift, whose perfection anticipates our mode of presence, surpasses our attention, dazzles our gaze, and discourages our lucidity. The Eucharist anticipates what we will be, will see, will love: *figura nostra,* the figure of what we will be, but above all ourselves, facing the gift that we cannot yet welcome, so, in the strict sense, that we cannot yet figure it. In this way, "sometimes the future lives in us without our knowing it" (Proust).[24]

6—From Day to Day

The memorial and *epektasis,* therefore, traverse the present from end to end. Far from being defined as two absences or blackouts of the *here and now,* their two absolutely originary temporalizations determine, as such, this simple interspace that we habitually privilege under the name of the present.

Henceforth what, exactly, becomes of the present? The initial demand—to think presence as a present, and the present as a gift—now finds an infinitely more concrete content. Presence must be received as the present, namely, as the gift that is governed by the memorial and *epektasis.* Each instant of the present must befall us as a gift: the day, the hour, the instant, are imparted by charity. This applies to the present time (gift given) as to manna: one must gather it each day, without ever being able to store it up or to amass it as far as to dispense with receiving it as a gift. The manna of time thus becomes daily for us. "Time is of a literal precision and entirely merciful" (Hölderlin).[25] The Christian names his bread "daily bread," first because he receives the daily itself as a bread, a food whose daily reception—as a gift—no reserve will spare. The daily quality of the bread given at each instant, of a gift that renders it (a) present, culminates in the request of the Pater: "Give us this day our daily bread," our bread of this day and which this day alone can give us, at the same time that this very day is given to us. The daily character of the bread constitutes it as a definitively provisory gift, always to be repeated and taken up again; it insures against any taking possession of the present: "really confining this bread to a single day, so that, because of the one who revealed this prayer to us, we will not have the audacity to extend our request to a second day" (Maximus Confessor).[26] Of time in the present, it can well be said that one must receive it as a present, in the sense of a gift. But this implies also that we should receive this present of the consecrated Bread as the gift, at each instant, of union with Christ.[27]

The eucharistic presence comes to us, at each instant, as the gift of that very instant, and, in it, of the body of the Christ in whom one must be incorporated. The temporal present during which the eucharistic present endures resembles it: as a glory haloes an iconic apparition, time is made a present gift to let us receive in it the eucharistically given present. Time and the eucharistic present endure in an apparent continuity only as long as in our myopic gaze the instants given and the instantaneous gifts are confused. Or rather, the consecrated Bread and Wine seem to us to borrow their indisputable permanence from a permanent present (according to the model of the *here and now*) because our charity does not have enough lucidity to deconstruct this subsisting present into a present gift, ceaselessly abandoned and taken up again, gone beyond and founded, thrown and projected between the memorial (temporalization by the past) and *epektasis* (temporalization by the future). The eucharistic present thus organizes in it, as the condition of its reception, the properly Christian temporality, and this because the eucharistic gift constitutes the ultimate paradigm of every present.

This interpretation presupposes a dispossession of the *here and now,* hence a critique of its primacy in the *"ordinary conception of time."* This critique rests in turn on the reinterpretation of the present on the basis of the memorial that gives it as a pledge and of the eschatological call that provokes its accomplishment. In addition, the importance of the memorial which renders present (given) time always anterior to itself depends on the irrepressible eschatological *epektasis:* we may say that temporalization by the future determines all, here as well.[28] This is a temporality where the present, always already anterior to and in anticipation of itself, is received to the extent that the past and the future, in the name of the Alpha and the Omega, give it. Which means: what is named (and wrongly criticized) under the name of "real presence" founders in the metaphysical idolatry of the *here and now* or else must be received according to the properly Christian temporality.

7—The Gift of Presence

Can the gap between this demand and our spontaneously idolatrous approach be overcome? In such an effort, would the theology of transubstantiation merit a privileged attentiveness? The first question will find the beginning of a response if prayer can transform our approach to the eucharistic present. But, before outlining in what sense this could be realized, one must satisfy a preliminary condition. I may transform my approach to the eucharistic present—and model myself by its dimensions—only if the eucharistic present itself is distinguished from me and from the consciousness that I have of myself (that we have of ourselves) on its occasion. One must admit a distance in order that the other may deploy in it the conditions of my union with him. Now, the theology of transubstantiation alone offers the possibility of distance, since it strictly separates my consciousness from Him who summons it. In the distance thus arranged, the Other summons, by his absolutely concrete sacramental body, my attention and my prayer. The response to the first question thus implies the second, settled in favor of the theology of transubstantiation. In order to advance, we must better understand the aporia, and, in a sense, construct it. The eucharistic present persists, according to the theology of transubstantiation, beyond our conscious attention, and yet this persistence is not amenable to the interpretation of time according to the (metaphysical) primacy of the *here and now.* Therefore one would have to conceive the factual irreducibility—this bread and this wine as Body and Blood—without for all that having recourse to the perdurability of the present. Would it be found as a deduction (in the Kantian sense) of the eucharistic persistence on the basis of the logic of charity (hence of the Cross), with neither borrowing nor detour? Perhaps. Let us outline it in three parts.

First, the Body and Blood persist in an otherness that goes as far as the species and the appearance of the bread and wine, most certainly not to assure any (idolatrous and imperialist) permanence—G~~o~~d "does not assure permanence," even that of History—but to continue to give themselves without return. The Son took on the body of humanity only in order to play humanly the trinitarian game of love; for this reason also, he loved "to the end" (John 13:1), that is, to the Cross; in order that the irrefutable demonstration of the death and resurrection not cease to provoke us, he gives himself with insistence in a body and a blood that persist in each day that time imparts to us.

He consecrates this wine as his blood only inasmuch as this blood is "shed for you" (Luke 22:20; see Matt. 26, 28; Mark 14:24). He consecrates this bread as his body only inasmuch as this body is "given for you" (Luke 22:20).[29] The commitment of Christ as far as the bread and wine, the risk thus run of blasphemy or of idolatry (which, in a sense, amount to the same), are uniquely the concern, as the whole of *kenosis,* of condescension and trinitarian "philanthropy." It is not a question of some "safety" that permanence would assure for man, but of the irrevocable commitment of the love that "endures all" (1 Cor. 13:1). In the eucharistic present, all presence is deduced from the charity of the gift; all the rest in it becomes appearance for a gaze without charity: the perceptible species, the metaphysical conception of time, the reduction to consciousness, all are degraded to one figure (or caricature) of charity: "Everything which does not lead to charity is figurative. The sole object of Scripture is charity. Everything that does not lead to this sole good is figurative" (Pascal).[30] The consecrated bread and wine become the ultimate aspect in which charity delivers itself body and soul. If we remain incapable of recognizing in it the ultimate advance of love, the fault is not its responsibility—love gives itself, even if "his own did not receive him" (John 1:11); love accomplishes the gift entirely, even if we scorn this gift: the fault returns to us, as the symptom of our impotence to read love, in other words, to love. Hence our tendency to reduce the eucharistic present to everything except to the love that ultimately assumes a body in it. Christ endures taking a sacramental body, venturing into the *here and now* that could blaspheme and/or idolize him, because already, he took a physical body, to the point of "not resisting, not recoiling . . ., not withdrawing (his) face from insults . . ., rendering (his) face hard as stone" (Isaiah 50:5–7). The sacramental body completes the oblation of the body, oblation that incarnates the trinitarian oblation—"You wanted neither sacrifice, nor oblation, but you fashioned me a body" (Psalms 40:7 according to the LXX, taken up again in Hebrews 10:5–10). In short, *the eucharistic present is deduced from the commitment of charity.*

8—The Urgency of Contemplation

Second, the eucharistic present does not persistently drive itself into the repeated interstices of our days to reside passively in them but rather to transform us, from glory to glory. For this bread—the contemporary deviancies are somewhat right to insist on this—is given only in order to feed; it is made present only to permit its consumption. But these same deviancies miss what to feed means here. In consuming this food, we do not assimilate the Christ—to our person or to our "social body," or whatever—like the food that finds in us its end and sole justification. On the contrary, we become assimilated through the sacramental body of the Christ to his ecclesiastical body. He who takes communion worthily "will not be transforming Christ into himself, but instead will be passing over into the mystical body of Christ."[31] The materiality that transubstantiation provokes aims only at uniting us, through the Spirit that brings it about, with the spiritual body of Christ constituted by the Church. A spiritual body, in other words a body infinitely more united, more coherent, more consistent—in a word, more real—than any physical body. The condescension of Christ as far as the materiality of the *here and now,* even at the risk of reification, aims at the spiritual incorporation par excellence: incorporation with the completed Body, this body which the Church permits us to "complete" (Col. 1:24) by the conformity, which it bestows on us, of our will to that of Christ accomplishing the design of the Father. The detour through the materiality of the eucharistic present plays a very precise role: as we spontaneously conceive it, the union called "spiritual" constrains us to less seriousness, fidelity, and commitment than "material" union; thus, by the violent and insurpassable fact of the eucharistic body—"this discourse is too hard!" a remark that reacts to the *Discourse on the Bread of life* (John 6:60)—Christ indicates to us a spiritual communion that is not less but even more close than any union that is, in our sense, "spiritual." The bread and the wine must be consumed, to be sure, but so that our definitive union with the Father may be consummated in them, through communion with the ecclesiastical body of his Son. *The eucharistic present is deduced from the real edification of the ecclesiastical body of Christ.*

Finally, the eucharistic present can be accommodated, under the double relation of sacramental commitment and of ecclesiastical edification, only when understood as mystical body. In its most traditional acceptation, in fact, the locution "mystical body" concerns the eucharistic body of the Christ—as opposed to his *corpus verum,* the ecclesiastical body. Modern semantics has transferred the first adjective to the second substantive.[32]

Indeed, we, who privilege the point of view of the *here and now* as the preeminent dimension of time and hence of (the) Being (of being), can hardly attribute reality but to an available and permanent thing. Or rather, we can hardly conceive that a reality should unfold outside of the available and permanent *here and now.* On the contrary, a properly theological gaze considers the eucharistic present as mystical, without this being a question of a reduction of its reality to some vague "mysticism"; the mystical character of the eucharistic present implies a full reality; thus one can speak of "the true manducation of the mystical flesh of Christ" (Anastasia the Sinaïte):[33] the flesh, though becoming mystical, remains nonetheless really edible. More, the mystical character of the eucharistic present not only does not destroy its reality, but carries it to a completion above suspicion, before which the reality of the *here and now* itself becomes a simple relay and support; common reality becomes mystagogy for the true reality, that of the eucharistic present as gift that itself is given as mystical. It is necessary to revive here the doctrine, common though fallen into disuse, of the couple *res et sacramentum.*[34] The bread and wine consecrated and transubstantiated into the Body and Blood are valid as *res*—Christ really given in the eucharistic present—but, at the same time, they still remain a *sacramentum* with respect to the ecclesiastical body of Christ, the Church, which they aim at and construct; only this ecclesiastical Body should be called purely *res.* What are we to understand if not that, from the point of view of the *here and now,* the distribution of the terms *res et sacramentum* would be radically inverted? For our naturally blind gaze, the bread and wine *are* real, the consecrated bread and wine *are* real as bread and wine, sacramental ("mystical" in the ordinary sense) as Body and Blood of Christ, whereas the ecclesiastical body remains purely sacramental ("mystical body," according to a modern acceptation). But only the inverse has a correct theological meaning. The real is exclusively "that which the eye has not seen, that which the ear has not heard, that which has not risen to the heart of man," but that "God revealed to us by the Spirit" (1 Cor. 2:9)—all the rest has only a sacramental and indicative function. The real is exclusively that which seems "mystical" to the ordinary gaze—the

Body of the Christ and his ecclesiastical body. Whoever fears that an idolatry of presence according to the *here and now* might ensue from the theology of transubstantiation admits by this very fact that he does not see that only the eucharistic present touches, in the consecrated host, the "real," and that what he fears as overvalued only plays there the role of *sacramentum.* In a word, the common objection can be raised only from the most radically nontheological point of view, the only one on the basis of which one can, even for a single moment, imagine that the theology of transubstantiation is interested in the *here and now* of the species, whereas through the species it attempts to approach the mystical *res* of the Body and of the blood. *The eucharistic present is deduced from theological, mystical "reality" alone.*

This triple deduction of the eucharistic present demonstrates, at least in outline, that its presence depends on charity, aims at the ecclesiastical body, and is amenable to a mystical reality. We thus rediscover the three temporalizations (kenotic commitment, anterior pledge of the Incarnation and Resurrection; mystical reality, *epektasis* of eschatological glory; ecclesiastical body, the daily gift of our days). The fundamental elements that permit the conjoining of our subjective approach with the objective demands of the eucharistic present reproduce in their turn the dimensions of a properly Christian temporality, so that each one of the justifications of the eucharistic present reinforces the originality of this temporality. From this we draw, provisionally, two conclusions.

That which separates a good number of Christians from a theologically correct (if not adequate) comprehension of the eucharistic present has to do with nothing less than the *"ordinary conception of time"* and hence with the metaphysical discourse of presence. That certain objections have the theology of transubstantiation in view as "metaphysical" does not prove that it belongs to metaphysics but, on the contrary, reveals criticisms so filled by the essence and the destiny of metaphysics that they cannot stop themselves from reducing a discourse even as radically theological as that of the eucharistic present/gift. There is nothing surprising in this: here, as in other less decisive but more visible domains (politics, epistemology, etc.), Christians confront, consciously or not, the test of the end of metaphysics. And as salvation does not cease to come first to them, the danger also increases first for them. Theological thought undoubtedly never experienced in such an imperative way the duty of formulating its own radically *theo*logical logic (which especially does not mean "dialectical theology," etc.); undoubtedly its responsibility never appeared as great with respect to all thought in expectation of a "new beginning"; but theological thought undoubtedly never stole away with so much fear from its theological task. The conversion of theological (and hence ecclesiastical) thought to its task and, here, to the meditation of the eucharistic present first requires prayer. In this sense, what we understand by the term "eucharistic contemplation" here assumes its true meaning: summoned to distance by the eucharistic present, the one who prays undertakes to let his gaze be converted in it—thus, in addition, to modify his thought in it. In prayer, only an "explanation" becomes possible, in other words, a struggle between human impotence to receive and the insistent humility of God to fulfil. And without defeat in this combat, thought will never carry the least speculative victory. Eucharistic contemplation, in this sense, would become an urgency: "Not only do we not sin by adoring Him, but we sin by not adoring Him" (Saint Augustine).[35]

7

THE LAST RIGOR

1—Predication

Faith does not cry. The cry, by its very violence, holds only an indiscernible anonymity in which nothing distinguishes pain from pleasure, jubilation from malediction. The higher it rises, the less it expresses itself. Its function of communication disappears as its vigor increases. Sincerity becomes more pronounced in barbarism. But, for all that, faith has nothing like a discourse, at least if discourse implies the succession of arguments, the assurance of an object that is defined precisely by the preeminence of a subject. Faith neither speaks nor states; it believes, and has no other end than to believe. Or rather, if it speaks and, in its way, states a meaning, so far as to be able, for a time at least, to follow the traces of a predicative language and to appear, as well, to say something about something, one must not forget the essential: faith would be worth nothing without charity—"if I have all the faith to move mountains, and I do not have charity, I am nothing" (1 Cor. 13:2). Fundamentally, faith must be absorbed in charity, of which it states, in its own way, the logic. Charity, "being the greatest of all" (1 Cor. 13:13), governs faith. Which means that one must rediscover in faith, and hence in its taking a turn to speak, the characteristics peculiar to charity. But these, or rather this characteristic, takes its bearing in the union of wills—"not my will, but yours." This is a union that accomplishes "all," in that it completes the trinitarian communion of persons, and this as far as the action of the Cross. How, then, are we to think faith in conformity with the union of wills or—what implies it—to discover that charity alone produces the logic of which faith makes use, contrary to every other logic, formal or otherwise?

Theology leaves its first presupposition, that which decides everything, radically unthought as long as it cannot justify by charity and, in the end, transcribe in charity, the discourse that faith utters in it. Without this operation, it founders in gnosis, or succumbs to the pretension of a scientificity that is all the more illusory when it reaches its goal. The question, then, comes down to knowing how faith can let charity speak, and how charity can regulate the discourse of faith. The answer lies in the confession of faith, which states that "Jesus [is] Lord."[1] But what does the mention of a "confession of faith" here indicate? Why not just have stated the elementary predicative proposition, and have modalized it by a verb of statement [*énonciation*]: "X confesses that . . ."? In fact, the addition of this argument reveals the divergence of the faith that speaks from the predicative statement. Thus the analysis of this divergence could lead us to specify in what way faith, when it states, obeys a logic of charity.

To validate an argument "X believes/confesses that P," where P stands for the predicative statement "Jesus [is] Lord," one would have to satisfy several conditions. That of designation: no empirical verification can assure, at least in the usually accepted sense, the truth of P that, in fact, lends itself to no repeatable or measurable confirmation (*Jesus* refers back to a past and unique historical event). This first condition suggests another, that of meaning: can one take a proposition like "Jesus [is] Lord," or "Jesus [is] the Christ," as endowed with meaning if *Lord* and *Christ* belong to the domain of a radically religious titulature, itself practiced in a sort of private language (though that of an entire people—Jews)? This double weakness leads to relating the attention of the predicative statement itself ("Jesus [is] Savior") to the argument that takes it up, and to asking:

what legitimacy permits a speaker to state a predication that satisfies entirely neither designation nor meaning? Legitimacy does not issue here intrinsically from the utterance [*énoncé*], as for a well-constructed proposition, endowed with meaning and actually provable. And yet, the utterance does not cease to find itself uttered by ceaselessly renewed speakers. Whence, if not the legitimacy of such a statement [*énonciation*], at least its pretension to such legitimacy? From the speaker himself. At least at first, in the sequence "X confesses that 'Jesus [is] Lord,' " the weight of validation bears on X. How and why would a given empirical individual take it on himself to be concerned with that X? By what right, and first by what audacity? For, the less the predicative utterance will be able by itself to establish its own rigor, the more the speaker [*énonciateur*] will have to carry the load of legitimating, with himself, the utterance. Hence a *displacement* from the utterance to the speaker, from validation and verification to legitimacy and qualification. The litigation is displaced from the utterance—whose strange and double weakness seems to turn every speaker away from taking up the challenge of such an utterance—toward the speaker. But, this being so, does not the debate regress from the theoretical domain to existential—because definitively singular—insignificance, indisputable because strictly irrational? To invoke the paradox of faith, the abyss of a profound decision, the inexplicability of a commitment, and so on, eventually permits the believer to pull himself out of a delicate situation—but on condition, simply, of avoiding the subject, the confrontation. The displacement of the scene of the litigation, in fact, does not simply lead from the utterance to the one who states it; or rather, by that very fact, it substitutes indisputable decision, hence also insignificant arbitrariness, for disputable rationality. To posit a fact in no way resolves the question, but dissolves it. How is it to be avoided that the attestation of faith should be valid only as a cry? Here, by terrorism. By simply saying "I believe . . . ," by making the validity of the utterance "Jesus [is] Lord" rest on the sole strength of its conviction, hence on its sole power of conviction, the Christian less justifies the utterance than he unmasks its inessential character. The lordship of the Christ becomes a "message"; that one dresses it up with the "evangelical" epithet hardly masks its status as slogan. Hence militancy, which shares a common characteristic with heresy: to modify as it wishes that which already no longer appears but as a content. What here determines the opportunity (according to whether such an aspect of the "message" "is accepted" or "is no longer accepted") or the "defense of the truth" (which one formulates and determines as he likes), or some other criterion, matters little—in any case, the relation of the speaker to the utterance remains that of effectiveness to indifference, of fact to the unverifiable, in a word a relation of mastery. But if a relation of mastery governs the confession of faith, restricting it to busy militancy and/or to conquering heresy, we are miles away from what we were seeking—to absorb the discourse of faith in the "logic" of charity.[2]

2—Performance

Does this failure leave us, however, without recourse? No, at least if it conceals within itself more than itself. The displacement of the litigation privileges the speaker. The speaker comes to interpret this privilege as a mastery. But can one not understand this same displacement in another way? What can the privilege of the speaker over the utterance indicate? The insignificance of the latter but also the actuality of the former. But what does the actuality of the speaker imply? We have not yet approached it except as an arbitrariness that affirms itself with complete indifference to the utterances, which are nevertheless supported. Hence the violence, the cynicism, the silence. It remains that effectiveness can not only be juxtaposed with the utterance but, no doubt also, assume it as such. For effectiveness would be able to penetrate, so to speak, the utterance itself, and the utterance flow back into effectiveness: a third term conjoins them, the statement [*énonciation*] itself. In some cases, statement permits the one who speaks to perform the utterance. The justice of the peace utters [*énonce*]: "I declare you united by the ties of marriage," and the betrothed are actually married; the policeman utters: "I arrest you in the name of the law," or the judge: "You are charged with . . .," and the citizen—free hitherto—finds himself actually arrested and charged. Bodily separation, refusal to obey, or evasion will not change these performances but rather underline their irreducible effectiveness. The performance allows the effectiveness to slip outside of the one who speaks (here the judge, the justice of the peace, the policeman are not valid on their own, but as representatives of other authorities), to the utterance itself that thus takes on the consistency of an effect. A supplementary proof of this effectiveness moreover appears immediately: only another performance (declaration of divorce, of charges dismissed, of acquittal) can undo what the first produced. Can one interpret on the basis of such performatives the confession of faith where X says "Jesus [is] Lord"? This is a premature question. Along the path that leads to it, in fact, a preliminary question arises: the performance becomes possible only when supported by a certain qualification of the one who speaks. Only the justice of the peace (or his duly confirmed representative) can marry, only the representative of the law can arrest (and with an arrest warrant), only a judge can indict. If not, marriage appears null, escape legitimate, evasion praiseworthy. No doubt there is still performance if one, in a private capacity, states "I promise," "I swear it," "I love you," "I curse you," etc., without any qualification needing to be added from outside to the private decision. But this does not dispense with a qualification in general; it remains, in these cases, precisely "private." Every man, in principle at least, carries within himself, and by himself, the power and the permanence that, alone, can validate a promise, a pledge, love, curse, and the like. Without them, he ceases, in a sense, to present the fullness of what man implies. One indeed sees that this qualification can be lost: thus, Don Juan, thus Iago, thus Sganarelle no longer possess all of their humanity—disqualified from their humanity, they *can* no longer perform certain statements. The performative therefore supposes a qualification, legal or natural. The one who speaks must benefit from this qualification to the very measure of what is stated performatively. To declare a war, one must have power and qualification as chief of state; to marry, as justice of the peace, a conventional, political, and in a sense circumstantial qualification is required. To promise, swear, love, curse, one must not be disqualified from one's humanity—

qualification that covers all the human essence, which can be lost but never recovered. But, to confess that "Jesus [is] Lord"—what qualification will suffice, and from where will it come? In other words, who indeed would be able to hold the role of an *I,* so that he may perform the utterance, hence so that he will be absorbed totally in the metalanguage of which he constitutes the first instance? So that he can also raise himself to the level of what it is a question of predicating in the predicative statement—". . . Lord"? The terminal equivalence, as it plays between the *I* and *Lord,* requires an *I* invested by an authority true to what *Lord* implies. What lordship will ever qualify the *I* for a lordly performance? In all rigor, only he who said: "Me, I am" (Exod. 3:14 = John 8:24, 58) can treat the statement that "Jesus [is] Lord" as a performative. And, in a sense, he did nothing other. But only in a sense, for he, as Son, never ceased to receive this lordly qualification from the Father. And, for Jesus, Christian dogmatics assures this qualification by acknowledging in him divinity, or better by acknowledging that the Father never stopped acknowledging it in him. Precisely through this Jesus appears as a Son.

To abolish (or more essentially to traverse) the gap between *I* and *Lord,* nothing less than the eternal Son is required. Who else would be able? Who other than the Lord would be able to perform that "Jesus [is] Lord"? If only the Son performs the kerygma, no one other than an adoptive son would be able to adopt, as his own, the pretension of such a performance. But this response still resolves nothing: who could ever know if he has the qualification of adoptive son? To this question, the response remains transhistorical, and no one can fulfill it if not he who adopts. Hence the difficulty must be approached obliquely. Only he who would respect its formal condition—*displacement* again, but no longer the same—could accomplish the performance. Displacement, now, from the speaker into the utterance that he performs and that marks the qualification to which this speaker must subscribe. No longer the absorption of the predicative utterance in the speaker, but the radical determination of the one who speaks by that which runs the game of statement. There is, therefore, an inversion of the displacement: no longer is there only the silent effectiveness of haughtiness, but above all the "semantic" qualification of the one who speaks through the utterance to be performed.

Far, then, from delivering us from the difficulties of the first displacement, the second redoubles them. If the first displacement led to the model of a militant discourse, indissolubly tied to the deviation of indifference (cynicism, opportunism, violence), the second displacement leads to the model of an ecstatic discourse, infallibly subject to its deviations. This, in other words, is the pretension to an absolute qualification, the certitude of an election, the assurance of having neither explanation to give nor account to settle, nor, at the extreme, words to make heard. The ecstatic discourse imagines itself to perform the confession of faith, because it imagines itself immediately sufficient. Thus it can founder, as much as militant discourse, in terrorism and violence. The passage from predication to performance thus does not allow us to progress one step. It simply disengages the demand of a second displacement, from the one who speaks to the utterance, after the first displacement, from the utterance to the one who speaks. Do these two topics of the discourse-object and of the metalanguage oppose one another? Or rather, do they not counterbalance one another?

3—Conversions

Two displacements, in inverse direction, and therefore, in appearance, opposed. But have we not already heard the orchestration of this theme, when metaphysics arrived at its summit (Hegel), though not at its completion (Nietzsche)? Must we not here consider the speculative proposition, in that it sets the subject and the predicate in dialectical movement? The predicate in the speculative proposition does not constitute an accidental or contingent addition to the subject, but a moment of the very manifestation of the subject. The subject passes entirely into the predicate to be figured essentially in it. To state that "the flower blooms," that "man speaks," does not amount simply to giving some supplementary information concerning the flower or man. A flower that could never be said to bloom simply would not *be* a flower (namely, the promise of a fruit) but the indication of a dead root. A man who never and in no way could be called speaking (namely, thrown in the world to constitute its "openness"), would not *be* a mute man (for the mute also speaks) but indeed an animal. The predicate—analytically or synthetically united to a subject does not matter here—receives the truth of the subject which, entirely, is displaced in it. But then, the simple logical relation of inherence of the predicate in the subject indicates more than a predicative tie: the predicate finds in the subject more than an inert substratum to which a copula would attach it. It finds itself in it, and, by transporting itself into the subject (by reintegrating itself in it through a movement that attests to an identity that is essential because dialectical), it recognizes in it nothing less than the essence of its manifestation. Does not the dialectical movement of the speculative proposition thus offer a model for the confession of faith, a model all the more powerful in that it integrates the two preceding models and their two displacements?

Before yielding to an easy identification, one would have to locate two distinctions between the speculative proposition and the confession of faith. Only by this location does an at least partial utilization of it become legitimate.

To begin with, the speculative proposition, as speculative as it becomes, and precisely because it posits that the subject *is* substance (and reciprocally), remains a pure proposition—I mean to say a purely predicative statement: the subject is displaced in the predicate, the predicate is displaced in the subject, in a play of the predicate and the subject. Every metalanguage must be reabsorbed in the propositional formula. Thus, moreover, does an absolute knowledge become thinkable—a knowledge that knows itself and includes the one who speaks in the statement. The confession of faith, on the contrary, unfolds entirely within the gap between the one who speaks and the statement, finding in it both its main difficulty and its first formal characteristic. In this sense, it would redouble the usage of the speculative models. First usage: "Jesus [is] Lord," where subject and predicate pass reciprocally one into the other; apologetically, at first, since, if he is not said *Lord, Kurios, Adonai,* Jesus simply does not coincide with himself, with his proper name, "he who saves" (Matt. 1:21 and Luke 1:31); and because inversely, the eschatological savior would save nothing if he did not take on a body in, or rather as, Jesus of Nazareth. Besides apologetics, dogmatic logic also imposes the speculative reversal: the subject (Jesus) must pass entirely into the predicate (*Lord*) in order that the exaltation of the Resurrected manifest absolutely the divinity of the crucified; inversely, it is necessary that the lordly Resurrection return, against chronology so to speak, to invest itself in the humanity of Jesus in order that the *kenosis* of the Incarnation should become envisageable. The speculative relation of the "subject" to the "predicate" conceals, here, the reciprocal implication of the Incarnation with the Assumption, at the heart of the same "once and for all" (Rom. 6:10, *ephapax;* Heb. 10:10).

Second usage: the speaker remains distinct from the utterance, by a gap through which pass the two displacements already located, without the repetition of transferences ever annihilating the gap. For, in fact, the one who becomes Christian is only he who comprehends, and then admits, that he will never cause to coincide, in a rigorous way, that which he states and that which, in him, states—not only, trivially, to reconcile what he is with what he says (sinister "authenticity"), but more radically he that he is with He that he says. Before knowing how to overcome this fault (or even whether it is necessary to attempt this), it is suitable to assign it to the dialectical model of the speculative proposition, in a double opposition. First, the confession of faith mobilizes here a proposition *and* a metalinguistic instance. Next, as one of the terms unbalances the relation by its (at least supposed) transcendence, the dialectical movement then becomes, if not impossible, at least highly subject to caution. Whereby a second rearrangement obviously seems here to become necessary.

Why, indeed, does the dialectical movement suffer no exception, whereas applied to the confession of faith, it seems to come to terms with another logic ("Jesus [is] Lord"), or to become problematic (as to the relation between the statement and the utterance)? It is because the dialectical movement is put to work by the "seriousness, the suffering, the patience, and the labour of the negative."[3] Now the negative rules the totality of being as universally as Spirit, to which, in a sense, it exclusively returns. But—and in our eyes the difficulty should not be underestimated—one doubtless would have to admit that the rigor of Love, hence that of the economy of salvation as that of the confession of faith, is distinguishable from the science of logic. Although such a thesis will not be established *here,* we might still be able to suspect it: in this case the profound motive of the insufficiency (for our purposes) of the speculative model immediately appears. To be sure, between the terms of the utterance, on the one hand, and between the one who speaks and the utterance, on the other, one must attempt to think a dialectical relation, or, more exactly here, to posit as noncontradictory the two above mentioned displacements. The dialectical instance permits one to continue beyond their apparent contradiction. But it undoubtedly does not suffice to conceive how and why these two displacements can and must reinforce one another. It certainly demonstrates that right at the point where logical understanding registers only contradiction, a(nother) logic can still work, without however showing us which one. Or rather it demonstrates that the logic set to work by the negative does not suit the rigors of charity. But, precisely, does charity develop the rigor of a logic? What one asks of charity, as regards logic, could be formulated in this way: to assure, by a tie between him who states and his utterance, the effectiveness (the designation) of that utterance and the qualification of him who states. Or even: to assure that he who confesses the faith does not contradict, by his simple presence, what he states, and that what he states ("Jesus [is] Lord") corresponds to a state of things. We thus ask for a double assurance, and to reach it we appeal to a logic of charity. But what does it mean to ask for an assurance from charity? Charity will give us assurances only if, like the Spirit acceding by the negative itself to the transparency of Absolute Knowledge, it produces, hence first *aims at* assurance. But charity maintains with assurance in general a relation that renders the validity of a request for assurances poorly assured.

Before continuing, let us remark that of the two assurances asked for, one already has the beginning of a response. The utterance "Jesus [is] Lord" acts, if not speculatively, at least in conformance to the demands that the speculative proposition attempts, on its part, to satisfy: dogmatically and apologetically, *Jesus* and *Lord* pass one into the other. They convert themselves one into the other. But such a logical conversion of the terms of the proposition is itself inscribed, and obviously, in the mystery of the Paschal *triduum*. As others have noted (A. von Speyr, H. U. von Balthasar, L. Bouyer, J. Guillet, etc.), Jesus gambles, upon the Cross, his Lordship. He gains it only in undertaking to lose it. This kenotic loss, going so far as death and, above all, the descent into hell, appears as the highest lordship—that, precisely, of love without reserve, universal and hence all-powerful. But it does not suffice to say of this lordship that in losing it the humanity of Jesus had no assurance of finding it again, in a game of loser wins. It does not suffice, since his very divinity cried out Psalm 22, attesting by that very fact, in one stroke, the *kenosis* and divinity as *kenosis*. When Jesus rises, he does not rise at all by himself but by the power and will of the Father. That this eternal and absolute will thus should have inspired the irreducibly constraining logic of love nevertheless does not imply in any way that Jesus may have benefited from assurances, nor even that his divine consciousness may have obtained *or even hoped for* any. The logic of love is developed with a constraining rigor without for all that giving any assurances—especially assurances formalizable in modal terms. We suspect henceforth that it belongs to the very rigor of a logic of love (in the figure of the *logos tou staurou*) not to assure conversion by any assurance at all.

What the first conversion teaches us can clear up the aporia of the second. This latter asks how he who states can not contradict that which he states by his own disqualification before the amplitude of what is in question with "Jesus [is] Lord." The one who speaks stands in need of an assurance on the validity, less of what he states (for, in a word, the Resurrection remains historically verifiable), than of his qualification to state. He asks for the assurance that he indeed has the right, himself, to confess the faith, and, by that very fact, that he "is indeed right" to do it. Now we face a question concerning the aporia: what meaning is there in demanding an assurance here? For it is a question of stating, we have just recalled in broad strokes, nothing less than the Paschal mystery of the death and resurrection, where the constraining advance is experienced humanly, and no doubt also divinely, as the failure of assurances. Just as the conversion of *Jesus* with *Lord* is stated all the more rigorously in that it is registered without any preliminary assurances, so too the conversion of the believer with the utterance in which he lets himself be recognized (if not qualified) as such must be founded all the more rigorously on the logic of love in that it does not rely upon an assurance. We must be understood: it is not a question here of the trivial conflict of self-justification before apostasy, which theatrically opposes "on my right" stubborn certainty, and, "on my left," authentic faith, without ready-made certainties, which lets itself be put in question, to the point of a purifying destitution, etc. It is a question of understanding that, if the logic here depends on love, the conversion must be understood as a conversion. Which means that if, in the Paschal *triduum,* the logical conversion of *Jesus* with *Lord* rests on the absolute conversion of the Son to the Father; if this conversion is completed triumphantly in the abandon without reserve or assurance of the Son to the Father; if finally love appears in the refusal to demand preliminary assurances, even in the refusal to assure oneself (to "save oneself," to "come down from the cross" Luke 23:35, 39 and Matt. 27:40)—then in order for the confession of faith, hence the conversion one into the other of the believer and the *kerygma,* to obey the logic of love, it must not pretend to found itself on a certain assurance. The obviousness, the serenity, and the confidence of its statement imply this rigor and grow with it. He who confesses that "Jesus [is] Lord" does not confess it in spirit and truth unless he expects from the lordship of Jesus alone his confirmation in his confession. Only Jesus can confirm to us that he [is] Lord, and that we confess him rightly, because he alone received from the Father both lordship (Phil. 2:11) and the quality of confessor (1 Tim. 6:12). The servant does not surpass the master: as Jesus received from an absolute spiritual conversion the absolute "logical" conversion of *Jesus* with *Lord,* the believer will never be able to receive his "logical" conversion with that which he states unless by a conversion—inchoate and tangential—that is fundamentally particular to Him who leads and precedes him. Hence, moreover, the principle of equivalence of conversions and confessions: "I say to you: whoever has confessed me before men, the Son of man will confess before the angels of God" (Luke 12:8). The Christian is not attested as such by calling himself Christian, but by saying: "Jesus [is] Lord," and expecting of Jesus alone that he confirm both the utterance and the one who speaks [*énonciateur*]—and, in the interval, he endures that the others call him *Christian* (Acts 11:26). He thus endures, as much as the suffering of an often persecuted minority, the pain of not knowing the one he names, and especially of knowing himself disqualified from every qualification to know him, and even to confess him.

But, from now on, does not the confession of faith find its logic only in finding its rigor? Does it find, in the logic of love drawn out in this way, only its dereliction? On the contrary, it discovers that, to confess the faith, love suffices. And of love, the Christian never stands in need, since the Spirit pours love out into the hearts that receive it (Rom. 5:5).

4—Martyrdom

The earlier displacements find their truth in the double conversion made visible by a double rearrangement of the speculative proposition. The essential of this critical rearrangement comes down in one case—"Jesus [is] Lord"—to substituting for dialectical assurance (negative, absolute knowledge) the Paschal abandon, in the other—the speaker/utterance [*énonciateur/énoncé*]—to noting that only the lordship of Jesus will (would) be able to qualify the speaker [*locuteur*] to perform such an utterance. Consequently, the difficulty of bringing the different terms of the discourse back to unity seems less to weaken or prohibit the confession of faith than, first, to characterize it exclusively. In a sense, the "difficulties" of the confession of faith take on the value of a definition: would the confession of faith be defined as a "difficult" discourse? Without doubt, as *the* "difficult" discourse: "Difficult is this discourse" (John 6:60). Difficult because it attempts to state the blessing of G~~o~~d: to bless G~~o~~d for blessing men in Jesus Christ. For our discourse, it is difficult to say the *eulogia*—the easy discourse of blessing. For blessing, preeminently, "puts at ease" (*eu-*) the one at whom it aims, by filling him with its grace. Blessing gives every comfort to the one whom it favors. But our discourse does not easily give these gifts, held as it remains in a model of mastery, limited by the hard need to have assurances. The "difficulty" that holds our discourse on the path of its conversion or confession of faith consists in nothing other than the conversion itself. Conversion does not indicate here, one must repeat, a recourse to the stickiness of ineffable states of mind (private language), but the substitution of certain rules of validation for others. *The rules of validation of the confession of faith, as "discourse of the cross"* (1 Cor. 1:18) *are the concern of charity,* as "charity of the truth, *agapē tēs alētheias*" (2 Thess. 2:10). Let us outline two preliminary elements that may help in determining these rules of validation.

Confession presupposes, in order to be absolutely valid, Jesus truly Lord, and the Christian who states, truly re-created in imitation of Christ. But these two conditions, by definition, cannot be fulfilled by the speaker himself, for neither one nor the other falls within the domain of his competence: only the Father can manifest the Lordship of Jesus, just as only Jesus can recognize a disciple for his own. In this sense, the confession of faith, while supremely implicating the believer, has nothing of a self-implication about it: not only does it not suffice to implicate oneself in it to verify it, but to pretend so would constitute the supreme imposture. The confession of faith passes through the one who speaks, but it comes from much further away and it goes much farther. It passes right through him: coming from the mystery, "hidden before the centuries," of adoption of men in the Son (Eph. 1:4–5), it aims at the recapitulatory lordship of the Son over the universe (Eph. 1:10). What is at stake in the confession of faith stems precisely from this: does the believer lend himself to this transition? Will he be able to lend himself to such a role of transition, which will allow him to pass between two instances definitively withdrawn from the assurance of any mastery whatsoever? To accept, or to refuse to take the turn to speak in such ("logical") conditions, is the concern of an apparently irrational decision, which one might name, out of kindness, existential. In fact, this existential decision would have no value if it were not inscribed in a logic of love. In refusing to perform and to predicate according to a model of mastery, he who confesses that "Jesus [is] Lord" *nevertheless already* performs an act of love, *nevertheless already* correctly predicates of the Word that he can love. Undoubtedly this confession remains inchoately constrained to charity. But this divergence itself does not at all escape charity. For divergence implies abandon and, above all, the endurance of that abandon. Thus confession finds itself taken up again by the martyr. For martyrdom, before speaking a putting to death, speaks a testimony. And, before even speaking a testimony, it speaks the renewal of the witness in the very figure of Christ and of his kenotically triumphant lordship. To the one who confesses, martyrdom gives, as it gave to Stephen, the occasion to enter into the place (and to know the conditions) where the confession of faith becomes absolutely correct. Martyrdom permits the confessor to see the trinitarian play—"filled with the Holy Spirit . . ., he saw the glory of God and Jesus who was seated to the right of God" (Acts 7:55).

Thus Lordship certainly belongs to Jesus, in a complete and reciprocal relation. Predication becomes perfectly legitimate. Next, martyrdom gives to the confessor the occasion to carry upon himself the characteristics of Christ and, in return, to find himself carried by them: to give up his spirit to God (Acts 6:59 = Luke 23:46), to pardon his tormentors (Acts 6:50 = Luke 23:34); thus qualification overcomes the martyr, when he accepts sharing in the passion, in other words in the logic of love. Performance also becomes perfectly legitimate. Martyrdom appears thus as the privileged instance where the confession of faith finds its first completion. Between confession, where the *I* puts his conversion to work in a discourse that always says too much for the one who states it, and martyrdom, where the *I* accepts abandoning himself silently in the figure of Jesus, to the Lord whose glory he contemplates, an *admirabile commercium* is established, where there is at play, with the destiny of our language, the eschatological interspace of the world. The one and the other—world and language—depend on the traverse of an identical distance.[4]

Notes

For bibliographic details of English translations used, see "English-Language Editions Cited," pages 233–36 below.

Preface to the English Edition

1. *Sur la théologie blanche de Descartes: Analogie, création des vérités eternelles et fondement* (Paris: Presses Universitaires de France, 1981; 2d ed., 1991), and *Sur le prisme métaphysique de Descartes* (Paris: Presses Universitaires de France, 1986). See the discussions of E. Jennifer Ashworth, *Studia Cartesiana,* 2 (Amsterdam, 1981), pp. 219–224; Charles Larmore, *Journal of Philosophy* 81/3, (1984): 156–62; John G. Cottingham, *Times Higher Education Supplement,* 29 November 1985; Richard A. Watson, *Independent Journal of Philosophy* 5/6 (1988): 147–49, etc. See also my essays, "The Essential Incoherence of Descartes' Definition of Divinity," in Amélie O. Rorty (ed.), *Essays on Descartes' Meditations* (Berkeley and Los Angeles: University of California Press, 1986), pp. 297–337; "On Descartes' Constitution of Metaphysics," *Graduate Faculty Philosophy Journal,* New School for Social Research, 11/1, pp. 21–34; and "The Idea of God," in M. Ayers and D. Garber (eds.), *Cambridge History of Seventeenth Century Philosophy* (Cambridge University Press, forthcoming).

2. In *L' idole et la distance* (Paris: Grasset, 1977; 2d ed., 1989; 3d ed., Paris: Hachette, "Poche-biblio," 1991).

3. Derrida takes up my theses in "Comment ne pas parler" in *Psyche* (Paris, 1987), pp. 535 ff. [trans. Frieden].

4. See *Réduction et donation: Recherches sur Husserl, Heidegger et la phénoménologie* (Paris: Presses Universitaires de France, 1989); and "L' interloqué," in "Topos: Who Comes After the Subject?" *Topoi: An International Review of Philosophy* 7/2 (September 1988): 175 ff.

5. See, for example, in France, reviews by J.-H. Nicolas, "La suprême logique de l'amour et la théologie," *Revue Thomiste,* October-December 1983, pp. 639–49; and J. D. Robert, "Dieu sans l'être: A propos d'un livre récent," *Nouvelle Revue Théologique,* 1983, pp. 406 ff. See also the discussions by R. Virgoulay, "Dieu ou l'être? Relecture de Heidegger en marge de J.-L. Marion, *Dieu sans l'être,*" *Recherches de Science Religieuses* 72/2 (1984): 163–98; and J.-Y. Lacoste, "Penser Dieu

en l'aimant: Philosophie et théologie de Jean-Luc Marion," *Archives de Philosophie* 50/2 (1987). This debate led to D. Dubarle's collection of studies, *Dieu avec l'être: De Parménide à Saint Thomas. Essai d'ontologie théologale,* introduced by J. Greisch (Paris: Beauchesne, 1986), and to the collective work, *L'être et Dieu.* Travaux du C.E.R.I.T. (Paris: Cerf, 1986) (D. Bourg, S. Breton, A. Delzant, C. Geffré, J. Grosjean, G. Lafon, J.-L. Marion, G. Vahanian, H.-B. Vergotte, etc.).

6. See E. Gilson, *L'être et l'essence* (Paris: J. Vrin, 1948, esp. 2d ed., 1962), as well as *Being and Some Philosophers* (Toronto, 1952). The record of the interpretation of the *Seinsfrage* by Gilson can be found in large part in M. Couratier (ed.), *Etienne Gilson et Nous: La philosophie et son histoire* (third section, P. Aubenque, J. Beaufret, J.-F. Courtine and P. Hadot) (Paris: J. Vrin, 1980).

7. Saint Thomas Aquinas, *In Boethii De Trinitate,* q.5, a.4, *resp.*

8. Saint Thomas Aquinas, *Summa Theologia,* Ia, q.45, a.2.

Envoi:

1. F. W. J. Schelling, *Zur Geschichte der neuren Philosophie,* in *Sämtliche Werke,* ed. Schröter, I/10, p. 22.

2. Throughout the translation, the capitalized "Being" will always signal an infinitival form (*l'être, être*) as distinguished from a participial form (*l'étant, étant*). At times this will mean losing Marion's distinction between *l'être* and *l'Etre,* but for the sake of clarity it seems the best solution.—Trans.

3. Y. Bonnefoy, *Dans le leurre du seuil* (Paris, 1975), p. 68.

4. *Hors-texte,* literally, "outside the text," the unpaginated plates added to the end of a book.—Trans.

Chapter One

1. P. Claudel, *Cinq grandes odes,* III, *Magnificat* in *Oeuvre Poétique,* Pléiade (Paris, 1967), p. 251.

2. Such a stopping of the gaze, which "fixes" it in an intentional lived experience finds its exemplary description in E. Husserl, for example in *Ideen I,* sec. 101, *Husserliana,* III, 254.

3. "[L]e point de *chute* du regard," literally, "the gaze's *falling-point.*"—Trans.

4. "[N]'y voyait que du feu," literally, "saw nothing but fire."—Trans.

5. P. Valéry, "Le cimetière marin," in *Oeuvres* I (Paris: Pléiade, 1960), p. 151 [trans. Paul, p. 277].

6. *Ibid.,* p. 147 [trans., p. 269], with which one might compare Aristotle, *On Divination in Sleep,* II, 464b8–10.

7. Baudelaire, "Harmonie du soir," in *Oeuvres Complètes* (Paris: Pléiade, 1961), p. 45 [trans. Fowlie, p. 57].

8. Term coined by Marion, the *invisable* indicates that which cannot be aimed at or taken into view (from the verb *viser,* to aim at).—Trans.

9. Cicero, *De Republica,* VI, 15 [trans. Keyes, p. 267]. This text is all the more significant in that here the *templum* has precisely no limit and extends to the universe; but it remains nonetheless defined, since determined by the human *conspectus.*

10. R. Walser, *Das Götzenbild,* in *Prosa* (Frankfurt: Suhrkamp, 1968), 129–30, which presents existentially the moments of our conceptual analysis: the visitor to an ethnological museum at first considers some statues with an interest that is as incontestable as it is external, to which is suddenly opposed an idol where his gaze freezes in order to read the divine impression that the idolatrous artist had consigned in it: "He stood there, suddenly, without knowing how, before a primitive wooden figure, which, frightful and crude as it was, made such a forceful impression on him that he succumbed, body and soul, to the magic of that rough idol—for it was one." This emotion has nothing "aesthetic" about it but incites—even more, physically constrains—one to adoration, certainly not of the image but of the very *Eindruck* that it exerts, and which is exerted as that very visibility: "a monstrous, dreadful desire suddenly took hold of him, to throw himself to the ground, to fall on his knees and to prostrate himself, in order to venerate with his body the dreadful image that had been taken from the deserts of Africa."

11. Heidegger, *Identity and Difference* [trans. Stambaugh p. 72].

12. Heidegger, *Nietzsche* (Pfullingen, 1961), 1, 251, p. 321 [trans. Krell, I, p. 66].

13. Kant, *Kritik der praktischen Vernunft,* Ak. A. V, p. 145 [trans. Beck p. 150].

14. F. Nietzsche, *Werke,* ed. Colli-Montinari, VIII/1, 217, fgt. 5 [71] [trans. Kaufmann, in *Will to Power,* sec. 55].

15. Feuerbach, *Das Wesen des Christentums,* in Gesammelte Werke (hereafter *G.W.*) (Berlin, 1968), V, p. 11, *"dass das Original ihres Götzenbildes der Mensch ist."*

16. Claudel, see n.1 above.

17. See Chantraine, *Dictionnaire étymologique de la langue grecque* (Paris, 1968), p. 354, which underlines that **eikō* first indicates the pearance [*la parence*] (if one might risk the expression) befalling the spectator starting from the thing itself in authentic ad-pearance [*adparence*] (hence the possible connotation of affinity of the thing thus related [*apparentée*] in appearance).

18. John of Damascus, "every icon manifests and indicates the secret," *Contra imaginum calumniatores orationes tres,* III, 17, in *Die Schriften des Johannes von Damaskos,* 3 (Berlin, 1975), p. 126. This formulation must no doubt be understood less as an echo of that from the *Timaeus, eikōn tou noētou theos aisthētos* (92c7), poorly verified moreover (the best manuscripts in fact give *poiētou*), than as a response to Colossians 1:15, explicitly glossed elsewhere: *hē tou aoratou eikōn kai autē aoratos* (*ibid.* III, 65, *loc. cit.* p. 170). This redoubling indicates, awkwardly no doubt, the reflux of the invisible upon the visible that itself, by this investment, becomes iconic (see below, sec. 7, "Visible Mirror of the Invisible").

19. Council of Nicea II, 787 (*Denzinger* [hereafter *Denz.*] 302). That the icon may be justified before the accusation of apparently inevitable idolatry only by a theology of hypostatic presence (radically distinct from the substantial presence in the Eucharist), hence by its christological reinterpretation, is demonstrated in masterly fashion by C. von Schönborn, *L'icône du Christ. Fondements théologiques élaborés entre le Ier et le IIe Conciles de Nicée (325–787)* (Fribourg [Switzerland], 1976). See also M.-J. Baudinet, "La relation icônique à Byzance au IXe siècle d'après Nicéphore le Patriarche: un destin de l'aristotélisme," in *Les Etudes Philosophiques,* 1978/1, 85–106.

20. See the formulation of John of Damascus cited above, n. 18.

21. Descartes, *Quintae Responsiones, Oeuvres,* ed. Adam-Tannery, VII, p. 368, 2–4; Clerselier translates: "Pour avoir une idée vraie de l'infini, il ne doit en aucune façon être compris, d'autant que l'incompréhensibilité même est contenue dans la raison formelle de l'infini"; Descartes, *Oeuvres Philosophiques,* ed. F. Alquié, 2 (Paris, 1957), p. 811 ["For the idea of the infinite, if it is to be true, cannot be grasped at all, since the impossibility of being grasped is contained in the formal definition of the infinite."—Trans. Cottingham, Stoothof, and Murdoch, p. 253].

22. René Char, "Contre une maison sèche," in *Le Nu perdu* (Paris: Nouvelle Revue Française, 1978), p. 125.

Chapter Two

1. Bossuet: "That is what is called an *epoch,* from a Greek word meaning to *stop,* because we stop there in order to consider, as from a resting place, all that has happened before or after, thus avoiding anachronisms, that is, the kind of error that confuses ages"; *Discourse on Universal History,* foreword [trans. Forster, p. 5]. One remarkable point: the epoch stops (*epekhō*), suspends, as it were, the flow of time,

as the idol stops the gaze, which cannot go beyond the farthest point where its capacity is filled. History as a succession of epoch-making idols? History can function therefore only inasmuch as the idols that make epoch in it still remain possible. Would the icon then institute the only possible end of history—its eschatological transgression (a traverse of distance, once again)?

2. Hölderlin, *Der Einzige,* 1, l. 48 f., "Herakles Bruder," 2, ll. 51–52: "Ich weiss es aber, eigene Schuld ists! Denn zu sehr, / O Christus! häng ich an dir, wiewohl Herakles Bruder / Und kühn bekenn'ich, du bist Bruder auch des Eviers," and 3, ll. 50–55 (*Gesamtausgabe* [hereafter G.A.], 2/1, pp. 154, 158 and 162). See our work, *L'Idole et la Distance,* Secs. 10 and 11 (Paris:Grasset, 1977).

3. C. Baudelaire, *Fusées,* XVII, in *Oeuvres complètes,* Pléiade (Paris, 1966), p. 1256. See P. Valéry, *Monsieur Teste:* "I confess that I have made an idol of my mind," *Oeuvres,* 2, Pléiade (Paris, 1960), p. 37 [trans. Mathews, p. 35].

4. There is nothing surprising in the transition from an "aesthetic" to a conceptual idol, since in one and the other case it is only a question of apprehension. Hence the famous sequence from Gregory of Nyssa: "Every concept [*noēma?*], as it is produced according to an apprehension of the imagination in a conception that circumscribes and in an aim that pretends to attain the divine nature, models only an idol of God [*eidōlon theou*], without at all declaring God himself" (*Vita Moysis,* II, par. 166, P.G., 44, 337b). On this point Nietzsche defends the legitimacy of an extension to the concept of the idol. Not only does he explicitly define it as an ideal—"Götzen (mein Wort für 'Ideale') umwerfen" (*Ecce Homo,* preface, sec. 2)—but he dedicates *Twilight of the Idols* to the "eternal idols" only inasmuch as he means "great errors," namely, concepts (cause, effect, freedom, etc.), those of metaphysics (*Twilight of the Idols,* foreword). These conceptual idols largely outlast religious idols and the "death of God." Hence their extreme danger.

5. L. Feuerbach, *Das Wesen des Christentums,* in *G.W.,* (Berlin, 1973), p. 11.

6. F. Nietzsche *Wille zur Macht,* sec. 55 [trans. Kaufmann].

7. *Das Wesen des Christentums,* 1/2, p. 93–95 [trans. Eliot, p. 46].

8. E. Kant, "moralischer Welturheber." See *Kritik der Urteilskraft* (hereafter, *K.U.*), sec. 87, "Folglich müssen wir eine moralische Weltursache (einen Welturheber) annehmen, um uns gemäss dem moralischen Gesetz einen Endzweck vorzusetzen . . . nämlich es sei so ein Gott. . . . d. i. um sich wenigstens nicht von der Möglichkeit des ihm [sc. a righteous man] moralisch vorgeschriebenen Endzwecks einen Begriff zu machen, das Dasein eines moralischen Welturhebers, d. i.

Gottes annehmen." ["Hence in order to set ourselves a final purpose in conformity with the moral law, we must assume a moral cause of the world (an author of the world) . . . in other words, that there is a God . . . i.e., so that he (a righteous man) can at least form a concept of the possibility of (achieving) the final purpose that is morally prescribed to him—assume the existence of a *moral* author of the world, i.e., the existence of a God." Kant, *Critique of Judgment* [trans. Pluhar, pp. 340, 342]. The [French] translation by A. Philonenko (Paris: Vrin, 1968) indeed reinforces precisely the idolatrous function of the "concept": "se faire au moins une idée de la possibilité du but final qui lui est moralement prescrit, admettre l'existence d'un auteur *moral* du monde, c'est-à-dire de Dieu" (p. 259). Likewise, "ein moralisches Wesen als Welturheber, mithin ein Gott angenommen werden müsse . . . ein moralisches Wesen als Urgrund der Schöpfung anzunehmen" (sec. 88) ["moral (being as author of the world), and hence a God . . . a *moral being* as the original basis of creation" (trans. Pluhar, pp. 345, 346)]. And "Nun führt jene Teleologie keineswegs auf einen bestimmten Begriff von Gott, der hingegen allein in dem von einem moralischen Welturheber angetroffen wird," sec. 91 ["But in fact physical teleology does not at all lead to a determinate concept of God. Such a concept can be found only in the concept of a moral author of the world" (trans, p. 346)]. (See, amongst others, *Kritik der praktischen Vernunft,* Ak. A. p. 145 [trans. Beck, p. 150]; *Religion innerhalb der Grenzen der blosson Vernunft,* III, 1 sec. 4 [trans. Greene and Hudson, p. 93], etc.). It remains to ponder over the motive that permits Kant thus to believe himself to have withdrawn from a danger that he expressly mentions, idolatry (*Idolatrie, K.U.,* sec. 89), and defines as "a superstitious delusion that we can make ourselves pleasing to the supreme being by means other than a moral attitude" [trans. p. 351]; for can one not ask how that which the practical attitude cannot not presuppose—that "God" is expressed according to morality, hence by a concept of morality—is still, and always will be, an idol? And his warning would turn on Kant himself: "For no matter how pure and free from images of sense such a concept of the supreme being may be from a theoretical point of view, practically the being is still conceived of as an *idol,* i.e., it is conceived of anthropomorphically in what its will is like" [trans., p. 351, n.57]. And if God did not subscribe to the categorical imperative? Kant's answer is well known: one would have to exclude God, and Christ as well, reduced to the simple role of an example of the moral law.

9. *Religion innerhalb der Grenzen der blossen Vernunft,* III, Ak. A., VII, p. 139 [trans. Greene and Hudson, p. 130].

10. Fichte, *Über den Grund unsers Glaubens an eine göttliche Weltregierung,* in *Fichtes Werke,* III, ed. F. Medicius, p. 130 [trans. Edwards, p. 25].

11. "Gott ist etwas Realeres als eine bloss moralische Weltordnung," *Untersuchungen über die menschliche Freiheit*. . ., ed. Schröter, I/9, p. 356 ["God is more of a reality than is a mere moral world-order." trans. Gutmann, p. 30].

12. Leibniz, *Textes inédits,* 1, ed. G. Grua (Paris: Presses universitaires de France, 1948), p. 287. This does not differ significantly from the reiteration by Husserl of "God" as "the subject possessing an absolutely perfect knowledge and therefore possessing every adequate perception possible" since it then is a matter of the pure and simple "idea of God," forged starting from requisites of *our* mind in the role of "a necessary limiting concept in epistemological considerations and an indispensable index to the construction of certain limiting concepts which not even the philosophizing atheist can do without" (*Ideen* I, secs. 43 and 79) [trans. Kersten].

13. M. Heidegger, *Identität und Differenz* (Pfullingen, 1957), p. 63 [trans. Stambaugh p. 71]. See "Insofern die Metaphysik das Seiende als solches im Ganzen denkt, stellt sie das Seiende aus dem Hinklick auf das Differente der Differenz vor, ohne auf die Differenz als Differenz zu achten"—"since metaphysics thinks beings as such as a whole, it represents beings in respect of what differs in the difference, and without heeding the difference as difference." (*ibid.,* p. 62 [trans., p. 70]). And *Über den "Humanismus", Wegmarken, G.A.,* 9., p. 322 [trans. Krell, pp. 202–203].

14. *Ibid.,* p. 63. "Sein als Grund und Seiendes als gegründetbegründendes . . ." [trans. p. 71].

15. *Ibid.,* p. 47 [trans., p. 56 (modified)].

16. *Ibid.,* p. 51 [trans., p. 60], then p. 64 [trans., p. 72]. One must hear in *Ursache* at once the cause [*la cause*], and that which metaphysically assures it, the primordial thing [*la chose primordiale*], *Ur-Sache.* See *Wegmarken, G.A.,* 9, p. 350 [trans. Krell, pp. 228–229]; and *Die Frage nach der Technik, Vorträge und Aufsätze* (Pfullingen, 1954), p. 26 [trans. Lovitt, p. 26]: "In the light of casuality, God can sink to the level of a cause, of *causa efficiens.* He then becomes, even in theology, the god of the philosophers, namely, of those who define the unconcealed and the concealed in terms of the causality of making, without ever considering the essential origin of this causality." The thinker accepts, in this way, running the risk of reproach for "atheism," since one can wonder to begin with, "might not the presumably ontic faith in God be at bottom godlessness [*im Grunde Gottlosigkeit*]? And might the

genuine metaphysician be more religious [*religiöser*] than the usual faithful, than the members of a 'church' or even than the 'theologians' of every confession?" *Metaphysische Anfangsgründe der Logik im Ausgang von Leibniz* (SS. 1928), *G.A.,* 26, p. 211 [trans. Heim, p. 165].

17. *Ibid.,* p. 64–65 [trans., p. 72 (modified)]. David, on the contrary, dances, naked, before the Ark. And, psalmist *par excellence,* sings. Also to the contrary, the experience related by R. Walser (Chap. 1, n.10 above).

18. *Nietzsche,* I (Pfullingen, 1961), p. 366 [trans. Krell, p. 106 (modified)]. See: "The ultimate blow against God and against the suprasensory world consists in the fact that God, the first of beings [*das Seiende des Seienden*] is degraded to the highest value [*zum höchsten Wert herabgewürdigt wird*]. The heaviest blow against God is not that God is held to be unknowable, not that God's existence is demonstrated to be unprovable, but rather that the god held to be real is elevated to the highest value. For this blow comes precisely not from those who are standing about, who do not believe in God, but from the believers and their theologians who discourse on the being that is of all beings the most in being [*vom Seiendsten alles Seienden*], without ever letting it occur to them to think on Being itself, in order thereby to become aware that, seen from out of faith, their thinking and their talking is sheer blasphemy if it meddles in the theology of faith [*die Gotteslästerung schlechtin*]" ("Nietzsches Wort 'Gott ist tot,' " in *Holzwege* [1950], pp. 239–240 = *G.A.,* 9, p. 260 [trans. Lovitt, p. 105]. Likewise "when one proclaims 'God' the altogether 'highest value', this is a degradation (*Herabsetzung*) of God's essence. Here as elsewhere thinking in values is the greatest blasphemy imaginable against Being" (*Über den "Humanismus", Wegmarken,* in *G.A.,* 9, p. 349 [trans. Krell, p. 228]). One question, by way of anticipation: blasphemy against "God" coincides here, and in several convergent ways, with blasphemy against Being; but could one not suspect that this very coincidence between the two blasphemies constitutes by itself a third and not lesser blasphemy, even though precisely it becomes possible, if only to anticipate it, on the exclusive condition of not thinking starting from and in view of Being?

19. J.-P. Sartre, *L'Etre et le Néant* (Paris, 1943), p. 703. The entire work (and therefore no doubt also Sartre's finally vulgar "atheism") rests on the assimilation of God to the *causa sui,* without any prudent distinction (Heideggerian or Pascalian) between the possible "gods." The fascination exercised by the "dignity of the *causa sui*" (p. 714, in a certainly involuntary echo of the debate between Descartes and Arnauld on the *causae dignitas, Oeuvres,* VII, p. 242, 5 [trans., vol. 2, p. 168])

invests not only the concept of "God," but even the elementary christology that the rhetoric must here fabricate for itself: "We have seen that desire is lack of being [*manque d'être*]. As such, it is directly *carried upon* the being which it lacks. This being, we have seen, is the *in-itself-for-itself,* consciousness become substance, substance become cause of itself, the Man-God" (p. 664); "the *Ens causa sui* that the religions name God. Thus the passion of man is the inverse of that of Christ, for man is lost as man in order that God be born" (p. 708). But whence comes the naïve and aggressive evidence that the highest name of the divine resides in the *causa sui,* if not from a half-conceptual and entirely uncriticized anthropomorphism?

20. Bossuet, *Discours sur l'Histoire Universelle,* II, 1 [trans. Forster, p. 115].

21. F. Nietzsche, *Werke,* ed. Colli-Montinari, VIII/3, p. 323, 17 [4] sec. 5 (and *Wille zur Macht,* sec. 1038) [trans. Kaufmann, sec. 1038].

22. *Uberwindung der Metaphysik,* sec. 12, in *Vorträge und Aufsätze,* I, p. 75 [trans. Stambaugh, p. 96].

23. *Über den "Humanismus", Wegmarken, G.A.,* 9, pp. 351, and 338–39 [trans. Krell, pp. 230 and 218]. The polemic provoked by these texts, or rather by the commentary of them that we persist in making, leads us to cite other parallels (without however pretending, as much as the thesis is constant, to exhaustiveness).

Thus: (a) "The turning of the age does not take place by some new god, or the old one renewed, bursting into the world from ambush at some time or other. Where would he turn on his return if men had not first [*zuvor*] prepared an abode for him? How could there ever be for the god an abode fit for a god, if a divine radiance [*en Glanz von Gottheit*] did not first begin to shine in everything that is? . . . The ether, however, in which alone the gods are gods, is their godhead [*ist ihre Gottheit*]. The element of this ether, that within which even the godhead itself is still present [*west*], is the holy. The element of the ether for the coming of the fugitive gods, the holy [*das Heilige*], is the track of the fugitive gods" (*Wozu Dichter?,* in *Holzwege,* 1950, pp. 249 and 250 = *G.A.* 5, pp. 270 and 272 [trans. Hofstadter, pp. 92 and 94]).

(b) "Whether the god lives or remains dead is not decided by the religiosity of men and even less by the theological aspirations of philosophy and natural science. Whether or not God is God comes disclosingly to pass from out of and within the constellation of Being [*ob Gott Gott ist, ereignet sich aus der Konstellation des Seins und innerhalb ihrer*]" (*Die Kehre,* in *Die Technik und die Kehre* (Pfullingen, 1962), p. 46 [trans. Lovitt, p. 49]).

(c) "The default of the unconcealment of Being as such releases the evanescence of all that is hale in beings [*alles Heilsmen im Seienden*]. The evanescence of the hale takes the openness of the holy [*das Offene des Heiligen*] with it and closes it off. The closure of the holy eclipses every illumination of the divine [*des Gottheitlichen*]. The deepening dark entrenches and conceals the lack of God [*den Fehl Gottes*]." Hence the consequence: "Because it is more essential, and older, the destiny of Being is less familiar [*unheimlicher*] than the lack of God [*unheimlicher als der Fehl Gottes ist . . . das Seinsgeschick*" (*Nietzsche,* II, pp. 394 and 396 [trans. Krell, IV p. 248]).

(d) "One could not be more reserved than I before every attempt to employ Being to think theologically in what way God is God. Of Being, there is nothing to expect here. I believe that Being can never be thought as the ground and essence of God, but that nevertheless the experience of God and of his manifestedness, to the extent that the latter can indeed meet man, flashes in the dimension of Being, which in no way signifies that Being might be regarded as a possible predicate for God" (*Séminaire de Zurich,* [French] trans. F. Fédier and D. Saatdjian, *Poésie* no. 13 (Paris, 1980), p. 61; see the [French] trans. of J. Greisch, in *Heidegger et la question de Dieu* (Paris, 1980), p. 334).

(e) "*Das Sein ist Gott,* now understood speculatively, signifies: *das Sein 'istet' Gott,* that is to say, *das Sein lässt Gott Gott sein. 'Ist'* is transitive and active. *Erst das enfaltete Sein selbst ermöglicht das Gott sein:* it is only *Being* developed unto itself (in the sense that it is in the *Logic*) which (in an aftershock) renders possible: *Being-God" (Séminaire du Thor 1968, Questions,* IV, p. 258). No doubt this last text must be utilized with more prudence than the preceding ones, on account of its commentary status and its mode of transmission; in the present context it remains significant. For the debate on the scope of these texts, see the "Note on the Divine and Related Subjects" at the conclusion of chap. 2.

24. See, before all else, two principal texts: *Der Ursprung des Kunstwerkes,* in *Holzwege,* particularly p. 29ff. = *G.A.*, 5, p. 25ff. [trans. Hofstadter, p. 39ff.]; and the conference *Das Ding,* in *Vorträge und Aufsätze,* I (Pfullingen, 1954), in which p. 51 [trans. Hofstadter, p. 178]: "When we say sky, we are already thinking of the other three along with it by way of the simple oneness of the four [*aus der Einfalt der Vier*]. / The divinities are the beckoning messengers of the godhead [*die winkenden Boten der Gottheit*]. Out of the hidden sway of the divinities the god emerges as what he is, which removes him from any comparison with beings that are present. / When we speak of the divinities, we are already thinking of the other three along with them by

way of the simple oneness of the four." To simplify things, or rather to exaggerate the formulation to the point of coarseness, one could even state that, since the "appropriating mirror-play of the simple onefold of earth and sky, divinities [*Göttlichen*] and mortals, we call the *world*" (*ibid.*, p. 52 = p. 179; emphasis added), and therefore since the world makes the four of the Fourfold, hence "makes" the gods, then—far from "God" creating the world—it would be up to the world to "make" the gods.

25. Postscript to *Was ist Metaphysik?* in *Wegmarken, G.A.*, 9, p. 307 [trans. Kaufmann, p. 261].

26. *Metaphysische Anfangsgründe der Logik* [1928], *G.A.*, 26, p. 20 [trans. Heim, p. 16]. Fortunately, this text radicalizes what the formulations of *Sein und Zeit*, sec. 4, might have held back too much.

27. *Ibid.*, p. 171 [trans, p. 136]; see secs. 10 and 11. These precocious analyses agree with the "neutrale tantum" which characterizes, later, the *Ereignis*, in *Zur Sache des Denkens*, 1969, p. 47 [trans. Stambaugh, p. 43].

28. Respectively, *Metaphysische Anfangsgründe der Logik, loc. cit.*, sec. 10, p. 177 [trans., p. 140], and *Prolegomena zur Geschichte des Zeitbegriffs* [1925], *G. A.*, 20, Frankfurt, 1979, p. 109–110 [trans. Kisiel, pp. 79–80]. The purely phenomenological atheism of Husserl, *Ideen* I, sec. 58, can serve, only to a certain extent, as a reference. On the permanence of the phenomenological method in the project of an analytic of *Dasein*, see the clarification by J.-F. Courtine, "La cause de la phenomenologie," in *Exercices de la patience* 3/4 (Paris, 1982).

29. *Vom Wesen des Grundes*, in *Wegmarken, G. A.*, 9, p. 159 [trans. Malick, p. 91]. In fact the text continues, and transforms the reduction of divine transcendence into its constitution on the basis of *Dasein*: "One must first gain an *adequate concept* of *Dasein* by illuminating transcendence. Then, by considering *Dasein*, one can *ask* [*nunmehr gefragt werden kann*] how the relationship of *Dasein* to God is ontologically constituted." The question of *Dasein*, that is to say the question that *Dasein* poses itself in relation to Being, determines in advance the possibility of any question of God: before the "turn," a preliminary already plays before and upon God; that it should be a question here of *Dasein*, and not of *Sein*, changes nothing for our present purposes.

30. Respectively, *Hölderlins Hymnen "Germanien" und "Der Rhein,"* *G.A.*, 39, p. 32; *Grundprobleme der Phänomenologie, G.A.*, 24, p. 110 [trans. Hofstadter, p. 79]; *Nietzsche*, II, p. 415 [trans. by Stambaugh p. 15]; *Vom Wesen und Begriff der* φύσις, in *Wegmarken, G.A.*, 9, p. 240

[trans. Sheehan, p. 222]. We are not taking account, of course, of the numerous texts that bring in the metaphysical interpretation of "God" as supreme being.

31. *Die Technik und die Kehre,* p. 45 [trans. Lovitt (modified), p. 47].

32. See, amongst others, *Nietzsche,* p. 324 [trans. Krell, II, p. 68], and *Identität und Differenz,* p. 65 [trans. Stambaugh, p. 72].

33. "[D]ans l'embarras d'une 'poule qui aurait trouvé une fourchette,'" literally, "in the straits of a hen who would have found a fork."—Trans.

34. "[U]n caquet de basse-cour," literally, "the cackle of a poultry yard."—Trans.

35. Report in *Berichte aus der Arbeit der Evangelischen Akademie Hofgeismar,* I, 1954 [trans. Hart and Maraldo, p. 65].

36. "[S]i la poule peut s'étonner de trouver une fourchette," literally, "if the hen can be surprised to find a fork."—Trans.

37. La Fontaine, *Fables,* I, 18, *Le renard et la Cigogne.*

Chapter Three

1. L. Wittgenstein, *Tractatus Logico-philosophicus,* no. 7, *Schriften,* I (Frankfurt, 1980), p. 83 [trans. Pears and McGuinness]. And M. Heidegger, *Identität und Differenz,* p. 45 [trans. Stambaugh, pp. 54–55].

2. Ignatius of Antioch, *To the Ephesians,* XV, 1; also see XIX, 1, and *To the Magnesians,* VIII, 2, as well as, in *Die Apostolischen Väter, griechisch und deutsch,* ed. Joseph A. Fischer (Darmstadt, 1956), p. 157, n. 86.

3. Aristotle, *Metaphysics* A, 3, 984b10 [trans. Barnes, p. 1557].

4. Origen, *On the Song of Songs,* P.G. 17, 272a.

5. Denys, *Divine Names,* I, 3, P.G. 3, 589b. See IV, 22, 724b; *Mystical Theology* I, 1, 997a; *Celestial Hierarchy,* XV, 9: "to honor by our silence that which, hidden, surpasses us," 340b. Likewise Maximus Confessor: "only faith receives these things [the incarnation and its modalities], honoring the Word by one's silence," *Ambigua,* P.G. 91, 1057a.

6. Gregory of Nazianzus, "honoring by a tribute without danger, that of silence," *Letter,* XCI, P.G. 37, 165a. See *Discourse* XXVII, 5, and XXXII, 14, P.G. 36, respectively 17b and 189b. On the theme and its difficulty, consult H.-U. von Balthasar, *"Wort und Schweigen," Verbum Caro* (Einsiedeln, 1960).

7. See above, chap. 1, secs. 1, 2, and 3.

8. One might consider, for instance, this curious paradox: "I certainly am not unaware of the fact that God is dead since Nietzsche: but

I believe in the virtues of an atheistic spiritualism in face of contemporary listlessness and resignation, something like an austere libertinage for a time of catastrophe" (B.-H. Lévy, *La barbarie à visage humain* (Paris: Grasset, 1977), p. 225). And to advance "the radical inexistence of the one that he [Jeremiah] calls his Lord" (*Le testament de Dieu*, (Paris, 1979), p. 274), without becoming incoherent, one would have otherwise to think further the status of both the existence and the nature of the "Lord" invoked here in so unreligious a manner.

9. Respectively, *Beyond Good and Evil,* II, sec. 53 [trans. Hollingdale, p. 62]; *Wille zur Macht,* sec. 55 = Nietzsche, *Werke,* ed. Colli-Montinari, 5 [71] 7, VIII, p. 217 (see secs. 151 and 1035, etc.) [trans. Kaufmann].

10. Respectively, *Ecce Homo,* "Genealogy of Morals," then *Genealogy of Morals,* I, 10 [trans. Kaufmann, pp. 312, 36].

11. *Wille zur Macht,* sec. 1038 = Nietzsche, *Werke,* 17 [4] 5, VIII/3, p. 323; then sec. 639 = [10] 138, VIII/2, p. 201 and sec. 712 [trans. Kaufmann (modified)].

12. *Tractatus logico-philosophicus,* 6.44: "Nicht *wie* die Welt ist, ist das Mystische, sondern *dass* sie ist" ["It is not *how* things are in the world that is mystical, but *that* it exists]; 6.522: "Es gibt allerdings Unaussprechliches. Dies *zeigt* sich, es ist das Mystische" ["There are, indeed, things that cannot be put into words. They *make themselves manifest.* They are what is called mystical." Trans. Pears and McGuinness].

13. *Wille zur Macht,* sec. 617 = Nietzsche, *Werke,* 7[154], VIII/1, p. 321 [trans. Kaufmann (modified)].

14. *Wille zur Macht,* sec. 693 = Nietzsche, *Werke,* 14[8], VIII/3, p. 52 [trans. Kaufmann].

15. *L'Hypothèque Ontologique.*—Trans.

16. *Séminaire de Zurich,* Fr. trans. by D. Saatdjian and F. Fédier, in *Po&sie,* 13 (Paris, 1980), p. 60–61. To be compared with the translation of J. Greisch, in *Heidegger et la question de Dieu,* p. 334. Let us cite, for once, the little-known original: "Wenn ich noch eine Theologie schreiben würde, vozu es mich manchmal reizt, dann dürfte in ihr das Wort 'Sein' nicht vorkommen. Der Glaube hat das Denken des Seins nicht nötig. Wenn er das braucht, ist er schon nicht mehr Glaube. Das hat Luther verstanden, sogar in seiner eigenen Kirche scheint man das zu vergessen. Ich denke über das Sein, im Hinblick auf seine Eignung, das Wesen Gottes theologisch zu denken, sehr bescheiden. Mit dem Sein, ist hier nichts anzusichten. Ich glaube, dass das Sein niemals als Grund und Wesen von Gott gedacht werden kann, dass aber gleich-

wohl die Erfahrung Gottes und seiner Offenbarkeit (sofern sie dem Menschen begegnet) in der Dimension des Seins sich ereignet, was niemals besagt, das Sein könne als mögliche Prädikat für Gott gelten. Hier braucht es ganz neue Unterscheidungen und Abgrenzungen." *Aussprache mit Martin Heidegger an 06/XI/1951,* privately issued edition by the Vortragsauschuss der Studentenschaft der Universität Zürich (Zurich, 1952). We thank Mr. Jean Beaufret for having permitted us access to this text [now published in *Seminare, G.A.,* 15 (Frankfurt, 1986), pp. 436–37].

17. *Berichte aus der Arbeit der Evangelischen Akademie Hofgeismar,* I, 1954 [trans. Hart and Maraldo, pp. 64–65].

18. *Nietzsche,* II, p. 132 [trans. Krell, IV, p. 88].

19. *Phänomenologie und Theologie,* in *Wegmarken, G.A.,* 9, p. 66 [trans. Hart and Maraldo, p. 20].

20. On philosophy as "foolishness" before God, *Einführung in die Metaphysik, G.A.,* 40, p. 9 [trans. Manheim, p. 7], and *Wegmarken, G.A.,* 9, p. 379 [trans. Kaufmann in *Existentialism from Dostoevsky to Sartre,* p. 276].

21. See *Nietzsche,* II, 132 [trans., Krell, IV, p. 88]; *Einführung, loc. cit.* One might consult in this regard J. Beaufret, "La philosophie chrétienne," in *Dialogue avec Heidegger,* 2 (Paris, 1973), "Sur la philosophie chrétienne," in *Etienne Gilson et nous: la philosophie et son histoire* (Paris, 1980), as well as "Heidegger et la théologie," in *Heidegger et la question de Dieu.* See finally J.-F. Courtine, "Gilson et Heidegger," also in *Etienne Gilson et Nous.*

22. *Berichte aus der Arbeit der Evangelischen Akademie Hofgeismer,* 1, [trans. Hart and Maraldo, p. 65].

23. *Hegels Begriff der Erfahrung.* In Holzwege, G.A., 5. 19 S, see p. 186–187. [trans. Dove, p. 135; see also pp. 145–148].

24. *Nietzsche,* p. 366 [trans. Krell, II, p. 106].

25. Respectively, *Holzwege, G.A.,* 5, p. 260 [trans. Lovitt in *The Question Concerning Technology,* p. 105], then *Über den "Humanismus,"* in *Wegmarken, G.A.,* 9, p. 349 [trans. Krell, p. 228].

26. *Der Satz vom Grund* (Pfullingen: Neske, 1957), pp. 53, 55, etc.

27. *Nietzsche,* pp. 251, 321, 333, etc. [trans. Krell, I, p. 217; II, pp. 66, 77].

28. *Identität und Differenz,* pp. 51, 64, 65 [trans. Stambaugh, pp. 60, 72]; see, to a lesser degree, *Die Frage nach der Technik, Vorträge und Aufsätze,* I, p. 26 [trans. Lovitt, p. 26].

29. *Nietzsche,* p. 324: "ob der Gott göttlicher ist in der Frage nach ihm oder dann, wenn er gewiss ist . . ." ["whether the god possesses

more divinity in the question concerning him or in the situation where we are sure of him"; trans. Krell, II, p. 68].

30. See *Identität und Differenz,* p. 46–47 [trans. Stambaugh, p. 56].

31. Respectively, *Holzwege, G.A.,* 5, p. 81, Eng. [trans. Lovitt in *The Question Concerning Technology,* p. 122]; then *Sein und Zeit,* sec. 3, p. 10 [trans. Macquarrie and Robinson, p. 30]. See: "Glaubens, dessen Auslegung die Theologie sein sollte," *Holzwege,* p. 203 = *G.A.,* 5, p. 220 ["faith, whose interpretation theology is said to be"; trans. Lovitt, p. 64], and the basic definition given in 1927 by *Phänomenologie und Theologie,* "Theologie ist die Wissenschaft des Glaubens," *Wegmarken, G.A.* 9, p. 55f. ["Theology is the science of faith"; trans. Hart and Maraldo in *Piety of Thinking,* p. 11].

32. *Phänomenologie und Theologie, Wegmarken, G.A.,* 9, p. 55 [trans. Hart and Maraldo, pp. 11–12].

33. *Sein und Zeit,* sec. 10, respectively p. 48 [trans. Macquarrie and Robinson, p. 74] and 48–49 [trans., p. 74 (modified)]. See again, sec. 40, *An.* 1, p. 190 [trans., pp. 234–35], where the theological description of anxiety, because it remains ontic, does not anticipate the ontological analytic of *Dasein* but retards it by pretending to substitute itself for it.

34. Respectively, *Phänomenologie und Theologie, G.A.,* 9, p. 56 [trans. Hart and Maraldo, p. 12; this version has "faith's conceptual interpretation of itself"] and *Sein und Zeit,* sec. 3, p. 10 [trans., p. 30].

35. *Sein und Zeit,* sec. 7, p. 37 [trans., p. 61].

36. *Metaphysische Anfangsgründe der Logik* [1928], *G.A.*, 26, p. 20 [trans. Heim, p. 16], which happily radicalizes the formulas of *Sein und Zeit,* sec. 4.

37. *Phänomenologie und Theologie, loc. cit.*, p. 48 and 49 [trans., p. 6]. On the theological situation of this text, see Y. de Andia, "Réflexions sur les rapports de la philosophie et de la théologie à partir de deux textes de Martin Heidegger," in *Mélanges de Sciences Religieuses,* 1975, 32/3, and 1976, 33/3.

38. *Phänomenologie und Theologie, loc. cit.,* p. 52 [trans., p. 9 (modified)] and 53 [trans. p. 10 (modified)]. Heidegger's emphasis. It is indeed a question of separating the "possibilities of existence," of which *Dasein* admits the mastery (*aus sich . . . mächtig*), from those of which it remains the slave (*Knecht*) by faith. Would the domain of the ontological be defined, here, at least, by mastery? Of what mastery would it be a question? By what dignity would faith find itself implicitly invested in order to oppose itself thereto?

39. *Ibid.,* p. 63 [trans., p. 18 (modified)].

40. *Ibid.,* pp. 64–65 [trans., p. 19]. Correction must be understood neither as a "punishment" nor as a redress but as a putting into relation with fixed coordinates, which permit a localization, a pinpointing, in short the measure of a drift.

41. Faith as "way, mode, *Weise*" of *Dasein; ibid.,* p. 55, 61, 68, as its believing variant [trans., pp. 12, 17, 22].

42. Respectively, *Prolegomena zur Geschichte des Zeitbegriffs* [1925], *G.A.,* 20, p. 109–110 [trans. Kisiel, pp. 79–80] and *Metaphysische Anfangsgründe der Logik* [1928], *G.A.,* 26, p. 177 [trans. Heim, p. 140]. No doubt, it is only a question, according to certain texts, of an appearance of atheism; but in phenomenology, appearance always manifests that which appears, even if it does not always correspond strictly with it. That atheism here should be "methodical" only renders it more rigorous: it refers in fact to the "disconnection" of God in the phenomenological reduction (Husserl, *Ideen* I, sec. 58) and is the concern of the radical neutrality of *Dasein* (commentary by E. Levinas, *En découvrant l'existence avec Husserl et Heidegger* (Paris, 1949, 1974), p. 167, 171, etc.). See above, chap. 2, nn. 27 and 28; and below, chap. 4, n.1.

43. This ambiguity could explain how Christian theology had been able, biographically, to serve as a path toward that which remains the most foreign to it. See *Unterwegs zur Sprache,* p. 96 [trans. Hertz, pp. 13–14], and the text from 1951, Fr. trans. in *Po&sie* 13, cited n. 16 above.

44. *"Seyn der Götter," Hölderlins Hymnen "Germanien" und "Der Rhein,"* WS 1934/35, *G.A.,* 39, pp. 271, 278. One indeed must read "Seyn" as the sign of a non-metaphysical thought of Being, otherwise written as *Sein;* this graphic change testifies to a decisive change in direction carried out in the first courses on Hölderlin.

45. *Die Technik und die Kehre,* p. 45 [trans. Lovitt in *The Question Concerning Technology*, p. 47 (modified)]; see chap. 2, n. 31 above.

46. *Über den "Humanismus,"* in *Wegmarken, G.A.,* 9, pp. 319–320 [trans. Krell p. 200].

47. *Holzwege,* p. 209 = G.A., 5, p. 227 [trans. Lovitt in *The Question Concerning Technology,* pp. 70–71]. The reduction of every *bonum* to *agathon,* hence to the *on* is even more developed in *Nietzsche,* II, p. 225 [trans. Krell, IV, pp. 168–169].

48. See A. Caquot, "Les énigmes d'un hémistiche biblique," in *Dieu et l'être. Exégèse d'Exode 3:14, et de Coran 20, 11–24* (Paris, 1978), pp. 20, 21; and H. Cazelles, "Pour une exégèse de Ex. 3:14," *ibid.,* pp.

31–32. It is known that the translation of the LXX deviates from literalness enough to make possible that of Aquila: "esomai ho esomai."

49. *L'athéisme difficile* (Paris, 1979), p. 59. To be compared with the commentary of P. Boutang: "this 'Being' . . . finds itself withdrawn, separated, by the divine declaration. Revelation is the institution of a secret"; *Ontologie du Secret,* (Paris, 1973), p. 458. Concerning the work by Saint Thomas on Exodus 3:14, the study of E. Zum Brunn, "La 'métaphysique de l'Exode' selon saint Thomas d'Aquin" in *Dieu et l'être,* pp. 245–269, indeed marks the innovative break in relation to the Fathers.

50. E. Zum Brunn, "L'exégèse augustinienne de 'Ego sum qui sum' et la 'métaphysique de l'Exode'," in *Dieu et l'être,* pp. 141–164. The recent study of D. Dubarle, "Essai sur l'ontologie théologale de saint Augustin," *Recherches augustiniennes,* XVI (Paris, 1981), as strong and convincing as it remains, relies no doubt on a solution that is a little too easy by dint of elegance—the distinction between the *esse commune* (of "Parmenidean" origin) and the *esse divinum* (authentically theological, Augustinian and soon Thomistic); but this very distinction remains to be established. We more willingly subscribe to the argument of J. S. O'Leary, "Dieu-Esprit et Dieu-substance chez Augustin," *Recherches de Sciences Religieuses* (July 1981), 69/3, if Augustinian thought there finds itself more explicitly taken up according to the onto-theo-logical constitution of metaphysics.

51. There is an excellent clarification by M. Harl, "Citations et commentaires d'*Exode* 3:14 chez les Pères grecs des quatres premiers siècles," in *Dieu et l'être,* pp. 87–108, which shows in particular how *ho ōn* intervenes, in the polemics against Eunomium, to challenge every pretension to giving *the* name of God, far from ever stating it (pp. 102, 108). In the end, one would have to grant J. Derrida's so incisive remark: "We can even go further: as a linguistic statement 'I am he who am' is the admission of a mortal"; *La voix et le phénomène* (Paris, 1967), p. 61 [trans. by Allison, p. 54].

52. On the link between the *agathon/agathotēs* and *agapē/erōs,* see Denys, *Divine Names,* IV, 7: "This very Good is praised by the holy theologians also as beautiful (*kalon*), as beauty (*kallos*), as the love that loves (*agapē*), as the beloved love (*agapēton*) and all the other divine nominations which are suitable to this splendor filled with grace, which renders everything beautiful" (P.G. 3, 701c); IV, 13, 712b–c; IV, 14, 712c., etc. See R. Roques, *L'univers dionysien. Structure hiérarchique du monde selon le pseudo-Denys,* (Paris, 1954), p. 114.

53. Respectively, *De Veritate,* q. 21, a.1 [trans. Schmidt, p. 5], then *Contra Gentes,* I, 38.

54. Respectively, *Itinerarium mentis in Deum,* VI, 1, then V, 2 [trans. Cousins, pp. 102, 95]. Obviously one must not neglect that the good itself does not offer, for Bonaventure, the proper name of G✗d. The ultimate moment, the *excessus* that actually makes one pass *in Deum* demands that one share the crucifixion of Christ: "transeamus cum Christo cruxifixo ex hoc mundo ad Patrem" (VII, 6) ["With Christ crucified let us pass out of this world to the Father"; trans., p. 116]. The only proper name thus would occur in the *fiat* by which, if the Christian speaks it in truth, he allows himself to be reappropriated by G✗d himself. See the strange commentary against this text by E. Gilson, "L'Etre et Dieu," *Revue Thomiste* (1962), p. 197.

55. Denys, *Mystical Theology,* 2, P.G. 3, 1000b. On the correspondance between *Aitia* and Requisite, see our study in *L'idole et la distance,* sec. 14. *Aitia* defies categorical expression since "everything is at once predicated of it and yet it is nothing of all these things," *Divine Names,* V, 9, 824b.

56. Respectively, *Divine Names* V, 7, 821b, then V, 8, 824a, finally V, 1, 816b. Concerning the discourse of praise, see *L'idole et la distance,* sec. 16.

57. *Summa Theologica,* Ia, q. 13, a.11, *resp.* [trans. Fathers of the English Dominican Province p. 70 (modified)]

58. Respectively, *Divine Names,* IV, 3, 697a, then IV, 7, 704b, and finally IV, 10, 705d–708a. See also V, 1, 816b (cited above in n. 56) and IV, 18, 716a.

59. "[*L*]*e moins que rien,*" a complete loss, a wash out.—Trans.

60. The reduction of the Dionysian *mē on* and *ouk onta* to simple matter without form arises as a major argument to avoid a larger confrontation; among the very frequent occurrences, we can bring up *In librum De divinis nominibus exposito,* ed. P. Caramello (Rome, 1950), nn. 226–29, 295–98, 355, etc. (and the commentary, pp. 98–99); *Summa Theologica,* Ia, q.5, a.2 *ad* 1; *Contra Gentes,* III, 20, etc.

61. *Addere,* says the *Commentary on the Sentences,* I, d.8, q.1, a.3, *resp.; superaddere,* says the *De Veritate,* q.21, a.1, *ad.* 1; *importare* says the *Summa Theologica,* Ia, q.5, a.2, *ad.* 1. The good implies the *ens,* to which it is "added" as if by importation.

62. Respectively, *Commentary on the Sentences,* I, d.8, q.1, a.3, *solutio,* then *Summa Theologica,* Ia, q.5, a.2, *resp.* [trans., I, p. 24]; which one might compare with this fragment: "all that participates in other participations, participates first in being itself: for something is first comprehended as a being, *prius intelligitur aliquod ens,* before being

comprehended as one, living, or wise"; *In Librum De Divinis nominibus expositio, loc. cit.* p. 236, n. 635.

63. *De Veritate,* q.21, a.1 *resp.* [trans., III, p. 6].

64. *Summa Theologica,* Ia, q.85, a.2, *ad* 3 [trans., I, p. 434, modified—the English version has "image" for *"idolum"*]. This disagreement between Denys and Saint Thomas, when it is not simply reduced to an "implicit" agreement (P. Faucon, *Aspects néo-platoniciens de la doctrine de saint Thomas d'Aquin,* [Lille/Paris, 1975], p. 236), becomes the pretext to celebrate a major progress of Christian thought. Denys, according to E. Gilson, "never rose above the primacy of the Good, never grasped the primacy of Being"; in this view, it is self-evident that, between the "primacy of the Good" and the "primacy of Being," the "Platonic" is the first and the "Christian" the second. For it never becomes worthy of question that it should be possible and *suitable* to "conceive God as identical to Being" (E. Gilson, *L'esprit de la philosophie médiévale,* [Paris, 1932], pp. 94–95 [trans. by A. H. C. Downes, *The Spirit of Medieval Philosophy* (New York: Charles Scribner's Sons, 1940), p. 93], commenting on the Thomistic debate with the *Divine Names,* V, 1). As much as the illustrious historian enlightens us in pointing out perfectly the disparity between Denys and Thomas, his assurance in seeing in it only a progress stifles the properly theological question that is involved here. This insufficiency indeed is found as well in A. Feder, "Des Aquinaten Kommentar zu 'Pseudo-Dionysius' *De divinis nominibus.* Ein Beitrag zur Arbeitsmethode des hl. Thomas," *Scholastik,* I, 1926 (which no more than mentions the Thomistic inversion), as well as in K. Kremer, *Die neuplatonische Seinsphilosophie und ihre Wirkung auf Thomas von Aquin* (Leyde, 1966) (where there is a mention without commentary of the reversal, p. 466).

65. Saurez, *Disputationes Metaphysicae,* I, s.1, n.19, 13, 26, etc. See our study *Sur la théologie blanche de Descartes* (Paris: Presses universitaires de France, 1981), pp. 128–139.

66. As undertake, in diverging directions, E. Levinas and J. Derrida; see our approach, *L'autre différant,* in *L'idole et la distance,* sec. 18, pp. 274–294.

67. Screen of Being (see above, chap. 2, sec. 4) implies that Being itself may have the value of an idol. But this idolatry cannot be confused with that idolatry which a being supports; beings are projected upon a screen, where they thus appear as the first visible; Being never appears as such, because to appear in perfect unveiling belongs only to beings; however, this constitutive unapparentness of Being (as retreat in unveiling itself) does not withdraw it from idolatry: Being, in

the capacity of a screen upon which every being is projected to appear in and as the visible, constitutes the condition of possibility par excellence of every idol that would be constituted as such—namely as apparent. Being opens the case [*écrin*] of idolatry as the screen [*écran*] of every idol.

68. The comparison of 1 Corinthians 1:22 with the *aei zetoumenon on* of *Metaphysics* Z, 1, 1028 b3, comes from Heidegger himself, of course (*Wegmarken, G.A.,* 9, p. 379; [trans. Kaufmann in *Existentialism From Dostoevsky to Sartre,* p. 276]).

69. Crampon translates: "qui appelle ce qui n'est pas comme étant (déjà)." The Vulgate renders it as "et vocat ea quae non sunt tanquam ea quae sunt"; Luther, as "und rufet dem, das nicht ist, dass es sei." A German (Catholic) translation offers more radically: "das nicht Seiende als seiend herbeiruft" (L. de Wette, *Die Bücher des Neuen Testaments,* [Heidelberg, 1832], 2d ed.).

70. See Aristotle, *Physics,* III, 1, 200b32–34 (the kinds of *metabolē*), and especially the discussion of absolute *genesis, On Generation and Corruption,* 318b3ff., which seems to distinguish absolute generation from relative generation only by a criterion itself relative: according to whether the substratum remains "unknown" (318b23) to sensation or not.

71. *Physics,* II, 1, 192b13–14.

72. See n. 20 above.

73. The Vulgate translates: "et ea, quae non sunt, ut ea quae sunt destrueret" (*destruere* renders, poorly moreover, *katargein,* to abolish). Luther understands "und das da nichts ist, dass er zu nichte mache, was etwas ist." Heidegger himself gave a translation of this passage: "Und so hat Gott das Abkunftlose der Welt, die Niedrigen, das Nicht-Seiende auserwählt, um das Seiende, das Herrschende zu vernichten" (*Metaphysische Anfangsgründe der Logik, G.A.,* 26, p. 222). This seems to us, with a slight addition (*das Herrschende*), the most precise.

74. Let us insist upon the fact that Paul uses *katargein,* conformably with its profane usage, in the sense not to destroy, annihilate, but to abolish, revoke, suspend (a decree, a law, *the* Law); similarly in Romans, 3:31; 4:14; 7:2; 1 Corinthians, 2:6; Ephesians 2:15, etc.

75. Aristotle, *Metaphysics*, VII, 1, 1028 b3.The guiding thread offered by *zētein* is found again in Luke 9:9 (where it is Herod who "seeks to see"), in Acts 17:27, where it is the pagans who "seek God," whereas on the contrary *agape* "does not seek its own things, *ou zētei ta heautēs*" (1 Corinthians, 13:5). In Titus 3:9, "searches" are thus characterized as "stupid." One might even hazard that "to seek" often con-

notes an aim of appropriation, which revelation, precisely, as *agape,* comes to abolish.

76. "Devenir fou, comme une roue, ou une poulie, devient folle, en tournant á vide, affranchie de toute accrochage effectif á l'axe: folle, donc désaxée."—Trans.

77. Nietzsche uses this term precisely after having cited 1 Corinthians 1:20–28, in the *Antichrist,* sec. 45.

78. "In Aristotle's time, when it already had a firm terminological meaning philosophically and theoretically, this expression *ousia* was still synonymous with property, possessions, means, wealth. The prephilosophical proper meaning of *ousia* carried through to the end. Accordingly *a being* [*Seiende*] is synonymous with an *at hand* [*extant*] *disposable*"; *Grundprobleme der Phänomenologie, G.A.,* 24, p. 153 [trans. Hofstadter, pp. 108–9]. See *Metaphysische Anfangsgründe der Logik, G. A.,* 26, p. 183 [trans. Heim, p. 145].

79. *Cratylus,* 386a: *ekhein . . . auta autōn tina bebaiotēta tēs ousias.*

80. "[A]u sens où l'on 'a du bien,' du 'bien au soleil.' "—Trans.

81. Let us add that the simple fact of asking for possession in place of the enjoyment of the gift implies the division of the *ousia* into two shares (which are unequal: the elder receives a larger share); hence possession supposes a loss of goods. The new modality of the goods is paid by their intrinsic diminution. In all rigor, the son exchanges something (the other part of the *ousia*) for nothing (another modality of his relation to the *ousia*). In philosophical terms: he exchanges the first category for the relation, an essentially inessential category (Aristotle, *Categories,* 8a13). In short, the son becomes mad and does not recognize the *ousia* the very moment he seizes it; he himself first, because in it he sees the means to glorify himself in the face of his father, distorts it, by the distorting that Paul, previously, pointed out.

82. The same verb reappears in Luke 16:1, to characterize the steward who "dissipates the goods, *ta huparkhonta*" of his master. On the contrary, according to John, Christ comes "to gather the sons of God" who had been "dissipated" (John 11:52).

83. "[T]o interpret . . . the primordial human condition, which makes us sensitive by dissipating Being or the Thing into pure diversity, as well as the refusal or annulment of a gift. The world could be the sediment or the precipitate of a first refusal"; M. Clavel, *Critique de Kant* (Paris, 1980), p. 206; see p. 254. Other texts and references in this direction in F. Gachoud, *Maurice Clavel. Du glaive à la foi,* (Paris: Presses universitaires de France, 1982), ch. 10, p. 173f.

84. *Es Gibt* in *Sein und Zeit,* secs. 43, 44, etc. And in *Zeit und Sein,*

passim, of which *Zur Sache des Denkens,* pp. 17–20, 23 25 [trans. Stambaugh, pp. 16–20, 23–24]. See our previous approach in *L'idole et la distance,* sec. 19.

85. Respectively, *Zur Sache des Denkens,* p. 17, then p. 19 [trans. Stambaugh (modified), pp. 17, 19].

86. *Zur Sache des Denkens,* p. 17 [translation of this passage, not used here, in Stambaugh, *On Time and Being,* p. 17].

87. See, for an essay on the "definition" of distance, in itself undefinable, *L'idole et la distance,* sec. 17.

88. *La relève:* Jacque Derrida's French rendering of the German *Aufhebung*—Trans.

89. Denys, *Divine Names,* IV, 2, P.G. 3, 696b.

Chapter Four

1. In fact, this capacity comes back to the *Ereignis* and not to Being and or time; *Zur Sache des Denkens,* p. 46–47 [trans. Stambaugh, pp. 43–44]. One nevertheless can consider here that which, in 1928, appears under the term of the *metaphysische Neutralität* of *Dasein* (*Metaphysische Anfangsgründe der Logik,* [1928], *G.A.* 26, pp. 171–172, 242, 246 [trans. Heim, pp. 136–137, 188, 190–191]). See above, chap. 2, n.27 and Chap. 3, n.42.

2. P. Valéry, *Oeuvres*, Pléiade (Paris: Gallimard, 1960), p. 26 [trans. Mathews, p. 24].

3. *Ibid.,* p. 32 [trans., p. 31].

4. *Ibid.,* p. 26 [trans., p. 22].

5. *Ibid.,* p. 74 [trans., p. 79].

6. *Ibid.,* p. 36 [trans., p. 35]

7. See chap. 2 above, *Double Idolatry,* n.3, and: "It seems to me that every mortal contains, very near the center of his machine and in a favored place among the instruments for navigating his life, a little mechanism of incredible sensitivity, which indicates the state of his self-love. It tells whether one admires oneself, adores, hates, or puts oneself out of existence; and some living *indicator,* quivering over the hidden dial, hesitates terribly quickly between the zero of being a beast and the maximum of being a god" (*Monsieur Teste, ibid.,* p. 50 [trans., p. 52]). Self-idolatry completes idolatry, but in exposing itself to the consequence of its logic, suicide by contempt for self.

8. *Ibid,* p. 45 [trans, p. 46]. See: "I was trying, then, to reduce myself to my *real* properties. I had little confidence in my abilities, and without any trouble I found within myself everthing necessary to hate myself" (*Ibid.,* p. 12 [trans., p. 5]); "if, in a soul already too much exer-

cised, such pride were not so bitterly turned against itself" (*Ibid.,* p. 33 [trans., p. 31]); "Center of strength, of contempt, of purity. / I sacrifice myself inwardly to what I would be!" (*ibid.,* p. 40 [trans., p. 39]); "I despise what I know—what I can do" (*ibid.,* p. 71 [trans., p. 76]).

9. See our study, "L'angoisse et l'ennui. Pour interpréter *Was ist Metaphysik?" Archives de Philosophie* (January–March 1980), 43/1.

10. "Repulsion" and "gesture" are David Farrell Krell's rendering of *Abweisung* and *Verweisung.* See "What is Metaphysics?" in *Basic Writings,* p. 105.—Trans.

11. *Wegmarken, G.A.,* 9, p. 307 [trans. Kaufmann, in *Existentialism from Dostoevsky to Sartre,* p. 261].

12. "[L']*étant donné,*" that is, the "supposing that."—Trans.

13. "P. Valéry, *Oeuvres,* p. 34 [trans. Mathews, p. 32].

14. This theme opens the book only because it gives, in advance, its conclusion (see 12:8). Thus all the intermediary development, in fact the *Qoheleth* itself, constitutes a commentary on that unique sentence.

15. See D. Lys, *L'Ecclésiaste ou Que vaut la vie?—Traduction, introduction générale, commentaire de 1/1 à 4/3* (Paris, 1977), p. 128.

16. *Wegmarken, G. A.,* 9, p. 113 [trans. Krell in *Basic Writings,* p. 104].

17. See Qoheleth, 2:11; 3:9; 3:22; 7:15; 9:1, and the commentary of D. Lys, *loc. cit.,* pp. 97–98. We will be careful not to introduce here the lexicon of value or of estimation; it is purely a question of "making the difference," even of a simple calculation of profitability.

18. See D. Lys: "it would be an error to understand *hbl,* 'vanity,' as 'nothingness' while it is a question of the image of the steam that is indeed present, but evanescent, in the air" (*op. cit.,* p. 75, see p. 275). Likewise A. Heher: "For *hbl* is, etymologically, steam, the ungraspable breath which only forms to be diluted. *hbl* is all that is doomed, by its very essence, to disappear. . . . Just as the breath passes before me to be confused with the impalpable atmosphere, where it no longer has any figure, I cannot but follow *hbl* with the gaze and see it lose itself" (*Notes sur Qohélet* [Paris, 1951], p. 72). The frequency of the verb *to be* and of the connected lexicon is all the more surprising that the explanation of the radically different semantic of *hebhel* is convincing.

19. "[Q]uod nos possumus vaporem sumi et auram tenuem, quae cito solvitur," *Commentarius in Ecclesiasten,* I, 2, in *Opera Exegetical* 1, CCSL, 78 (Turnhout, 1959), p. 253. As to Gregory of Nyssa, he first defines the vain / *mataion* as *anupostaton,* "that which does not reside, and only has being in the sole utterance of the word," in short, that which flies away, like words. From this, other, more current meanings are obtained: "Another vanity is applied to the uselessness of things produced through an effort that attains no goal, like children's

structures in the sand, and firing arrows toward the stars, the pursuit of winds, or the race to catch up to one's own shadow" (*Commentarius in Ecclesiasten* I, P.G. 44, 620c–d).

20. *Atmis* usually translates *hebhel,* only the LXX make an exception in preferring *mataiotēs*—the point in common of translations consists in indicating that the thing does not hold; either it dissipates (*atmis*), or it is distracted, as a magnetized needle or a free wheel (*mataiotēs*). James 4:14 therefore is closest to the Qoheleth in saying: *atmis . . . pros oligon phainomenē epeita kai aphanizomenē;* which the Vulgate retranscribes—Jerome very logically using the same Latin term to render *atmis* and to render *hebhel*—as *vapor . . . ad modicum parens et deinceps exterminabitur.*

21. Saint Jerome: "Caducum et nihil universitatis ex hoc verbo ostenditur" (*op. cit.,* p. 253). For "there is an irremediable weak spot attached to human designs; it is mortality. All can fall that way in a minute: which forces us to confess that as the most inherent vice, if I might so speak, and the most inseparable of human things, it is their own caducity" (J.-B. Bossuet, *Discours sur l'Histoire Universelle,* III, 6). Caducity does not at all consist in falling but in being able to fall—rather in not being able to avoid falling; all falls under the blow not of a fall, but of an impossibility. [The English "caduke," which has fallen into disuse, most accurately renders the French *caduc* as used in this context. In addition to the English senses of "liable to fall, fleeting, transitory, perishable, corruptible, and (of persons) infirm or feeble," one should also bear in mind the juridical sense of the French *caduc* as indicating that which is null. Note also the related "caducous."—Trans.]

22. See above, chap. 3, sec. 4, discussion of *as if.*

23. Saint Jerome, *op. cit.,* pp. 252–53; which in his own way—so precisely and delicately distorted—E. Renan confirms: "We can find him [Qoheleth] skeptical, materialistic, fatalistic, pessimistic above all; what he certainly is not, is atheistic. To deny God, for him, would not be to deny the world, it would be folly itself. If he sins, it is because he makes God too large and man too small. . . . In sum, God interests himself in man"; *L'Ecclésiaste traduit de l'hébreu. Etude sur l'âge et le caractère de ce livre* (1882), in *Oeuvres Complètes,* ed. H. Psichari, 7 (Paris, 1955), p. 538.

24. Pascal, *Pensées,* Br. sec. 161, L. sec. 16; see Br. sec. 164, L. sec. 36: "Anyone who does not see the vanity of the world is very vain himself" [trans. Krailsheimer, pp. 35, 38].

25. Genesis 1, 4, 12, 18, 21, 25, 31.

26. To be precise, *Melancholia I,* a line-engraving dating from 1514.

Some henceforth classic studies—E. Panofsky and F. Saxl, *Dürers 'Melancholia I'. Eine quellen—und typengeschichtliche Untersuchung* (Leipzig/Berlin, 1923), then developed by R. Klibansky, E. Panofsky and F. Saxl, *Saturn and Melancholy* (London, 1964 and Oxford, 1979)—have shown the debt of this engraving, among others, to M. Ficino, *De vita triplici* (1489, which distinguishes three melancholies: (1) *imaginativa,* here illustrated by Dürer; (2) *rationalis;* (3) *mentalis*), and to Agrippa of Nettesheim, *De occulta philosophia* (Würzburg, 1510). But here we will retain only the remark that the engraving presents the "unfocused eyes typical of profound thought," or, according to Melanchthon here cited, "vultu severo, qui in magna consideratione nusquam aspicit" (*loc. cit.,* p. 319 and n. 117). An unfixed gaze, which directs itself nowhere if not toward the vanishing point [*point de fuite*] where the visible flees.

27. Marion is playing here upon *fuite* and *fuire* in a manner that defies translation: "flight-lines" (*lignes de fuite*), "vanishing point" (*point de fuite*) "flight," "escape" and "leak" (*fuite, fuire).*—Trans.

28. *Summa Theologica,* II*a*–II*ae,* q.35, a.3, resp. [trans., p. 1346].

Chapter Five

1. Pascal, *Pensées,* Br. sec. 799, L. Sec. 303 [trans., Krailsheimer, p. 123]. With Athenagoras of Athens as counterproof: "each one thinking himself fit to know what concerns God not from God himself (*ou para theou peri theou*), but from himself alone," *A Plea Regarding Christians,* VII, P.G. 6, 904b.

2. *Father* constitutes the first word that we say to G~~o~~d in the very sense that G~~o~~d says it (to G~~o~~d, as Son to Father, precisely): "But, one day, somewhere, he was praying. When he had finished, one of his disciples asked him: 'Lord, teach us to pray, as John taught it to his disciples.' He said to them: 'When you pray, say: Father . . .'" (Luke 11:1–2). *Father,* we cry (Romans 8:15; Galatians 4:16), only because first Christ says it himself (Mark 14:36; Matthew 11:25; 26:39; Luke 23:34, 46; John 11:41; 12:27, 28; 17:1, 5, 11, 21, 24, 25; etc.).

3. (Romans 10:14.) One should listen here to R. Bultmann: "[R]evelation is not illumination or the communication of knowledge, but rather an occurrence. . . . Thus revelation must be an occurrence that directly concerns *us,* that takes place in us ourselves; and the word, the fact of its being proclaimed must itself belong to the occurrence. The preaching is itself revelation"; 'Der Begriff der Offenbarung im Neuen Testament," *Glauben und Verstehen,* 3 (Tübingen, 1960), p. 21 [trans. Ogden, p. 78]. As to the limits of this position, they are well

known (see, among others, our outline, "Remarques sur le concept de révélation chez R. Bultmann," *Résurrection,* 27, [Paris, 1968]).

4. One thus would have to speak of a sort of textual Sindon or, in another sense, of a literary veil of Veronica: the impression made by the paradoxically visible glory of G~~o~~d upon a shroud of inert words, of dead letters.

5. It is therefore a question, for once in a strict sense, of a literary event: an event produces effects, leaves traces, imposes monuments under the figure of texts. Not that the texts themselves make the event (in the sense of the usual "literary event of the season"), but, inversely, in the sense that, precisely, they *do not* make the event, since the event alone makes them. Proof being that taken in themselves, they cannot lead back to the event, nor reconstitute it. This very gap between texts and event, far from removing us forever from the Paschal event (Bultmann, and others), indicates to us on the contrary (a) that with Easter it indeed is a question of an event and not of the effect of meaning or of a play of interpretation, and (b) that the full repetition of this event by an other/the same opens the texts to us—right to the Eucharist.

6. On the different acceptations of the closure of meaning and their theological implications, we refer to the whole of the published works of M. Constantini, and primarily to "Celui que nous nommons le Verbe," *Résurrection,* 36 (Paris, 1971); "Du modèle linguistique au modèle chrétien du langage," *Résurrection,* 46 (Paris, 1975); "La Bible n'est pas un texte," *Revue Catholique internationale Communio,* I/7 (Paris, 1976); "Linguistique et modèle chrétien de la parole," in *Confession de la foi* (series edited by C. Bruaire) (Paris, 1977).

7. Gregory of Nazianzus, *Orationes,* XXXI, 8, P.G. 36, 141b. In other words, and on a whole other register: "Now, we are going to speak a bit, no longer of God, but of theology. / What a fall!" (M. Bellet, *Théologie Express* [Paris, 1980], p. 77). Despite its title, more trivial than intriguing, if only because of its insolent and mystical tone, this essay, which is right on target, should receive a meditative welcome.

8. Gregory of Nazianzus, *Orationes,* XXXI, 3, P.G. 36, 136a.

9. Augustine, *In Johannis Evangelium,* IX, 3, CCSL, vol. 36 (Turnhout, 1954), p. 92. No doubt one mustn't attribute to chance that this text is invoked by Hamann, to center his *Aestheticain Nuce* (Fr. trans. J.-F. Courtine, in *Poétique,* 13 [Paris, 1980], p. 41).

10. Guillaume de Saint-Thierry, *Super Cantica Canticorum,* n.21, ed. J.-M. Déchanet, "Sources Chrétiennes" (Paris, 1962), p.96 [trans. (here modified) Mother Columba Hart, p. 16].

11. "[S]ur des chemins qui ne mènent nulle part," an allusion to the French translation of Heidegger's *Holzwege.*—Trans.

12. See "De l'éminente dignité des pauvres baptisés, "*Revue catholique internationale Communio,* IV/2 (Paris, 1979).

13. Denys, *Divine Names,* II, 9, P.G. 3, 648b, and the authorized commentaries of Maximus Confessor (or John of Scythopolis) *Scholia in lib. De Divinus Nominibus* P.G. 4, 228b, and from Thomas Aquinas: "non solum discens, sed et patiens divina, id est non solum divinorum scietiam in intellectu accipiens, sed etiam diligendo, eis unitus per affectum" (*Expositio super Dionysii De Divinis Nominibus* II, 4, *ad fin.*). We could not put it better than to say that the love of Love constitutes an epistemological condition of theology as *theo*logy.

14. Doubtless it would be useful here to take up again certain passages from Heidegger, *Phänomenologie und Theologie, Wegmarken, G. A.,* 9, pp. 54 and 56 [trans. Hart and Maraldo, pp. 10–11, 12–13.]

15. Denys *Divine Names,* III, 1, P.G. 3, 680d.

Chapter Six

1. *"[E]xplication,"* which in the French indicates not only an explanation of or for something, but also a discussion, argument, or fight.—Trans.

2. Theology has nothing in common with scientificity and its processes of objectivation. See M. Heidegger, *Phänomenologie und Theologie, Wegmarken, G.A.,* p. 68–77 [trans. Hart and Maraldo, pp. 22–30). In another style, see L. Bouyer, "Situation de la théologie," in *Revue catholique internationale Communio,* I/1 (Paris, 1975).

3. Besides the translation of *ousia* (in Luke 15:35–36) by *substantia* (see above chap. 3, sec. 4, text at note 78), one should bear in mind Fauste of Riez (452–478) (Pseudo-Saint Jerome, *Ep.* XXXVIII, P.L. 30, 272b). "Visibilis sacerdos visibiles creaturas in substantiam corporis et sanguinis sui, verbo suo secreta potestate convertit, ita dicens . . ."; the confession imposed by the Sixth Council of Rome, in 1079, on Bérenger: "Panem et vinum . . . substantialiter converti in veram et propriam ac vivificatricem carnem et sanguinem Jesu Christi . . . non tantum per signum et virtutem sacramenti sed in proprietate naturae et veritate substantiae" (Mansi, *Collectio* XX, 524; Denz. 355), etc.

4. Council of Trent, Session 13, c.4 (*Denz.* 877 and 884). *Metabolē:* Cyril of Jerusalem, *Mystagogical Catecheses,* IV, 2, and V, 7 (P.G. 33, 1097b and 1116a); Justin, *First Apology,* 66, 2 (P.G. 6, 429a), etc.

5. Respectively, the *Letter* of Innocent III to the Bishop of Lyon, 1202 (*Denz.* 414) and the Fourth Lateran Council, 1215 (*Denz.* 430; Mansi XXII, 982s).

6. See J.-R. Armogathe, *Theologia Cartesiana. L'explication physique*

de l'Eucharistie chez Descartes et dom Desgabets (The Hague, 1977), in particular pp. 6, 8, 11, 31–32, etc. It is important to underline, even more than does J.-R. Armogathe, that Saint Thomas and Duns Scotus (a fortiori the Fathers) propose no explanation or "eucharistic physics" that would claim to take up the mystery of the body of Christ within a non-theological theoretical corpus. Only Descartes and Leibniz will take this step. This is why the equivalence of the logics of the Eucharist that J. Guitton assumes ("Logique de l'Eucharistie," in *Revue catholique internationale Communio,* II, 5, 1977) seems disputable. For there is an obvious unevenness and an obvious original displacement of the discourse: from contemplation, it passes to explanation.

7. The liturgy thus would honor the eucharistic presence as the Third Estate would honor Louis XVI on the holiday of the Federation: the king, mute, sanctions by his real presence a fraternity sure of itself, and which, in acclaming him, comprehends that it holds him in its power, that he lives only by that fraternity. Thus Talleyrand was able alone to celebrate a Eucharist even more profane than profaned.

8. S. Mallarmé, *Igitur ou la folie d'Elbehnon,* I, Le Minuit, *Oeuvres complètes,* Pléiade (Paris, 1945), p. 435 [trans. Wooley, p. 155]. One will be surprised to see Mallarmé cited here only if one underestimates certain eucharistic texts that would merit a thorough theological reading: *Catholicisme,* in *Variations sur un sujet, loc. cit.,* pp. 390–95, which contains a sequence as remarkable as theologically correct, p. 394. E. Pousset denounced this risk in measured and precise terms: "L'Eucharistie, présence réelle et transsubstantiation," in *Recherches de Sciences Religieuses,* 1966, 2.

9. To reintegrate transsignification and transfinalization in transubstantiation in order to consolidate them was the effort of J. de Baciocchi ("Présence eucharistique et Transsubstantiation," in *Irenikon,* 1959 and *L'Eucharistie* (Tournai, 1964); E. Pousset (*loc. cit.*), F.-X. Durrwell (*L'eucharistie, présence du Christ,* [Paris, 1971]); and J.-H. Nicolas, ("Présence réelle eucharistique et transsignification," *Revue Thomiste,* 1981). We had taken up this aim, whose recent theological evolution no doubt has shown its limits, in "Présence et distance," *Résurrection,* 43/44 (Paris, 1974).

10. *In Persona Christi,* see John-Paul II, *Dominicae Cenae,* II, 8: "The priest offers the holy sacrifice 'in persona Christi,' which means more than 'in the name' or 'in place' of Christ. 'In persona': that is to say in the specific, sacramental identification to the 'great priest of the eternal Covenant,' who is the author and the principal subject of his own sacrifice, in which he cannot be replaced by anyone" (Fr. trans. *Sur le mystère et le culte de la sainte eucharistie* [Paris, 1980], p. 28).

11. We can understand then why celebrating Eucharists on condition became inevitable: the unanimity of the community is no longer here a fruit of communion but, as collective consciousness of self, its condition. All the schismatic "fundamental communities," on one side and the other, have this common trait: the eucharistic celebration reflects first the determination of the group; it is celebrated *against* an adversary. Political pruritus does not rot certain eucharists to the same extent that, on the contrary, a distorted theology of the Eucharist delivers these communities to political pruritus.

That one might *pray against* (despite the theological non-sense of the expression) is what is undertaken by some of the "eucharistic prayers" collected by H. Oosterhuis (in *Autour de la table,* Fr. trans. [Paris, 1974], p. 109). That one should say in them: "We pray to you against ourselves / against our preference not to know / against the laziness of our economic politics . . ." does not diminish the aggressiveness of the request but on the contrary reinforces it, by interiorizing the accusation—so far as to illustrate emblematically the reactive comportment analyzed in the *Genealogy of Morals* I, secs. 10–11 and II, secs. 11–12. All hatred begins with self-hatred. See R. Brague, "Si ce n'est ton frère, c'est donc toi," *Revue catholique internationale Communio,* II/4, 1977.

12. Respectively, L. Charlot, "Jésus est-il dans la hostie?" in *Foi à l'épreuve,* no. 5, CRER (Angers, 1977), p. 20, and R. Berset, *De commencement en commencant, Itinéraire d'une déviance* (Paris:Seuil, 1976), pp. 176 and 179. Despite the simultaneously unpolished and loose writing, one will have recognized, in this text, the doctrine of *res/sacramentum,* but strictly inverted: here the species become *res,* the sacramental communion becomes *res/sacramentum,* the communion with "God" (and not with Christ, a detail of some importance!), *sacramentum tantum.* And thus, the body that makes the Church (here, the deviant community) gives consistency, through the sacramental body, to the glorious (and hence historically risen) body: taken up again, inverted, from the doctrine of the *corpus triforme.*

At an entirely other level of seriousness and competence, C. Duquoc: "La notion de presence risque d'évacuer le substrat humain en lequel elle se réalise: le repas ou le pain partagé," in *Revue des Sciences philosophiques et théologiques* (Paris, 1969/3), p. 427. But precisely: (a) Is it a question of a human substratum? Is it not a question, even more than of the shared meal or bread, of the gift of the Christ, free and independent of our substrata? (b) Is it indeed a question of a *substratum?* Do not presence and substratum (*substratum, hupokeimenon*) coincide, sometimes even as early as Aristotle, so that from one to the other there is no progression, but indeed strict equivalence? See R. Boehm, *La Métaphysique d'Aristote, Le Fondamental et l'Essential* (Paris, 1976; Fr. trans., original edition [The Hague, 1965]).

13. See B. Besret, *De commencement,* p. 46. Hence the facility, in those apparently "incarnational" theologies, in admitting that one may substitute the bread and wine with other species (rice, tea, etc.): the singularity of the historical contingency of Jesus disappears as easily as the concrete moment of *any* consecration here and now is rendered null and void.

14. See B. Besret, *op. cit.,* pp. 182–183. With the forgetting or the end of expectation (subjective disappearance of the present in immediate consciousness) ends the reality of the eucharistic presence in the species. Not that there is not any presence at all, but it remains subjected to the praying consciousness; it is not by chance that B. Besret speaks of *burning* the unconsumed bread after "consecration": the icon, which includes no substantial presence (but only hypostatic; see M.-H. Congourdeau, "L'oeil théologique," in *Revue catholique internationale Communio,* II, 5, 1977), had to burn when the physical medium (wood) was becoming undone or was decomposing. The consecrated bread here plays the role of the painted wood, neither less nor more. The confusion of the two presences, hypostatic (icon) or substantial (Eucharist), either likens the icon to the Eucharist (iconoclasm: see Ch. von Schönborn, *L'icône du Christ* [Fribourg, 1976], in particular pp. 223–226), or else reduces the Eucharist to the icon (contemporary deviancies, idolatry of sense); in both cases one falls short of a correct understanding of the incarnation (see M.-H. Congourdeau, *loc. cit.*).

Let us remark finally that the deviant and reductionist interpretation of the eucharistic present (Besret, Charlot, "Dutch Catechism," etc.) give to it the function that, in the faith of earlier times, came back to the blessed bread: offered by a member of the community, this sacramental, blessed before the consecration, was distributed to all in sign of the union of the community with itself, without replacing or rivaling the eucharistic gift. Let this pious custom be reestablished if it would avoid reducing the *conversio realis* of the Bread and of the Wine!

15. Hegel, *Encyclopaedia,* sec. 552 [trans. Wallace and Miller, pp. 284–285]. As replacement for the Catholic host, morality will become the highest divine presence but comprehended in the present of consciousness: "The ethical life (*Sittlichkeit*) is the divine spirit as indwelling in self-consciousness, as it is actually present (*wirklicher, Gegenwart*) in a nation and its individual members" (*ibid.* [trans., p. 283]).

One would have to give all the Hegelian parallels to this text, which make it much more than one incident. In the *Lectures on the Philosophy of History* (IV, II, 1), Hegel notes that the host forbids that "the presence of Christ [should be] essentially established in representation and spirit" (*Jubiläumsausgabe,* 11, p. 480) and that "for the Catholic, the process does not take place in the spirit, but by the intermediary of the thingness that mediates it" (*ibid.*). Likewise, in the *Lectures on the Philosophy of Religion* (III, III, 3), he underlines remarkably that "this exteriority is the foundation of the whole Catholic religion" (16, p. 339 [trans. Brown, Hodgson, and Stewart, p. 480]). See also the *Lectures on the History of Philosophy* (III, II, II, B; 19, p. 146). See, from the same perspective, Feuerbach, *The Essence of Christianity,* II, 7. One must certainly recognize that Catholicism attempts to preserve this gap, criticized by Hegel to the benefit of Lutheranism and in view of absolute knowledge; indeed we attempt nothing other, here, under the name of "distance."

16. *Sein und Zeit,* Secs. 81–82, from which the famous note 1, p. 432–433 [trans. Macquarrie and Robinson, pp. 483–484], but previously paragraphs 6 and 65. Obviously it is not by chance that Hegel completes the metaphysical ("ordinary") conception of time *and* rejects the Catholic real presence; this presence, at a distance from consciousness (of self and of time), disqualifies by its independence and its great perpetuity the two fundamental characteristics of the "ordinary concept of time": the primacy of the *here and now* and the reduction of time to the perception of it that consciousness experiences.

17. One must neither maximize nor minimize that Heidegger should have begun to envisage an alternative to the "ordinary conception of time" after the privileged reading of the Letters of Saint Paul, particularly of 1 Thessalonians 4 and 5 and of 2 Corinthians 12:1–10. See O. Pöggeler, *La pensée de Heidegger* (Paris, 1967), p. 43f. (Fr. trans.), citing a still unpublished course from 1921–1922. One might consult Y. de Andia, *Présence et eschatologie dans la pensée de Martin Heidegger,* PUL, (Lille/Paris, 1965), as well as K. Lehmann, "Christliche Geschichtserfahrung und ontologische Frage beim jungen Heidegger," in *Philosophisches Jarbuch der Görresgesellschaft* (1966), 74/1.

18. See J. Jeremias, *La dernière cène, les Paroles de Jésus* (Fr. trans., Paris, 1972), pp. 283–304; L. Bouyer, *Eucharistie* (Paris, 1966), pp. 87–88, 107, etc.; *Le Fils éternel* (Paris, 1973), pp. 140–152; and "Liturgie juive et Liturgie chrétienne," *Istina,* 1973/2. Inversely, *L'Introduction à la foi chrétienne* ("Dutch Catechism") (Paris, 1968): "the essential rea-

son for which the Church itself does what the Lord did. It does it in memory of Him, to think of Him" (p. 429); and B. Besret, *op. cit.,* p. 50. On the contrary, the *Memorial* of Pascal spontaneously obeys theological requirements: certainly, Pascal always keeps it to himself, "to retain the memory of a thing that he always wanted present to his eyes and his mind" (note by P. Guerrier, in the 3d collection, cited in Pascal, *Oeuvres complètes,* ed. L. Lafuma [Paris, 1963], p. 618). But this subjective memory concerns an absolutely real fact of salvation (union with God which reaches him in the very midst of separation), which radically determines the present instant of recollection (the "little parchment" maintains fidelity) and aims at an eternal completion: "Eternally in joy for a day of exercise on earth. *Non obliviscar sermones tuos.* Amen." One could find a definition of the memorial such as it culminates with the eucharistic present in the Pascalian approach to hope, hence to Christian temporality: "The Christian's hope of possessing an infinite good is mingled with actual enjoyment as well as with fear, for, unlike people hoping for a kingdom of which they will have no part because they are subjects, Christians hope for holiness, and to be freed from unrighteousness, and some part of this is already theirs" (*Pensées,* Br. sec. 540, L. sec. 917) [trans., Krailsheimer, p. 312].

19. Jewish prayer on the eve of Passover, cited by J. Jeremias, *La dernière cène,* pp. 300–301, and L. Bouyer, *Eucharistie,* p. 87, after B. Italiener, A. Freimann, A. L. Mayer, A. Schmidt, *Die Darmstädter Passach Haggadah* (Leipzig, 1928), fol. 32b–33a.

20. "[*D*]*onne,*" a deal or distribution, in the sense of a hand of cards.—Trans.

21. See J. Jeremias, *op. cit.,* pp. 301–5.

22. John of Damascus: "This bread offers the first-fruits of the bread to come, which is *epiousion. Epiousion* means either that which is to come, the time to come, or that which we do to safeguard our being"; (*De la foi orthodoxe,* IV, 13; see Fr. trans. by E. Ponsoye, (Paris, 1966), p. 175. Ambrose understands the bread "of this day" as bread "that is coming": "The Latin names *daily* this bread that the Greeks say is to come (*advenientem)"; De Sacramentis,* V, 4. G. Martelet developed this theme with vigor and rigor in *Résurrection, Eucharistie, Genèse de l'homme* (Paris, 1972).

23. Ignatius of Antioch, in *Die Apostolischen Väter,* ed. J. A. Fischer, (Darmstadt, 1956), pp. 158–61. See Cyril of Jerusalem, *Catéchèses mystagogique,* V, 15, "Sources Chrétiennes" 126 (Paris, 1966), pp. 162–63.

24. M. Proust, *A la recherche du temps perdu,* Pléiade, 2, (Paris, 1954), p. 639.

25. Hölderlin, *Letter to his mother,* no. 307, *G.A.,* 6, 1, p. 467.

26. Maximus Confessor, *Expositio orationis dominicae,* P.G. 90, 900c–d.

27. Saint Cyprian: "And this is why we ask that we be given each day our bread, that is to say the Christ, in order that we who live by Christ and reside in Him should not regress far from his sanctification and from his body" (*De dominica oratione,* XVIII, P.L. 4, 531a).

28. See Heidegger, *Sein und Zeit,* sec. 65: "The primary phenomenon of primordial and authentic temporality is the future" [trans., p. 378]. We obviously do not claim here to maintain the least agreement. However, it is certainly not by chance that the Catholic theology of the eucharistic present leads, in its break with the metaphysical conception of time, to taking a path not unknown to the "destruction of the history of ontology." But the influence is not necessarily exerted here in a unilateral manner.

29. First Corinthians 11:24 gives, according to the variations, "body broken/crushed/given/delivered." Delivered, or even betrayed: the Christ gave his body for us, in the sense that a traitor, who represented us all, "gave" him away. The liturgy of Saint Basil says: "This is my body, which is broken for you in remission of sins" (see A. Hamman, *Prières eucharistiques des premiers siècles à nos jours,* coll. "Foi Vivante" [Paris, 1969], p. 20). Canons II, III and IV (in this way more traditional than the "Roman" canon I) all mention the "body delivered for you" (*ibid.,* pp. 120, 125, 132).

30. Pascal, *Pensées,* Br. sec. 670, L. Sect. 270 [trans. Krailsheimer, p. 112] (see Br. sec. 665, L. sec. 849 [trans., p. 292]). On the commitment of charity in the present, see John of Damascus: "The bread and the wine are not the symbol of the body and the blood (far from me!); it is the very body of the deified Lord" (*loc. cit.*), and Theodore of Mopsuestia: "It was not said: 'This is the symbol of my body, this is the symbol of my blood,' but indeed: 'this is my body and my blood' " (*Fragments on Matthew 26,* P.G. 66, 713b).

31. Saint Bonaventure, *Breviloquium,* VI, 9, 6 [trans. de Vinck, p. 256]. This text echoes the famous one of Saint Augustine: "Cibus sum grandium: cresce et manducabis me, nec tu me in mutabis sicut cibum carnis tuae, sed tu mutaberis in me" (*Confessions,* VII, 10, 16) ["I am the food of full-grown men. Grow and you shall feed on me. But you shall not change me into your own substance, as you do with the food of your body. Instead you shall be changed into me"; trans. Pine-Coffin, p.147]. See also Guillaume de Saint-Thierry, *De Natura et Dignitate Amoris,* XIII, 38 (P.L. 184, 403); Richard of Saint-Victor, *Declarationes . . . ad B. Bernardum* (P.L. 196, 262), etc.: and the texts cited by H. Lubac, *Corpus Mysticum,* 2d ed. (Paris, 1949), pp. 200–202.

32. See the demonstration given by H. de Lubac, *op. cit.,* p. 55.

33. *In Hexameron,* XII (P.G. 89, 1069c), cited in H. de Lubac, *op. cit.,* p. 55.

34. See the *Letter* of Innocent III to the Bishop of Lyon (*Denz.* 415); Saint Thomas, *Summa Theologica,* IIIa, q.73, a.3, *ad. resp.;* a.6, *ad. resp.* Lucid explanations in H. de Lubac *op. cit.,* p. 189f.; and *Catholicisme* (Paris, 1938), pp. 63–65.

35. Saint Augustine, *Commentary on Psalm 98:9* (P.L. 37, 1264).

Chapter Seven

1. Under certain conditions, this formula is the equivalent, as to linguistic status, of the vetero-testamentary formula that it completes: "Jahweh is our only God." We will be able, in what follows, to make use of this tacit equivalence.

2. On this deviance, see our outline, "De l'éminente dignité des pauvres baptisés," in *Revue catholique internationale Communio,* IV/2 (Paris, 1979).

3. *The Phenomenology of Spirit* [trans. Miller, p. 10]; see G. W. F. Hegel, *G.W.,* 9, *Phänomeologie des Geistes* (Hamburg, 1980), p. 18.

4. See *L'idole et la distance, loc. cit.* sec. 16, and "Droit à la confession," in *Revue catholique internationale Communio* I/1 (Paris, 1975).

English-Language Editions Cited

Aristotle. *Metaphysics.* In *The Complete Works of Aristotle,* ed. Jonathan Barnes. Princeton: Bollingen, 1984.

Augustine. *Confessions.* Trans. R. S. Pine-Coffin. New York: Penguin, 1961.

Baudelaire, Charles. "Harmonie du Soir." In *Flowers of Evil and Other Works,* trans. Wallace Fowlie. New York: Bantam, 1964.

Bonaventure, Saint. *Breviloquium.* Trans. José de Vinck. Paterson, NJ: St. Anthony Guild Press, 1963.

———. *Itinerarium mentis in Deum. The Soul's Journey into God.* Trans. Ewert Cousins. New York: Paulist Press, 1978.

Bossuet, Jacques-Bénigne. *Discours sur l'Histoire universelle. Discourse on Universal History.* Trans. Elborg Forster. Chicago: University of Chicago Press, 1976.

Bultmann, Rudolph. "Der Begriff der Offenbarung im Neuen Testament." "The Concept of Revelation in the New Testament." Trans. Schubert M. Ogden. In *Existence and Faith,* ed. Schubert M. Ogden. New York: Meridian, 1960.

Cicero. *De Republica,* 6.15. Trans. Clinton Walker Keyes. Cambridge, MA: Harvard University Press, 1966.

Derrida, Jacques. "Comment ne pas parler." "How to Avoid Speaking: Denials." Trans. Ken Frieden. In *Languages of the Unsayable,* ed. Sanford Budick and Wolfgang Iser. New York: Columbia University Press, 1989.

———. *La voix et le phénomène. Speech and Phenomena.* Trans. David B. Allison. Evanston, IL: Northwestern University Press 1973.

Descartes, René. *The Philosophical Writings of Descartes,* vol. 2. Trans. John Cottingham, Robert Stoothof, and Dugald Murdoch. Cambridge: Cambridge University Press, 1984.

Feuerbach, Ludwig. *Das Wesen des Christentums. The Essence of Christianity.* Trans. George Eliot. Buffalo, NY: Prometheus Books, 1989.

Fichte, Johann Gottlieb. *Über den Grund unsers Glaubens an eine göttliche Weltregierung.* "On the Foundation of Our Belief in a Divine Government of the Universe." Trans. Paul Edwards. In *Nineteenth Century Philosophy,* ed. Paul Gardiner. New York: Macmillan, 1969.

Gilson, Etienne. *L'esprit de la philosophie médiévale. The Spirit of Medieval Philosophy.* Trans. A. H. C. Downes. New York: Charles Scribner's Sons, 1940.

Guillaume de Saint-Thierry. *Super Cantica Canticorum. Exposition on the Song of Songs.* Trans. Mother Columba Hart. Spencer, MA: Cistercian Publicans, 1970.

Hegel, G. W. F.. *Encyclopaedia.* Part 3. *Philosophy of Mind.* Trans. William Wallace and A. V. Miller. Oxford: Oxford University Press, 1971.

———. *Lectures on the Philosophy of Religion.* Trans. R. F. Brown, P. C. Hodgson, and J. M. Stewart. Berkeley: University of California Press, 1988.

———. *Phänomenologie des Geistes. The Phenomenology of Spirit.* Trans. A. V. Miller. Oxford: Oxford University Press, 1977.

Heidegger, Martin. *Berichte aus der Arbeit der Evangelischen Akademie Hofgeismar.* Vol. 1. "Conversation with Martin Heidegger." Trans. James G. Hart and John C. Maraldo. In *The Piety of Thinking.* Bloomington, IN: Indiana University Press, 1976.

———. *Das Ding.* "The Thing." In *Poetry, Language, Thought,* trans. Albert Hofstadter. New York: Harper and Row, 1971.

———. *Einführung in die Metaphysik. An Introduction to Metaphysics.* Trans. Ralph Manheim. New Haven: Yale University Press, 1987.

———. *Die Frage nach der Technik. The Question Concerning Technology and Other Essays.* Trans. William Lovitt. New York: Harper and Row, 1977.

———. *Grundprobleme der Phänomenologie. The Basic Problems of Phenomenology.* Trans Albert Hofstadter. Bloomington, IN: Indiana University Press, 1982.

———. *Hegel's Begriff der Erfahrung. Hegel's Concept of Experience.* Trans. Kenneth Royce Dove. New York: Harper and Row, 1970.

———. *Identität und Differenz. Identity and Difference.* Trans. Joan Stambaugh. New York: Harper and Row, 1969.

———. *Die Kehre.* "The Turning." In *The Question Concerning Technology and Other Essays,* trans. William Lovitt. New York: Harper and Row, 1977.

———. *Metaphysische Anfangsgründe der Logik im Ausgang von Leibniz. The Metaphysical Foundations of Logic.* Trans. Michael Heim. Bloomington, IN: Indiana University Press, 1984.

———. *Nietzsche.* Trans. David Farrel Krell. New York: Harper and Row; vol. 1, 1979; vol. 2, 1984; vol. 4, 1982.

———. *Nietzsche II.* Trans. Joan Stambaugh. In *The End of Philosophy.* New York: Harper and Row, 1973.

———. *"Nietzsches Wort 'Gott ist tot.'" "The Word of Nietzsche, 'God Is Dead.'" In The Question Concerning Technology and Other Essays,* trans. William Lovett. New York: Harper and Row, 1977.

———. *Prolegomena zur Geschichte des Zeitbegriffs. History of the Concept of Time: Prolegomena.* Trans. Theodore Kisiel. Bloomington, IN: Indiana University Press, 1985.

———. *Phänomenologie und Theologie.* "Phenomenology and Theology." Trans. James G. Hart and John C. Maraldo. In *The Piety of Thinking.* Bloomington, IN: Indiana University Press, 1976.

———. *Sein und Zeit. Being and Time.* Trans. John Macquarrie and Edward Robinson. Oxford: Basil Blackwell, 1962.

———. *Über den "Humanismus."* "Letter on Humanism." Trans. Frank A. Capuzzi, in collaboration with J. Glenn Gray and David Farrell Krell. In *Basic Writings,* ed. David Farrel Krell. New York: Harper and Row, 1977.

———. *Überwindung der Metaphysik.* "Overcoming Metaphysics." Trans. Joan Stambaugh. In *The End of Philosophy.* New York: Harper and Row, 1973.

———. *Unterwegs zur Sprache. On the Way to Language.* Trans. Peter D. Hertz. New York: Harper and Row, 1971.

———. *Der Ursprung des Kunstwerkes.* "The Origin of the Work of Art." In *Poetry, Language, Thought,* trans. Albert Hofstadter. New York: Harper and Row, 1971.

———. *Vom Wesen des Grundes. The Essence of Reasons.* Trans. Terrence Malick. Evanston, IL: Northwestern University Press, 1969.

———. *Vom Wesen und Begriff der phusis.* "On the Being and Conception of *phusis* in Aristotle's *Physics* B.1." Trans. Thomas J. Sheehan. In *Man and the World.* Vol. 9. 1976.

———. Postscript to *Was ist Metaphysik?* "Postscript to 'What is Metaphysics?' " In *Existentialism from Dostoevsky to Sartre,* ed. Walter Kaufmann. New York: Penguin, 1975.

———. *Wozu Dichter?* "What are Poets For?" In *Poetry, Language, Thought,* trans. Albert Hofstadter. New York: Harper and Row, 1971.

———. *Zur Sache des Denkens. On Time and Being.* Trans. Joan Stambaugh. New York: Harper and Row, 1972.

Husserl, Edmund. *Ideen . . . I. Ideas.* Vol. 1. Trans. F. Kersten. The Hague: Martinus Nijhoff, 1983.

Kant, Immanuel. *Kritik der Urteilskraft. Critique of Judgment.* Trans. and intro. Werner S. Pluhar. Indianapolis: Hackett, 1987.

———. *Kritik der praktischen Vernunft. Critique of Practical Reason.* Trans. Lewis White Beck. New York: Macmillan, 1985.

———. *Religion innerhalb der Grenzen der blossen Vernunft. Religion within the Limits of Reason Alone.* Trans. Theodore M. Greene and Hoyt Hudson. New York: Harper and Row, 1960.

Klibansky, R., E. Panofsky, and F. Saxl. *Saturn and Melancholy.* London, 1964.

Mallarmé, Stéphane. *Igitur ou la folie d'Elbehnon.* Trans. Grange Wooley. In *Stéphane Mallarmé.* Madison, NJ: Drew University Press, 1942.

Nietzsche, Friedrich. *Jenseits von Gut und Böse. Beyond Good and Evil.* Trans. R. J. Hollingdale. London: Penguin, 1972.

———. *Zur Genealogie der Moral. Ecce Homo and the Genealogy of Morals.* Trans. Walter Kaufmann. New York: Random House, 1967.

———. *Wille zur Macht. The Will to Power.* Trans. Walter Kaufmann. New York: Random House, 1967.

Pascal, Blaise. *Pensées.* Trans. A. J. Krailsheimer. New York: Penguin, 1966.

Schelling, F. W. J. *Untersuchungen über die menschliche Freiheit. Schelling: Of Human Freedom.* Trans. James Gutmann. Chicago: Open Court, 1936.

———. *Summa Theologica.* Trans. Fathers of the English Dominican Province. New York: Benziger Brothers, 1947.

———. *De Veritate. Truth.* Vol. 3. Trans. Robert W. Schmidt. Chicago: Henry Regnery Company, 1954.

Valéry, P. "Le cimetière marin." Trans. David Paul. In *Paul Valéry,* ed. James R. Lawler. London: Routledge and Kegan Paul.

———. *Monsieur Teste.* Trans. Jackson Mathews. Princeton: Princeton University Press. 1973.

Wittgenstein, Ludwig. *Tractatus Logico-philosophicus.* Trans. D. F. Pears and B. F. McGuinness. London: Routledge and Kegan Paul, 1961.

Sources

Chapter 1, "The Idol and the Icon," develops a text whose initial version appeared first in the *Revue de Métaphysique et de Morale,* 1974/4, then in a translation by L. Wenzler, in *Phänomenologie des Idols,* a collection edited by Bernhard Casper (Freiburg/München: Alber Verlag, 1981).

Chapter 2, "Double Idolatry," resumes and completes an article that initially appeared under the title "La double idolâtrie. Remarque sur la différence ontologique et la pensée de Dieu," in *Heidegger et la question de Dieu,* a collection edited by R. Kearney and J. Stephen O'Leary (Paris: Grasset, 1980).

Chapter 3, "The Crossing of Being," completes and modifies a lecture on "La vanité d'être et le nom de Dieu," given November 22, 1980, by invitation of the doctoral seminar organized by the Facultés de Théologie des Universités de Suisse romande (dir. Ph. Secretan and P. Gisel) and published in *Analogie et Dialectique,* edited by P. Gisel (Geneva: Labor et Fides, 1982). It was taken up again at the invitation of l'Escuela Asturina de Estudios Hispanicos (dir. O. Gonzalez de Cardedal), August 6, 1981, at Avila.

Chapter 4, "The Reverse of Vanity," and chapter 5, "Of the Eucharistic Site of Theology," were first published in the French edition of the present book (1982).

Chapter 6, "The Present and the Gift," reproduces (and modifies) an article published in the *Revue catholique internationale Communio,* II/6 (Paris, November 1977) and reprinted in *L'Eucharistie, pain nouveau pour un monde rompu* (Paris: Fayard, 1980).

Chapter 7, "The Last Rigor," reproduces (and modifies) a contribution to *La confession de la foi,* edited by C. Bruaire (Paris: Fayard, 1976); in that first form it was translated by L. Wenzler in *Gott nennen. Phänomenologie Zugänge,* edited by Bernhard Casper (Freiburg/Munich: Alber Verlag, 1981).

The texts reproduced here that were first published elsewhere have, of course, been subject to significant revisions.

Index